# SHAKESPEARE'S MYSTERY PLAY

## A STUDY OF "THE TEMPEST"

BY

COLIN STILL

LONDON
CECIL PALMER
OAKLEY HOUSE, BLOOMSBURY STREET, W.C.1

**Kessinger Publishing's Rare Reprints**
**Thousands of Scarce and Hard-to-Find Books!**

· · ·
· · ·
· · ·
· · ·
· · ·
· · ·
· · ·
· · ·
· · ·
· · ·
· · ·
· · ·
· · ·
· · ·
· · ·
· · ·
· · ·
· · ·
· · ·

We kindly invite you to view our extensive catalog list at:
http://www.kessinger.net

# SHAKESPEARE'S MYSTERY PLAY

TO

MY WIFE

# PREFACE

THIS work, as its title sufficiently indicates, is primarily a study of one of the plays of Shakespeare; but I may, perhaps, be allowed to express the hope that no one will treat it exclusively as such and without reference to its wider implications.

I take this occasion to offer my sincere thanks to the Rev. E. W. Badger, M.A., Rector of Bradenham, Buckinghamshire, and to Major W. Melville Lee, of Oxford, to both of whom I am especially indebted for helpful criticism and advice.

COLIN STILL.

RUISLIP, MIDDLESEX.
1921.

# CONTENTS

## PART I

# PART I

# Shakespeare's Mystery Play

## CHAPTER I

### *IS THERE A MYSTERY ?*

EVERYONE who is familiar with the course and the tone of modern Shakespearean discussion is aware that during recent years there has been a considerable lapse from the higher standards of controversy; and to the unprejudiced observer the orthodox school appears to be as guilty in this respect as its opponents. The nature of the decline can be stated quite briefly. On the one hand, innumerable theories of an extraordinary and often fantastic character have been advanced by people who seem for the most part habitually to mistake vigour of assertion for force of argument; and, on the other hand, those who adhere to the strictly orthodox standpoint have been so exasperated by much that is perverse and ill-argued that very few of them can now approach a new theory with unaffected impartiality and a genuine willingness to be convinced.

Let me say quite frankly at the outset that the case put forward in the present work is of such a kind that it must (if accepted) necessitate some reconsideration of Shakespearean values. In the circumstances just noted, therefore, it may be well to begin with some general observations addressed more especially to the orthodox school.

In the first place, I venture to remind the reader that a mood of disdainful impatience with all novel

# Shakespeare's Mystery Play

Shakespearean theories, even though it may be to some extent excused on the grounds of past experience, is quite contrary to the spirit of all true criticism; and, moreover, that it must have the unfortunate effect of placing at a serious disadvantage many new and original ideas which are deeply interesting and worthy of the most careful consideration. Secondly, so that there may be no misconception in this respect, I hasten to declare in the clearest possible terms that this study has no concern whatever with questions relating to the authorship of Shakespeare's works, and certainly is not written with any desire to assist, openly or otherwise, the Baconian hypothesis. Thirdly, I may say that my purpose is simply to offer an interpretation of *The Tempest* which is based upon a volume of cumulative evidence in the text of the Play, and which meets its many and obvious difficulties. And lastly, I may ask whether anyone really believes that the results achieved up to the present time by students of the Play are of so definite and comprehensive a nature as to exhaust the subject entirely and to render further investigation unnecessary.

As a matter of fact, the study of this Play has hitherto been singularly unproductive. Writing at a comparatively recent date, Dr. Garnett remarks:

> The source of the plot of *The Tempest* has until lately been a mystery, and even the most recent writers seem unacquainted with the important discovery, by Edmund Dorer, of a Spanish novelette, from which it is evidently derived, unless Shakespeare and the Spaniard resorted to a common source. The story, a most dull and pedantic production, occurs in a collection entitled *Noches de Invierno* ("Winter Nights") by Antonio de Esclava, Madrid, 1609.*

Now, this clearly implies that, in the opinion of so eminent an authority as Dr. Garnett, Esclava's story

* See *English Literature, an Illustrated Record*, by Richard Garnett and Edmund Gosse, 1903, vol. ii., p. 251.

# Is There a Mystery?

is the only discovery that has been made which throws any light upon the problem of *The Tempest*. In other words, unless we accept the Spanish novelette theory, the question of what was in Shakespeare's mind when he framed the broad plan of the Play remains the mystery it was before Dorer's discovery.

What, then, are the essential features of Esclava's story, and how far does it carry us in respect to *The Tempest?* Dr. Garnett, citing Ander's *Shakespeare's Books*, gives a summary of the novelette, as follows:

> Dardanus, King of Bulgaria, a virtuous magician, is dethroned by Niciphorus, Emperor of Greece, and has to flee with his only daughter, Seraphina. They go on board a little ship. In mid-ocean Dardanus, having parted the waters, rears by art of magic a beautiful submarine palace, where he resides with his daughter till she becomes marriageable. Then the father, in the disguise of a fisherman, carries off the son of Niciphorus to his palace under the sea. The youth falls in love with the maiden. The Emperor having died in the meantime, Dardanus returns with his daughter and his son-in-law to his former kingdom, which he leaves the latter to rule over, while he withdraws into solitude.

" This," Dr. Garnett concludes, " is unquestionably the groundwork of the plot of *The Tempest*." But surely the circumstances hardly warrant a statement of such finality ? However interesting and important Dorer's discovery may be, " unquestionable " is a very strong term to use in a matter of this kind. Even if it were necessary (which it is not) to assume that Shakespeare obtained the idea for his story from any other source than his own imagination, there is nothing very remarkable in this Spanish novelette theory. It has undoubtedly a certain plausibility, which is enhanced by the fact that there is no alternative theory worthy of notice; but it is by no means irresistible on its own intrinsic merits. It is based upon a resemblance which is certainly not so striking and exact, not so well sustained in respect of many important details, as to warrant the assertion (implied by Dr. Garnett) that the discovery of anything more remarkable and convincing is beyond all reasonable expectation. Moreover, on a weighing of probabilities, is it much more difficult to believe that the slender resemblance which exists between Esclava's story and the Play occurred quite fortuitously than to assume that Shakespeare not only understood the Spanish language but actually read Spanish novelettes—including those of a " dull and pedantic " character—almost as soon as they were published ?

But even those who are disposed to accept the theory provisionally, partly on such intrinsic merits as it possesses and partly because they know of nothing better to take its place, must admit that it does not carry them very far. They must acknowledge that it refers only to the " groundwork " of *The Tempest*, and that the Play contains a number of strange and obscure features upon which Esclava's story does not shed any light whatever. In these circumstances, no serious person is likely to deny that there is ample room for further inquiry; and a thesis which, like the one I am about to offer, deals frankly and faithfully not only with the Play as a whole, but also with practically all the many difficulties presented by the text, ought to be assured of a close and impartial examination, however unorthodox it may be.

Now, I contend that there are abundant grounds for the opinion that *The Tempest* is not a pure fantasy, but a deliberate allegory—not a work in which the Poet gives free rein to the caprice of imagination, but a work in which a clear and dominant idea transcends the nominal story and determines the action, the dialogue, and the characterisation. The Play is certainly not so self-sufficient that it does not need to be explained or interpreted. On the contrary, shrewd

6

analysis of the text reveals numerous peculiarities which would be defects in the province of fantasy, but which are of the kind that is practically inevitable in the construction of an allegory. Furthermore, as I shall show, there are many important features which, on a purely literal reading, are strained and unconvincing, ridiculous, or wholly inexplicable. What is wanted is some conception of the Play that will enable us to explain all the peculiarities; to " resolve every the happened accidents " in such a manner that (as Prospero says) each of them will " seem probable "; to define accurately the nature of the various characters and their relation to the action and to each other; and to perceive an underlying unity of idea in much that is to outward appearance inconsequent and disconnected.

Nothing but an allegorical interpretation can achieve all this; and I claim that the thesis formulated in the present study carries us considerably farther in these several respects than any that has yet been put forward. *The Tempest* has, of course, often been treated as an allegory. For example, Prospero has been held to be a personification of Aristocracy, Caliban of Democracy, Ariel of the Religious Principle, and so on; and this conception is clearly presupposed in Ernest Renan's sequel to the Play. But commentaries which proceed on such lines as these are open to many fatal objections. They are arbitrary; they solve none of the difficulties; they have neither an initial presumption in their favour nor any circumstantial textual evidence to support them; they are based upon resemblances which are far too broad and vague to be significant, and which are not apparent at all unless the critic's own philosophical standpoint be accepted. In short, such commentaries are entirely worthless as expositions of the Poet's conscious purpose.

# Shakespeare's Mystery Play

The interpretation I have to offer is of a very different kind. It does not, as these others do, ascribe to the Play a narrow and arbitrary meaning that is quite unlikely on *a priori* grounds to have been intended by the Poet; nor is it precariously established by selecting a few convenient passages and construing them without regard for the context in which they occur. On the contrary, the present interpretation imputes to the Play the widest and greatest of all epic themes; and it rests upon a mass of internal evidence which practically exhausts the whole of the text and renders the charge of special pleading inadmissible. Indeed, the evidence is of such a nature, and is so well sustained through every phase of the Play, that to reject the theory of deliberate intention on the part of the Poet implies the occurrence of a long series of amazing and quite incredible coincidences. In other words, if my view of the Play be a mistaken view, every canon of probability is violated by the circumstances from which it is derived.

What, then, is the substance of my argument? Until a number of points have been explained and developed, it is somewhat difficult to state the full scope of this study in a few comprehensive sentences; but the key to the mystery of *The Tempest* may be said, broadly and paradoxically, to lie in the fact that *The Tempest* is a Mystery. What I shall seek to prove by textual evidence is—

(*a*) That the Play belongs to the same class of religious drama as the mediaeval Mysteries, Miracles, and Moralities;

(*b*) That it is an allegorical account of those psychological experiences which constitute what mystics call Initiation;

(*c*) That its main features must, therefore, of necessity resemble those of every ritual or ceremonial

8

initiation which is based upon the authentic mystical tradition; and

(d) That actually the resemblance to initiatory rites, and more especially to those of the pagan world, is so consistent and exact that, if we do not accept the foregoing three propositions in explanation of it, we must assume either the occurrence of an incredible series of coincidences or the perpetration by the Poet of an equally incredible literary freak.

As to the ultimate purpose and value of the Play I make no comment at the moment, because a true estimate in this respect depends very largely upon considerations which cannot be intelligibly summarised until the major portion of my case has been stated.*

For reasons of convenience in the handling of a great volume of complicated evidence, I shall begin by comparing the incidents of the Play with the principal features of the pagan rites. Thereafter I shall attempt first to interpret the ancient ceremonies of initiation in terms of psychological experience, and then to show that the moral philosophy which these ceremonies symbolically expressed is precisely what is intended in *The Tempest*. In this latter endeavour the heart of the whole problem will be reached; and it is here that the real force and scope of my theory, together with all the important implications involved in the Poet's method, will become fully apparent.

For the purposes of the first part of the argument, wherein the Play is compared with the ancient ceremonies, I shall accept (provisionally, and subject to proof by new means at a later stage) the theory

---

* The reader who wants a full summary of my conclusions before studying carefully the detailed evidence on which they are based may refer to the first part of the final chapter (" Concluding Remarks ").

propounded by Bishop Warburton and endorsed by Thomas Taylor with regard to the Sixth Book of Virgil's *Aeneid*—namely, that the description of Aeneas' "Descent into Hell" corresponds to the outward forms of the pagan initiatory rites. In this connection, it is only fair to state that a few of my earlier points have already been noted by Mr. W. F. C. Wigston in his *Bacon, Shakespeare, and the Rosicrucians*. I profoundly disagree with the general conception of *The Tempest* put forward by Mr. Wigston, who contends that the Play dramatises the relation of the Poet to his art and to the world. This theory, which is avowedly written in the interest of the Baconian hypothesis, certainly cannot be said to solve all the problems presented by the text. It ignores many of the more difficult passages and wrongly interprets others. It entirely misses the essential idea underlying the Play; and its failure to make any impression whatever in authoritative quarters may be taken as the measure of its weakness and inadequacy. Nevertheless, Mr. Wigston's study ought undoubtedly to be mentioned here, as the only one (so far as I know) which contains any suggestions of the kind put forward in the present work.

One other comment may here be made. The strength of the evidence in support of my thesis lies in the cumulative effect of a very large number of resemblances, not one of which would be of any great importance if it stood alone; and, in judging a work of this kind, the reader must bear in mind the fact that every piece of evidence, however slender in itself, is enhanced in value as the volume of proof increases. In the same way, the possibility that these resemblances are the accidental result of some quite meaningless coincidence is gradually diminished and finally eliminated; for, as their multiplication continues, so the assurance irresistibly emerges that they are the result either of deliberate design on the Poet's part or of some necessity inseparable from the intended purpose of the Play. And for these reasons I ask the reader's forbearance in the earlier stages of the argument, and especially at the outset, until the effect of the evidence has begun to accumulate.

# CHAPTER II

## *THE PLAY AND THE PAGAN RITES*

THE first step in the presentation of my thesis consists in a comparison of the chief features of the Play with certain known features of the ancient ritual initiation, as recorded mainly in the literature of the Greeks and Romans. This may be called the mechanical proof; and, to be quite frank, it is neither so striking nor so comprehensive as the argument that follows in the second part of this study. Nevertheless, the demonstration of a very large number of similarities between the Play and the ancient records does establish a *prima facie* case; and this preliminary justification of a thesis which must have far-reaching implications, and must in some measure affect the general course of Shakespearean criticism, should at least serve to secure a patient hearing for the more intricate argument in which an attempt is made to elucidate the real and ultimate meaning of the Play.

Let me begin by emphasising again, in the clearest possible terms, the purpose of the comparisons I shall make between the Play and the pagan rites. The success of my main contention with regard to *The Tempest* does not depend wholly, or even at all, upon my being able to prove to the reader's satisfaction that Shakespeare deliberately contrived the resemblances to which I am about to draw attention. Indeed, even if it could be established beyond dispute that the Poet was totally unaware of these resemblances, no pre-

# The Play and the Pagan Rites

sumption would thereby be created against the more important part of the theory I have to offer. It must be quite clearly understood that the present work is primarily an essay in interpretation. My concern is certainly not to represent *The Tempest* simply as an ingenious jigsaw puzzle constructed out of fragmentary records relating to the mystery-cults of the ancients, but to prove that it is a masterpiece of epic drama which is true to the experience of all mankind. In this endeavour I shall first point out that a very remarkable similarity does in fact exist between the Play and the pagan rites of initiation. I shall then attempt to show that the inner theme of the Play is one which is expressed in countless works of art and literature, in ancient myth and popular tradition, and in all authentic initiation rites (more especially those of the pagan world); and that many, if not all, of the resemblances now in question would result automatically and of necessity—*without any conscious effort whatever on Shakespeare's part*—from the development of this theme through the only allegorical medium which would command the approval of a sound æsthetic judgment.

If my main purpose be distinctly understood in this sense at the outset, there can be no offhand dismissal of the theory on the grounds that comparisons with the mystic rites of initiation involve a fantastic and improbable view of the Play. That *The Tempest* does in fact correspond with significant accuracy to the pagan ceremonies will be demonstrated beyond question. That Shakespeare consciously intended it to correspond to those ceremonies is quite another matter, upon which I offer no opinion.

Now, the first thing to observe about the pagan Mysteries is that they were divided into the Lesser and the Greater Mysteries, and must therefore have involved a Lesser and a Greater Initiation. The exact difference between the two initiations is a point I defer for the present. But if the reader will now turn to *The Tempest*, he will find that Prospero expressly enjoins Ariel to land the men from the ship in different groups:

> As thou bad'st me,
> In troops I have dispersed them 'bout the isle.
>
> (Act I., Scene 2.)

There are three parties—namely, (1) Stephano and Trinculo, (2) the Court Party, and (3) Ferdinand. I propose to demonstrate the following three propositions:

(i) That the experiences of Stephano and Trinculo represent a failure to achieve Initiation;

(ii) That the experiences of the Court Party constitute the Lesser Initiation; and

(iii) That the experiences of Ferdinand constitute the Greater Initiation.

The first of these propositions is incapable of any considerable proof by the " mechanical " method; but a notable case can be made out for the other two by the simple process of comparing the experiences of the Court Party and of Ferdinand with what is known concerning the incidents which occurred during ceremonial admission to the pagan Mysteries. This is the task I shall first attempt; and thereafter the three propositions will be amplified and proved by means that will simultaneously indicate the ultimate significance of the Play.

## 1. STEPHANO AND TRINCULO.

As stated above, I contend that the story of Stephano and Trinculo represents a failure to achieve Initiation. It forms an important and illuminating part of the wider scheme with which I deal later on; but, because these men do not go through all the successive experiences to which the pagan aspirant was submitted, there is naturally no consistent and sustained parallel between what happens to them in the Play and what happened to the candidate during ritual initiation. Comparison of the text with the ancient records does not, therefore, carry us very far in the case of Stephano and Trinculo; and the proposition I have stated above must await proof by other means at a later stage in this study.

One point, however, may here be noted. In his work on the Magic Oracles of Zoroaster, Pletho tells us that—

It is the custom in initiations to present before the initiates *spirits in the shape of dogs*. . . .

These are the very words used in the Play, when Stephano and Trinculo are driven away from the entrance to Prospero's cell:

Enter divers *Spirits in the shape of hounds*, and hunt them about.
(Act IV., Scene 1.)

The passage from Pletho is referred to both by Thomas Taylor and by Dr. Warburton in connection with the aspect of Virgil's *Aeneid VI.* as an account of initiation. Warburton (mistakenly, I think) quotes it to explain the encounter of Aeneas with the dog Cerberus; but Taylor (more correctly, as I shall have occasion to show) is clearly of opinion that the ritual practice recorded by Pletho is alluded to in Virgil's reference to certain dogs which Aeneas hears howling in a wood. It will be noticed that at this point the Sibyl who is conducting Aeneas exclaims: " Hence, far hence, O ye profane "; which was the cry used in the Mysteries to expel the uninitiated. She then tells him that he must " march boldly forward." This he does, ignoring the dogs. It is reasonably clear, therefore, that the encounter with the ghostly dogs is a test of constancy; and, had Aeneas been dismayed or turned from his purpose by them, he could not have achieved initiation. In the Play, Stephano and Trinculo do not show such firmness when the " spirits in the shape of hounds " appear. They flee incontinently, and are ignominiously hunted about.

Stephano and Trinculo, indeed, are not aspirants. They have neither the mind nor the heart to achieve initiation. They fail at every test—with consequences that will presently be examined in detail.

## 2. THE COURT PARTY.

From a large volume of testimony it is evident that in the ceremonies of formal admission to the pagan Mysteries the candidate passed, by ritual representation, through the abodes of the dead. In this well-authenticated principle the argument which Warburton formulated, and which Taylor endorsed and amplified, with regard to Aeneas' " Descent into Hell," has its natural starting-point. The exact sense in which the principle is to be understood will presently be discussed. For the moment, it may safely be assumed as a working hypothesis; and I now set myself to show, by the simple process of mechanical comparison, that there is a striking and sustained resemblance between (*a*) the story of the Court Party in the Play, and (*b*) initiation records in general and Virgil's *Aeneid VI.* in particular.

Speaking of the trials to which the pagan initiate was submitted, Dr. Warburton declares:

These trials were of two sorts: the encountering of *real* labours and difficulties, and the being exposed to *imaginary and false terror*. This latter was objected to all the initiated in general; the other was reserved for chiefs and leaders (*Divine Legation*, ii., 4).

16

# The Play and the Pagan Rites

The italics are his. The fact that Ferdinand is compelled by Prospero (who corresponds to the hierophant or initiator) to carry loads of heavy logs—a " real labour "—marks him out as one of the " chiefs or leaders." Dr. Warburton is not very explicit as to what he intends by this latter phrase; but if he means that they were the initiates into the higher degrees, we have here a provisional warrant for treating the case of Ferdinand as distinct from that of the Court Party. That such differentiation is fully justified will be seen in due course.

The nature of the " imaginary terrors " which the lesser initiates experienced is indicated to some extent, and for the rest can be inferred, from the ancient records; and that there is a remarkable resemblance between these ritual " terrors " and certain occurrences in the Play will appear in the ensuing examination of the incidents that befall the Court Party after the imaginary wreck.

For it was no more than an imaginary wreck. In the first scene the vessel is said to split, and the belief of all those who land upon the Island is that she sank and that they had a narrow escape from drowning. Yet, as we are told in Ariel's report to Prospero (I. 2), and again at the end of the Play (V. 1), the vessel was actually safe and sound, with the mariners all clapped under hatches and in a heavy sleep, while the main action of the Play was going forward. Nevertheless, although the wreck was imaginary, the text is clear enough that all the travellers except the mariners (with whom we are not concerned) were immersed in the water. Ariel says:

> All, but mariners,
> Plunged in the foaming brine . . .
>
> (Act I., Scene 2.)

# Shakespeare's Mystery Play

In view of this explicit statement that these men plunged into the water, an exceptional importance must attach to the fact that Gonzalo, after landing upon the Island, calls attention no less than four times to the unblemished condition of his clothes. The Poet seems to be emphasising some highly significant circumstance. Let us look at these curious passages:

> GON. But the rarity of it is, which is indeed almost beyond credit—
> SEB. As many vouched rarities are—
> GON. That our garments, being, as they were, drenched in the sea, hold, notwithstanding, their freshness and glosses; being rather new-dyed, than stained with salt water (Act II., Scene 1).

A moment later he repeats:

> GON. Methinks our garments are now as fresh as when we put them on first in Afric (*ibid.*).

Shortly after, he recurs to the same point:

> GON. Sir, we were talking that our garments seem now as fresh as when we were at Tunis (*ibid.*).

And, for the fourth time:

> GON. Is not, sir, my doublet as fresh as the first day I wore it? I mean, in a sort (*ibid.*).

In the last lines Gonzalo clearly means to say that, although the garments show that they have been worn before, they bear no stain of salt water.

There is even a fifth reference to the point in question, for Ariel remarks to Prospero:

> On their sustaining garments not a blemish,
> But fresher than before.
> (Act I., Scene 2.)

It is remarkable enough that, although these men are said to have plunged into the sea, their garments are nowise impaired; but what is very much more remarkable is that both Gonzalo and Ariel declare the garments to be fresher than before. The fact is, the immersion in the water is not to be understood in a strictly physical sense. Like baptism in the Christian Church and the " washings " in the pagan rites, it is. represented as a physical occurrence; but its significance is entirely subjective. It corresponds to the first definite stage in initiation—namely, the preliminary purification, whereby the aspirant is cleansed of the grosser kinds of sin. Hence the improvement referred to by Gonzalo and Ariel—which is otherwise totally inexplicable.

I shall presently return to this point with a fuller explanation; but it may be noted here that Ariel tells Ferdinand:

> Full fathom five thy father lies;
>   Of his bones are coral made;
> Those are pearls that were his eyes:
>   Nothing of him that doth fade,
> But doth *suffer a sea-change*
>   *Into something rich and strange.*

(*Ibid.*)

We cannot, of course, take this song literally. It is quite true, according to Gonzalo and Ariel, that the immersion has in some way improved the state of Alonso and his companions. But it certainly is not true that any of them have been transformed into coral and pearl; and why Ariel should be made to say this of Alonso is not at all clear—unless we assume that the Poet here seeks in some measure to dissemble by a palpable extravagance the nature of the symbolical " sea-change " suffered by the Court Party. In any case, since a transformation into coral and pearl does not occur, there is no need to explain it; but we cannot equally pass over the statement that there has been " a sea-change into something rich and strange," for this is elsewhere confirmed by both Gonzalo and Ariel.

# Shakespeare's Mystery Play

How, then, is it to be explained? It is difficult to see what possible alternative there is to the present suggestion—viz., that the immersion in the sea corresponds to a degree in ritual, involving a betterment in the state of the candidate.

The conversation which punctuates Gonzalo's several efforts to call attention to the condition of the garments is also full of significance. We read:

GON. Methinks our garments are now as fresh as when we put them on first in Afric, at the marriage of the king's fair daughter Claribel to the King of Tunis.

SEB. 'Twas a sweet marriage, and we prosper well in our return.

ADR. Tunis was never graced before with such a paragon to their queen.

GON. Not since widow Dido's time.

ANT. Widow! a pox o' that! how came that widow in? Widow Dido!

SEB. What if he had said "Widower Aeneas" too? Good lord, how you take it!

ADR. "Widow Dido," said you? you make me study of that: she was of Carthage, not of Tunis.

GON. This Tunis, sir, was Carthage.

ADR. Carthage?

GON. I assure you, Carthage.

(Act II., Scene 1.)

And, a few lines later, the same allusion recurs:

GON. Sir, we were talking that our garments seem now as fresh as when we were at Tunis at the marriage of your daughter, who is now queen.

ANT. And the rarest that e'er came there.

SEB. Bate, I beseech you, widow Dido.

ANT. O, widow Dido! ay, widow Dido.

(*Ibid.*)

What are we to make of these two passages? We have a direct reference to Dido and Aeneas; and the very manner of forcing it into the dialogue is commented upon in the dialogue. "How came that widow in?" And again, "What if he had said widower Aeneas, too?" These are leading questions put to us by the

# The Play and the Pagan Rites

Poet himself. We have to answer: how came this reference in, not once and casually, but twice and each time with peculiar stress laid upon it?

The first fact to be noticed is that the travellers are returning from Tunis to Naples. Tunis, we are told in the Play, was the ancient Carthage—a fact of which it is inconceivable that any of the party could be ignorant, although the comments they make (*q.v.*) throw the statement into the greatest prominence. They would assuredly be acquainted with this elementary fact concerning the place of which Alonso's daughter was now queen. We may therefore conclude that this piece of information is inserted into the text for the guidance and benefit of the reader, and that there is some ulterior purpose in the curious way it is emphasised.

Now, Virgil's *Aeneid VI.* (which by hypothesis is an account of initiation) begins with the arrival of Aeneas in Cumæ from Carthage, whence he had fled from the amorous Dido. Cumæ was a harbour in Italy, in the province of Naples and only a few miles west of the town of Naples itself; and it was here that Aeneas made his " Descent into Hell." His initiation was, therefore, a feature in his journey from Carthage to Cumæ—practically we may say from *Tunis to Naples.*

There is thus a pronounced resemblance between the circumstances associated with the initiation of Aeneas and those associated with the initiations in the Play. Dido, queen of Carthage (Tunis), was connected with the Tunis-Naples journey of Aeneas, which ended with initiation; and in the Play she is mentioned by the Court Party in a context that refers to the Queen of Tunis and to their Tunis-Naples journey—which journey, as I am contending, includes initiation. Here is ample answer to the Poet's leading question— " How came that widow [Dido] in?"

21

# Shakespeare's Mystery Play

There are, moreover, other similar points of contact with *Aeneid VI.* For during his "Descent into Hell" Aeneas meets Leucaspis, who was drowned in the Tyrrhenian Sea. This sea lies outside the Bay of Naples, and might quite properly be held to be the scene of the imaginary wreck in the Play. Again, Aeneas meets in Hell his pilot Palinurus, who was drowned during the voyage from Carthage (Tunis) to Cumæ (say Naples).

Why should Shakespeare, having all the seas of the world to choose from, select one with these *Aeneid VI.* associations? The supposition that he did so quite fortuitously, and then, recalling the case of Aeneas, mentioned his name and Dido's simply as a *jeu d'esprit*, with no ulterior purpose, is totally inadequate, for this particular parallel does not stand alone.

Consider the oddness of the allusion to Aeneas— "*what if he had said widower Aeneas too? how you take it!*" And consider, too, the stress laid upon the reference to Dido—"*O, widow Dido! ay, widow Dido!*" May we not conclude that the Poet is deliberately drawing our attention to the extraordinary parallel between the case of the Court Party in the Play and that of Aeneas?*

At a later stage in this study I shall give reasons for equating the immersion of the travellers in the sea with the crossing of the River Styx—both representing that passage through or over water which has an important place in the symbolical scheme of initiation. It will be recalled that, when Aeneas

---

\* In Dryden's version of the *Aeneid* there is a double verbal coincidence that accentuates the parallel. Freely translating the references to Leucaspis, the Lycian crew, and Palinurus, Dryden uses the word *tempest*, and speaks of Palinurus sailing from *Afric* to the Latin shore. This should suggest the above comparisons to any alert mind familiar with the Play.

crosses the infernal river, he is told by Charon the ferryman that he has come to the realm of sleep:

This is the place of Ghosts, of Sleep, and drowsy Night.
(*Aen.* vi. 390.)

To the same effect Dante, in his account of a visit to the abodes of the dead, says that when he had passed over the water with Charon the ferryman—

I
Down-dropped, as one with sudden slumber seized.
(*Inferno,* iii. *fin.*)

Both of these ideas occur in very definite form in the story of the Court Party. We read:

GON. Will you laugh me asleep, for I am very heavy?
ANT. Go asleep, and hear us.
    [*All sleep but* ALON., SEB., *and* ANT.
ALO. What, all so soon asleep?
(Act II., Scene I.)

And a few lines later:

ALO. Thank you, wondrous heavy.
      [ALONSO *sleeps.*
SEB. What a strange drowsiness oppresses them!
ANT. It is the quality o' the climate.
(*Ibid.*)

And, a few lines later again, Antonio comments upon the suddenness with which they were seized with slumber:

They fell together all, as by consent;
They dropped, as by a thunder-stroke.
(*Ibid.*)

This may be compared with the words of Dante, who says that what caused him to " down-drop with sudden slumber " was the conquering of his senses by a loud shaking of the earth and the flash of lightning. In the

23

# Shakespeare's Mystery Play

Play Sebastian and Antonio do not fall asleep. It is obvious, of course, that if they also had been shown to drop in the same way, the action of the Play would have come to an awkward halt. But, although they do not actually sleep, they accuse each other of being in a sort of sleep:

> ANT. My strong imagination sees a crown
> Dropping upon thy head.
> SEB.          What? art thou waking?
> ANT. Do you not hear me speak?
> SEB.                I do; and, surely,
> It is a sleepy language, and thou speak'st
> Out of thy sleep. What is it thou didst say?
> This is a strange repose, to be asleep
> With eyes wide open; standing, speaking, moving,
> And yet so fast asleep.
> ANT.          Noble Sebastian,
> Thou let'st thy fortune sleep, die rather; wink'st
> Whiles thou art waking.
> SEB.         Thou dost snore distinctly:
> There's meaning in thy snores.
>
> *(Ibid.)*

Let us now consider the circumstances in which the sleepers awake. Sebastian and Antonio having drawn their swords against Alonso and Gonzalo, Ariel enters and sings in Gonzalo's ear; whereupon the sleepers all awake, and Alonso cries:

> Why, how now, ho! awake! Why are you drawn?
> Wherefore this ghastly looking?
>
> *(Ibid.)*

The traditional practice in ritual initiation of confronting the candidate with men carrying drawn swords is well known. I do not unduly insist that it is this practice that is here reflected, because in the Play the armed men are (according to the present thesis) themselves two of the several candidates. But observe the replies of Sebastian and Antonio to

24

the demand for an explanation of their being " drawn ":

> SEB. Whiles we stood here securing your repose,
> Even now, we heard a hollow burst of bellowing
> Like bulls, or rather lions; did it not wake you ?
> It struck mine ear most terribly.
> ANT. O, 'twas a din to fright a monster's ear,
> To make an earthquake: sure, it was the roar
> Of a whole herd of lions.
>
> *(Ibid.)*

It may be said that these two men are simply improvising a plausible excuse for having their swords drawn. This is no doubt true as far as it goes, although we are not told that they positively did not hear a fearsome noise. In any case, it is curious that in putting this particular excuse into the mouths of Sebastian and Antonio the Poet should seem at the same time to have made an allusion to the *rhombos* which was used in the Greek initiations.

What, then, was the *rhombos ?* It was no more than what is known to boys in England as the " bull-roarer." I quote as follows from an essay of the late Mr. Andrew Lang:

> Beginning low, with a kind of sharp tone thrilling through a whirring noise, it grows louder till it becomes a sort of fluttering windy roar. . . . Boys have known the bull-roarer in England as one of the most efficient modes of making hideous and unearthly noises. . . . In all probability the presence of the *rhombos*, or bull-roarer, in Greek Mysteries was a survival from the time when Greeks were in the social condition of Australia. In the first place, the bull-roarer is associated with mysteries and initiations. . . . (on " The Bull-Roarer ").

Another Greek name for the bull-roarer was *konos*. Quoting from Lobeck's famous work on the Greek Mysteries, Mr. Lang goes on to identify this noise-producing instrument with the turndun of the Australians:

> The ancient scholiast on Clemens writes: " The *konos* is a little piece of wood to which a string is fastened, and in the Mysteries it

was whirled round to make a roaring noise."* Here, in short, we have a brief but complete description of the bull-roarer, of the Australian turndun. No single point is omitted. The *konos*, like the turndun, is a small object of wood, it is tied to a string, when whirled round it produces a roaring noise, and it is used at initiations (*ibid.*).

To sum up, the *rhombos* or *konos* used in the Greek initiations is the same as the turndun used in the Australian initiations, and both are nothing more than our English " bull-roarer." Now, if the present view of *The Tempest* be correct, we may reasonably look through the Play for some reference to a hideous and alarming noise, such as that produced by the *rhombos ;* and the idea is certainly well expressed in the words of Sebastian and Antonio just cited. Their account of a hideous roaring as of bulls or lions is apt enough; but the matter seems to be clinched by a remark of Gonzalo which reflects one of the peculiar features of the *rhombos*. For, as Mr. Lang says, the noise which this instrument emits " begins low, with a kind of sharp tone thrilling through a whirring noise "; so that, before the sound rises to a roar as of bulls or lions, it resembles exactly the " strange humming " of which Gonzalo speaks:

> I heard a humming,
> And that a strange one, too, which did awake me.
> (Act II., Scene 1.)

True, Ariel had been singing in his ear. But is it pure coincidence that Gonzalo's somewhat curious remark, emphasising the " strangeness " of the " humming," serves as a final and identifying reference to the *rhombos* of the Greek initiations ?

The lines with which I have been dealing practically terminate the first Scene of the second Act; and we hear no more of the Court Party until the Scene which

---

* Lobeck, *Aglaoph.*, i., p. 700: Κῶνος ξυλάριον οὗ ἐξῆπται τὸ σπαρτίον καὶ ἐν ταῖς τελεταῖς ἐδονεῖτο ἵνα ῥοιζῇ.

opens in "*Another Part of the Island.*" The Poet loses no time with preliminaries, but opens the dialogue with these words:

> Gon. By'r lakin, I can go no further, Sir;
> My old bones ache: here's a maze trod, indeed,
> Through forthrights and meanders ! By your patience,
> I needs must rest me.
> Alo.                                    Old lord, I cannot blame thee,
> Who am myself attached with weariness
> To the dulling of my spirits.
> (Act III., Scene 3.)

These are the men who, when we last saw them, had just awakened from a heavy sleep. We must therefore suppose that their arrival now in " another part of the island " thoroughly wearied with their wanderings marks the lapse of a considerable period, during which they have been laboriously searching about the Island.

Now, Dr. Warburton quotes a passage from an ancient writer, preserved by Stobaeus, in which death is likened to initiation. In the course of this passage we read:

> The first stage is nothing but errors and uncertainties, laborious wanderings. . . . (*Sermo* cxix.).

Plutarch likewise refers to " errors and wanderings "; in fact, the practice of circumambulation during ritual initiation is too well known to need extensive proof here. Later on I shall show that the ritual wanderings occurred in the Lesser Initiation—as, indeed, the passage preserved by Stobaeus says that they belong to " the first stage." Hence in the Play we find them in the story of the Court Party, but not in the story of Ferdinand.

While I defer inquiry into the origin and significance of this idea of " errors and wanderings," a word with regard to their ritual expression may be said at this

27

juncture. The *Encyclopædia Britannica* (9th edition), dealing with the matter on the basis of a number of classical references, speaks of—

> The wanderings (of the candidate) by night round the shores and plain of Eleusis with torches in search of the lost Cora (*sub voce* " Mysteries ").

The wanderings of initiation are always a search for that which is lost. In the Eleusinian rites the lost Cora is, of course, Persephone; and, although I do not suggest that the lost Ferdinand represents Persephone, yet it is significant that the wanderings of the Court Party " round the shores and plain " of the Island are explicitly a search for one who is lost; for, when the men start on their wanderings, Ariel says:

> So, king, go safely on to seek thy son.
>> (Act II., Scene 1.)

From the article in the *Encyclopædia Britannica* which I have just quoted, we gather that after the wanderings on the shores the candidate was admitted to the holy building, where he saw " strange apparitions." And we are told that—

> It is also certain that figures, probably of great size, were introduced by machinery (*sub voce* " Mysteries ").

Monstrous apparitions were undoubtedly presented before the initiate, as the writer of the article says; but their monstrosity consisted in unnaturalness of shape rather than in magnitude of proportions. Celsus tells us that—

> Monsters and terrors were introduced in the Bacchic initiations (*Orig. contra Cels.* iv.).*

---

* Τοῖς ἐν ταῖς Βακχικαῖς τελεταῖς τὰ φάσματα καὶ δείματα προεισάγουσι; cited by Warburton, whose translation, however, I do not use above as it is free and somewhat misleading.

28

# The Play and the Pagan Rites

And Virgil depicts Aeneas as encountering a number of hybrid monsters during his "Descent into Hell." Pletho likewise, in his work on the Magic Oracles of Zoroaster, alludes to these monstrous apparitions. He says:

It is the custom in initiations to present before the initiates spirits in the shape of dogs, and other apparitions of monstrous shape.*

I have already had occasion, in the case of Stephano and Trinculo, to allude to the "spirits in the shape of dogs." Later pages will show that these ghostly dogs appear in a stage of initiation different from that in which the "monstrous apparitions" are encountered. For the moment, let the reader compare the "monsters" of Celsus and the "monstrous shapes" of Pletho with the "strange shapes" which appear to the Court Party in the Play:

*Solemn and strange music ; and Prosper above, invisible. Enter several strange shapes, etc.*

ALO. What harmony is this ? my good friends, hark !
GON. Marvellous sweet music !
ALO. Give us kind keepers, heavens !  What were these ?
SEB. A living drollery.

(Act III., Scene 3.)

And, a few lines later, Gonzalo describes the strange shapes:

If in Naples
I should report this now, would they believe me ?
If I should say I saw such islanders
(For, certes, these are people of the island)
Who, though they are of *monstrous shape*, yet, note,
Their manners are more gentle-kind than of
Our human generation you shall find
Many, nay, almost any.

(*Ibid.*)

---

* Εἴωθε τοῖς πολλοῖς τῶν τελουμένων φαίνεσθαι κατὰ τὰς τελετὰς κυνώδη τινὰ καὶ ἄλλως ἀλλόκοτα τὰς μορφὰς φάσματα ; cited by Warburton.  In this case also the translation given above is not his.

29

# Shakespeare's Mystery Play

Comment is needless; but attention may be drawn to the fact that the Court Party evinces no sign of terror when the shapes appear. "A living drollery," exclaims Sebastian; and Gonzalo describes their manners as " gentle-kind "—a point to which I shall recur in due course.

That the " monstrous " nature of these creatures, like that of the hybrids which confronted Aeneas, consists not so much in their great size as in their unnatural shape is proved by Gonzalo's words:

> Who would believe that there were mountaineers
> Dew-lapped like bulls, whose throats had hanging at them
> Wallets of flesh ? or that there were such men
> Whose heads stood in their breasts ? which now we find
> Each putter-out of five for one will bring us
> Good warrant of.
>
> (*Ibid.*)

The phrase " each putter-out of five for one " refers to a crude system of insurance that was practised in Shakespeare's time. It was a sort of wager laid by someone who stayed at home, the odds being quoted according to the nature of an intended journey and the traveller's prospects of a safe return. " Five for one " would be long odds, implying a small prospect of return. The fact that even the " putter-out " of these odds would now attest the existence of such creatures as are here described confirms that Gonzalo's words are a literal description of the " monstrous " shapes. This is illuminating; and I shall subsequently use this passage as one of the means of identifying the creatures and of determining what it is they represent. Meantime it may be noted that Virgil, in speaking of the " monstrous shapes " which Aeneas encounters, expressly calls them " monsters ":

Multaque praeterea variarum monstra ferarum. . . .

(*Aen.* vi. 285.)

30

# The Play and the Pagan Rites

Notwithstanding the customary renderings, the phrase "variarum monstra ferarum" might be construed as conveying that the monsters were *hybrids*, like the men with throats of bulls who appear to the Court Party. In any case, the "monsters" which Virgil proceeds to name were certainly hybrids.*

Now, this Scene in which the "monstrous shapes" are introduced into the Play contains many other allusions that support the initiation hypothesis. These others, being of a symbolical character, cannot be adequately dealt with until I have examined the symbolical basis of initiation; but one further comparison may be made at this stage. We are told that the Shapes bring in a banquet, which vanishes when the King and his companions approach to partake of it:

> Thunder and lightning. Enter Ariel like a Harpy, claps his wings upon the table, and, with a quaint device, the banquet vanishes (Act III., Scene 3).

There is here a notable resemblance to one of the passages in *Aeneid VI*. I give it in Davidson's translation:

> And full in their view are banquets furnished out with regal magnificence; the chief of the Furies sits by them, and debars them from touching the provisions with their hands; and starts up, lifting her torch on high, and thunders over them with her voice. . . . (lines 604-7).

And this is not all; for Virgil's next two lines tell us that:

> Here are those who, while life remained, had been at enmity with their brothers, had beaten a parent, or wrought deceit against a client (lines 608-9).

What were the misdeeds of the "three men of sin" in the Play? Antonio has "been at enmity with his

---

* The same phrase, "variarum monstra ferarum," occurs in Ovid, *Metam.* xiv. 414.

31

brother " Prospero, and has usurped his throne. Sebastian has just conspired to kill his own brother Alonso and to usurp his throne. And Alonso, twelve years before, wrought deceit against the too trustful Prospero. The fact that commentators have not noted and developed this parallel is the more curious in that Dryden, in his extremely well-known rhymed version of the *Aeneid*, rather arbitrarily renders the lines 608-9 thus:

> Then they who brother's better claim disown,
> Expel their parents, and usurp the throne,
> Defraud their clients. . .

Dryden's interpolated reference to the usurping of the throne accentuates the parallel with the Play; and, whatever may have been his reason for inserting this, the version he gives should have suggested the main lines of the present argument.

According to Virgil, Aeneas sees the prohibiting of the banquet *in Tartarus*. In the Play the like incident occurs while the Court Party is (as I shall presently show) *in Purgatory*. This divergence from the *Aeneid VI*. involves no sacrifice of essential symbolical principle, and does not therefore call for explanation. But in the comparison I have just made there is one small difference that is well worth notice. I refer to the fact that in *Aeneid VI*. the banquet is prohibited by a Fury, whereas in the Play it is prohibited by a Harpy. Virgil rarely differentiates Furies and Harpies; but Servius and Cordanus declare that the Fury in the lowest region becomes the Harpy in the middle region. And it is certainly suggestive that Shakespeare, submitting his characters *in Purgatory* to an experience which Virgil assigns to *Tartarus*, has employed a Harpy instead of a Fury, and thus appears to have conformed to the principle stated by both Servius and Cordanus.*

It may now be convenient, in view of the several parallels already made with Virgil's work, to call attention to a point which the reader should bear in mind as the case is carried farther. If *The Tempest* describe (as I contend it does) a pilgrimage through Purgatory to Paradise, its essential theme is precisely the same as that of Dante's *Divina Commedia* ; and these recurrent resemblances to *Aeneid VI.* suggest the interesting possibility that Shakespeare followed, in a sense, the example of Dante in *taking Virgil as his guide.*

Of the *Divina Commedia* I shall have much to say later. For the moment, let it suffice to remind the reader that Rossetti firmly believed this work to have been consciously intended as an account of Dante's initiation into the Order of the Knights Templar. We may think that Rossetti carried his argument too far; but we cannot deny that he presented a formidable case for his theory—as Warburton presented a formidable case for a similar theory in respect of *Aeneid VI.* Including *The Tempest*, therefore, we have here three great works, all of which contain numerous points of resemblance to the rites of initiation. How does this happen ? Must we conclude that a remarkable series of pure coincidences has been three

* " Apud inferos Furiae, in medio Harpyiae, in caelo Dirae et Jovis Canes dictae "; Carolus Ruaeus, 1759, London edition of Latin-annotated *Aeneid* iii. 212 and xii. 845, note based on authority of Servius and Cordanus.

I am not prepared to insist that Shakespeare consciously and deliberately copied the incident of the banquet from Virgil's work; but if he did, he must have understood the three regions as being Tartarus (for Furies), Purgatory (for Harpies), and Paradise (for Dirae and Jovis Canes). Whether this is what Servius and Cordanus really meant is another matter.

times repeated, or that the resemblances in question are due in all three cases to deliberate design? It is not absolutely necessary to accept one or other of these two conclusions. For (as I shall presently show) the theme which is expressed in these and many other works is one which is expressed also in the mystic rites of initiation; and hence resemblances of the kind noted by Rossetti and Warburton and in the present study may quite well have occurred automatically, on the simple principle that " things which are equal to the same thing are equal to one another."

Reverting to the story of the Court Party, I refer to the first Scene of the last Act. Here the Poet makes a marked distinction between the state of mind of Alonso, Sebastian, and Antonio on the one hand, and that of their Attendants on the other. Ariel says:

> The king,
> His brother, and yours, abide *all three distracted*,
> And the remainder mourning over them,
> Brimful of sorrow and dismay.
>
> (Act V., Scene 1.)

And a little later on in this same Scene we read:

Re-enter Ariel: after him, Alonso, *with a frantic gesture*, attended by Gonzalo; Sebastian and Antonio *in like manner*, attended by Adrian and Francisco. . . . (*ibid.*).

It is quite clear that the " frantic gesture " is made only by Alonso, Sebastian, and Antonio—the three who are said to be " distracted." The attendant courtiers are " brimful of sorrow and dismay "; but there is no suggestion that they are " distracted," nor do they make the " frantic gesture " made by the others.

This is a notable distinction. In his *Divine Legation* Dr. Warburton tells us (without, unfortunately, giving the exact reference) that Plutarch, dealing with the Mysteries, mentions a drug called *leucophyllus* which

# The Play and the Pagan Rites

was used in the Mysteries of Hecate. It drove the initiate into a frenzy, during which he was made to confess all the wickedness he had done or intended; and Warburton adds that " confession was one necessary preparative for initiation." The drug was doubtless administered to the initiate in order to produce in him a state of super-excitation, by which the effect of his ritual experiences would be intensified; and if, as Plutarch implies, the purpose was to provoke him to confession, the drug would be used more particularly in the case of " men of sin."

Now, this is in some sort reflected in the Play. In the third Scene of the third Act there is a long speech in which Ariel soundly rates the " three men of sin," and in which he says to them—

> I have made you mad. . . .

After the Shapes have carried out the table, Prospero (still " above, invisible ") remarks aside:

> And these, mine enemies, are all knit up
> In their distractions: they now are in my power;
> And in these fits I leave them. . . .
>
> (Act III., Scene 3.)

The " enemies " are clearly the three men in question. The preceding long speech was addressed by Ariel to them, and there is nowhere in the Play any hint of hostility towards the other men—indeed, quite the contrary is the case. Moreover, when Alonso, stung by Ariel's reference to Prospero, rushes out, followed by Sebastian and Antonio, we find Gonzalo exclaiming to the others:

> All three of them are desperate; their great guilt,
> Like poison given to work a great time after,
> Now 'gins to bite the spirits—I do beseech you
> That are of suppler joints, follow them swiftly
> And hinder them from what this ecstasy
> May now provoke them to.
>
> (*Ibid.*)

Here is a distinct allusion to the working of a poison. True, the allusion is only by way of a simile; but the frenzy is real enough. Furthermore, the reference is made only in the case of the " three men of sin," who, before their ecstasy has subsided, do in fact confess and repent their sins, I do not, of course, suggest that *leucophyllus,* or any similar drug, was actually administered to Alonso, Sebastian, and Antonio; but, having regard to all the other points of resemblance to the pagan rites, it is curious (to say the least) that a simile of poison should occur in connection with an ecstasy leading to confession and repentance.

When Alonso, Sebastian, and Antonio enter " with a frantic gesture," followed by their attendant courtiers, we read that—

> They all enter the circle which Prospero has made, and there stand charmed (Act V., Scene 1).

Whereupon Prospero, who has just called forth some " heavenly music," speaks as follows:

> A solemn air, and the best comforter
> To an unsettled fancy, cure thy brains,
> Now useless boiled within thy skull! There stand,
> For you are spell-stopped.
>
> *(Ibid.)*

It will be noticed that this Scene is laid " before the cell of Prospero "; and that, shortly after the men have been spell-stopped, Prospero throws open the door of the cell:

> The entrance of the cell opens, and discovers Ferdinand and Miranda playing at chess (*ibid.*).

Now, Themistius has given an account of initiation which corresponds in a remarkable degree to the above passages. This account is cited by many authorities; and I give it in the closest possible translation, together with the original Greek, so that there can be no suggestion that I have strained its meaning in order to secure a point. Themistius says:

The man at the moment of approaching the innermost sanctuary was filled with a shuddering and a swimming in the head, and was held by dismay and complete perplexity, and was unable to take a step or to lay hold of any beginning leading inwards (*i.e.*, to make any start towards entering); and when the hierophant, having thrown open the entrance to the temple, . . . (*Orat. in Patrem*).*

The parallel with the Play is remarkably close. The " shuddering and dismay " of the initiate is expressed by the " frantic gesture " of the distracted three and the " dismay " of their attendants. The " complete perplexity and a swimming in the head " is reflected in the reference to " brains useless boiled within the skull." The figurative inability of the initiate to take a step towards entering appears in the Play as an actual physical incapacity for movement (" spell-stopped "), which is doubtless more than Themistius means to convey; but this is a difference of degree rather than of essence. Moreover, just as in the Play all this happens immediately outside the cell, which Prospero subsequently throws open, so, according to Themistius, these sensations were experienced by the initiate immediately outside the temple, whose entrance the hierophant subsequently throws wide open.

It should further be noticed that the throwing open of the gates of the temple, which Themistius describes, terminated the wanderings on the shore at Eleusis in search of " the lost child "; and that in the Play the opening of the entrance of the cell, " discovering Ferdinand," obviously terminates the wanderings of the Court Party in search of " the lost son." The

* Ὁ μὲν ἄρτι προσιὼν τοῖς ἀδύτοις, φρίκης τε ἀνεπίμπλατο καὶ ἰλίγγου ἀδημονίᾳ τε εἴχετο καὶ ἀπορίᾳ συμπάσῃ, οὐδὲ ἴχνους λαβέσθαι οἷός τε ὤν, οὔτε ἀρχῆς ἡστινοσοῦν ἐπιδράξασθαι εἴσω φερούσης, ὁπότε δὲ ὁ προφήτης ἐκεῖνος ἀναπετάσας τὰ προπύλαια τοῦ νεὼς . . .

correspondence I am suggesting is, therefore, complete at every point; and it will presently be still further emphasised by a demonstration that the inner meaning of this part of the Eleusinian rites is clearly implicit in the text of the Play.

Let us now consider what Ariel says to Alonso, Sebastian, and Antonio in the long speech wherein he accuses them of being " three men of sin."     We read:

> They [the powers] . . . do pronounce by me
> Lingering perdition, worse than any death
> Can be at once, shall step by step attend
> You and your ways; whose wraths to guard you from,
> Which here, in this most desolate isle, else falls
> Upon your heads, is nothing, but heart's sorrow
> And a clear life ensuring.
>
> (Act III., Scene 3.)

This surely confirms almost to the point of proof the view for which I am contending?  Observe that it is precisely " here in this most desolate isle " that these men must face the wrath of " the powers " and receive the appalling sentence of " lingering perdition," unless they repent their misdeeds.  Clearly, then, the Island is for them a desolate place wherein the guilty expiate their sins by suffering, from which there is no escape (as Ariel says) save by the way of genuine repentance. In other words, the Court Party is *in a Purgatory.*

Ariel, of course, is obviously striving to bring these men to penitence and a new resolve; and here again there is a marked resemblance to the pagan rites. If it had contained nothing else, his speech condemning the men of sin and exhorting them to repentance and amendment would amount simply to a statement of the moral principle; and, as such, it would constitute no very valid evidence that an initiation is in progress. But his implicit identification with Purgatory of the place wherein this principle is spoken at once establishes

# The Play and the Pagan Rites

a direct and particular correspondence with the ancient initiation; for, in so far as the pagan aspirant was virtually represented as passing through Purgatory, the practical and ostensible purpose of this experience was undoubtedly the same as that for which Ariel is striving in the Play. Epictetus says that everything in the Mysteries was devised to secure amendment of life;* and Plato's approval of the Eleusinian Mysteries was based upon the fact, which Andocides and Diodorus confirm, that the initiate generally did lead a better life as a result of the great effect produced upon him by his ritual experiences.† Indeed, all the available records relating to the pagan ceremonies, certainly those that refer to Eleusis, point to the conclusion that the ritual "Descent into Hell" had for its practical object that of leading the aspirant through penitence to self-mastery by foreshadowing to him the "lingering perdition" which awaits the unrepentant in Purgatory.

That this is exactly what happens in the case of the Court Party is intimated quite plainly in the text. For these men, passing into a Purgatory, are warned of the fate which there awaits the guilty among them, who are exhorted to save themselves by "heart's sorrow and a clear life ensuing." As a result of this experience, the three who are definitely men of sin are brought to repentance, while all of them "find themselves":

> In one voyage
> Did Claribel her husband find at Tunis,
> And Ferdinand, her brother, found a wife,
> Where he himself was lost; Prospero his dukedom,
> In a poor isle; and all of us ourselves,
> When no man was his own.
>
> (Act V., Scene 1.)

---

* *Arrian. Dissert.* iii c. 21; cited by Warburton.

† Andocides, *De Myst.* 31; Diodorus Sic., *Hist.* vol. xlviii. Cf. *Ency. Brit.*, 9th ed., *sub voce* "Mysteries."

# Shakespeare's Mystery Play

What is this self-finding but the achievement of that same self-mastery which the pagan ceremonies were designed to inculcate? In subsequent pages I shall go very closely into the whole matter; but the broad significance of Gonzalo's speech is clear enough. Previous to their " Descent into Hell " these men were not " their own." They were in the grip of the lower impulses; and it is their victory over these that constitutes the self-finding of which Gonzalo speaks. As with the aspirant in the pagan rites, their achievement of self-mastery is the direct outcome of a passage through Purgatory. It is the fulfilment of the purpose of the Lesser Initiation, whereby the candidate was purged of unworthy impulses and rendered fit for the Greater Initiation which followed later.* And, quite appropriately from the standpoint of the present theory, the story of the Court Party closes on this note of repentance and self-finding.

One of the privileges to which formal initiation gave access was that of consulting the oracle. Warburton writes:

> Now, amongst the uses of initiation, the advice and direction of the *oracle* was not the least: and an oracular bureau was so necessary an appendix to some of the Mysteries, as particularly of the Samothracian, that Plutarch, speaking of Lysander's initiation there, expresses it in a word that signifies *consulting the oracle* (*Div. Legation*).

The italics are Warburton's. The point in question seems to be directly referred to in the Play, for Alonso says:

> This is as strange a maze as e'er men trod;
> And there is in this business more than nature
> Was ever conduct of: some oracle
> Must rectify our knowledge.
>
> (Act V., Scene 1.)

---

* All authorities are agreed that the Lesser Mysteries were no more than a preparation for the Greater.

# The Play and the Pagan Rites

Thus, at the very end of those experiences which have constituted his initiation, Alonso in a manner proposes to consult some oracle. True, the allusion is made in the Play only by way of a figure of speech; but the fact remains that the reference is there. And observe what Prospero replies:

> Sir, my liege,
> Do not infest your mind with beating on
> The strangeness of this business; at picked leisure,
> Which shall be shortly, single I'll resolve you
> (Which to you shall seem probable) of every
> These happened accidents; till when, be cheerful
> And think of each thing well.
>
> (*Ibid.*)

Now, this is a remarkable promise for Prospero to make. Unless the present theory be accepted, he must seem to be committing himself to a needlessly precise and comprehensive undertaking; for he implies that at " picked leisure " he will explain (" resolve ") every one of the " happened accidents " in such a way that each will be seen to be completely relevant and intelligible (" seem probable "). Furthermore, to the literalist the promise must seem exceedingly difficult to fulfil, for the incidents are strange and astonishing, as Alonso says:

> There is in this business more than nature
> Was ever conduct of.
>
> (*Ibid.*)

How, then, is it all to be explained? And if (as is ordinarily supposed) the Play be but a fantasy, what need is there for explanation at all? Surely Prospero means that each of the many incidents which have befallen the Court Party has some symbolical significance and is accordingly capable of reasoned interpretation? What else can he mean?

As a matter of fact, the entire phrasing of Prospero's

41

promise clearly suggests that the Play is a sustained allegory. So also, by common consent, was the ritual of the pagan Mysteries. The writer in the *Encyclopædia Britannica*, from whom I have already quoted several times, appears to accept the view that the ancient ceremonies were theological and philosophical enigmas. He remarks that from certain of the records—

we may infer the belief of the writers that important truths were enigmatically expressed in the Mysteries, and that the intellect which could penetrate beneath the surface was able to apprehend them (*sub voce* " Mysteries ").*

He also cites Plutarch to the effect that it required a philosophical training and a reverent religious frame of mind to understand the Mysteries.† It is evident, therefore, that what happened in the Mysteries was capable of being " resolved " into an intelligible philosophy; and I shall presently show that the ideas enigmatically expressed in the initiation ritual are precisely those allegorised in the incidents which Prospero promises to explain.

It may be taken for granted that at some time the pagan aspirant was told the meaning of what had occurred during his initiation. As to when and how he was so informed I shall have something to say later. For the moment I suggest simply that such explanation has its counterpart in the interpretation which the Court Party is to receive " at picked leisure." Pending this promised discourse, Prospero charges these men to " be cheerful " and to " think of each thing well "— which is exactly the tone the hierophant would be likely to adopt towards the initiate at the close of his strange and disturbing experiences.

* In a footnote he adds that " the word *enigma* is used by Sopater, *Diaer. Zetem.*, p. 120; Clem. Alex. *Strom.*, p. 658; and in Christian writers frequently; Lobeck, pp. 143, 189."

† *De Isid.* lxviii.

# The Play and the Pagan Rites

The preliminary survey of the story of the Court Party, from the angle to which I have confined myself in this chapter, is now completed. The case that has resulted from a mechanical comparison with the records concerning the pagan initiation rites is not, I think, a negligible one; but it will be heavily reinforced in the course of the wider examination that will follow when the story of Ferdinand has also been dealt with on the present lines.

## 3. FERDINAND.

The proposition I stated at the outset with regard to Ferdinand was that his experiences constitute the Greater Initiation. This proposition is, for two reasons, more difficult to prove by the " mechanical " method than that relating to the Court Party. In the first place, as a consequence of the stricter secrecy imposed upon the higher initiates, the records bearing upon the Greater Initiation are somewhat meagre; and, secondly, commentators on the Mysteries are not unanimous as to the exact position of the dividing-line which determines whether any given record shall be held to refer to the Greater or to the Lesser of the pagan initiations.

In the later phases of my argument both of these handicaps are to some considerable extent mitigated by a reconstitution of the esoteric basis of the ancient ceremonies, which not only furnishes the data whence all the main features of the Greater Initiation can be deduced, but also supplies a positive warrant for the dividing-line as I have drawn it. The force of that warrant proceeds from the symmetrical form and perfectly rational meaning of the initiation scheme thus reconstituted. And, in so far as the views of some other writers as to what the Greater Initiation comprised do not wholly accord with the view presumed in the present chapter, my own opinion can be justified by pointing to a more consistent and comprehensive interpretation than any which those who differ from me have been able to offer. I beg, therefore, that any criticisms which this present section may provoke shall (if they be of a kind covered by either of the two difficulties I have mentioned) be deferred until the whole of my case has been stated.

Now, it is commonly agreed that the aspirant for the pagan Greater Initiation was placed upon a spartan diet for a period before the ceremony. The limited duration of the Play does not permit us to see this discipline in actual operation; but the point seems to be referred to by Prospero, who tells Ferdinand:

> Sea-water shalt thou drink; thy food shall be
> The fresh-brook mussels, withered roots, and husks
> Wherein the acorn cradled.
>
> (Act I., Scene 2.)

Such was not, of course, in a literal sense the diet to which the pagan candidate was restricted; but it is curious that a discipline of this sort should be suggested for Ferdinand, and for no one else in the Play. Moreover, it is upon Ferdinand alone that certain heavy labours are imposed:

> *Enter Ferdinand, bearing a log . . .*
> I must remove
> Some thousands of these logs, and pile them up,
> Upon a sore injunction.
>
> (Act III., Scene 1.)

The difference between this kind of ordeal and the kind to which the Court Party is submitted is precisely the difference between " real labours " and " imaginary terrors "; and, according to Warburton's definition, it marks out Ferdinand as a " chief or leader "—

# The Play and the Pagan Rites

description which, when used in connection with the Mysteries, can refer only to the higher initiates.

For the immediate purpose, and subject to full proof hereafter, it may be premised that, whereas in the Lesser Initiation the candidate passed through Purgatory, in the Greater Initiation he was ritually represented as attaining to Paradise. That such is broadly the distinction between the case of the Court Party and that of Ferdinand is almost self-evident. Certainly Ferdinand does not pass through Purgatory, for his experiences differ entirely in character from those of the Court Party; but that he does attain to Paradise, in the particular sense implied in the ancient rites, is not difficult to demonstrate from the evidence contained in the text.

Let us consider in what sense the pagan aspirant was supposed to enter Paradise. In the first place, it should be noted that after his formal admission to the Greater Mysteries the candidate was called *epoptes*, which means " a seer." This title was conferred in allusion to the revealing vision accorded to him in the Greater Initiation. What was it, then, which the candidate saw and which constituted a revelation?

Thomas Taylor, in his work on the *Eleusinian and Bacchic Mysteries*, declares that what was presented was a vision of the gods by means of magical evocation on the part of the hierophant. He writes:

> That magical evocation formed a part of the sacerdotal office in the Mysteries, and that this was universally believed in by all antiquity, long before the era of the Platonists, is plain from the testimony of Hippocrates, or at least Democritus, in his treatise *De Morbo Sacro*, p. 86 f. (*op. cit.*, p. 69 ff., edit. J. Weitstein, Amsterdam).

He cites Proclus as saying that " in all initiations and mysteries the gods exhibit many forms of themselves " (*In Plat. Repub.*); and he refers to the words of Plato that " in consequence of the divine initiation we become spectators of entire, simple, immovable, and blessed visions " (In *Phaedrus*). Taylor adds—

This doctrine, too, of divine appearances in the Mysteries is clearly confirmed by Plotinus, *Ennead* I., lib. vi., p. 55, and *Ennead* IX., lib. ix., p. 700 (*op. cit.*, p. 69).

And he states his conclusion as follows:

From all this it may be inferred that the most sublime part of *epopteia*, or inspection, consisted in *beholding the gods themselves* (*op. cit.*, p. 68).

From these testimonies it would seem that in one of the stages of his initiation—viz., in the last stage, called *epopteia*—the pagan aspirant was granted a sight of the gods; and it was in this coming into the very presence of the gods that his advent into Paradise was implied.

Now, it is assuredly not without reason that in the Play the Ceres Masque is witnessed only by Ferdinand and Miranda. For the moment, let the reader ignore Miranda; her case is dealt with in the later part of this present section. It will be noticed that she makes no comment during or at the end of the Masque, nor does she seem to be in any way affected by it: two significant facts. Ferdinand, on the other hand, exclaims:

This is a most majestic vision. . . .
(Act IV., Scene 1.)

And Prospero thus addresses him at the close of it:

You do look, my son, in a moved sort,
As if you were dismay'd. . . .

(*Ibid.*)

This contrast, emphasising the effect of the vision upon Ferdinand, suggests that it is primarily, if not solely, for him that the vision is called forth.

The similarity between the case of Ferdinand and

46

that of the pagan initiate is obvious.   For the Masque
accords to Ferdinand (and Miranda) a direct sight of
some of the deities, amongst whom we find Ceres, who
was the presiding deity of the Eleusinian cultus; and
the correspondence is accentuated by the fact that
Ferdinand is made to exclaim, while the Masque is in
progress:

> Let me live here ever;
> So rare a wondered father and a wise
> Makes this place Paradise.

(Ibid.)

Thus Ferdinand, being come into the very presence
of the gods, declares himself to be in Paradise; and
this is the particular sense of the ancient rites.   As for
the fact that Miranda is with him in this experience,
it is enough for the moment to remark that Dante,
when he attained to Paradise, was accompanied by
Beatrice.

It may be added that the Masque not only introduces
(Demeter) Ceres, who was the presiding deity of
Eleusis; it also contains an allusion to the carrying off
of her daughter Persephone by Pluto (Dis):

> Since they did plot
> The means that dusky Dis my daughter got. . . .

(Ibid.)

Since much of the mystic teaching of the Eleusinian
rites revolved around the myth of the abduction of
Persephone, this gratuitous reference to the matter
in the course of the Masque is not without value as
a hint of the purpose of the Play.

In one of the passages just cited from his work
on the Mysteries, Taylor affirms that " magical evocation [of the gods] formed a part of the sacerdotal office ";
and in the Play Prospero, being asked by Ferdinand

whether those who appear in the Masque are spirits,
replies:

> Spirits, which by mine art
> I have from their confines called to enact
> My present fancies.

(Ibid.)

In other words, Prospero, who represents the hierophant, claims to have called forth the deities by magic.
Observe that Taylor explicitly adds that the pagan
world almost universally credited the hierophant with
the power of magical evocation; but, although Shakespeare represents Prospero as making this claim, we
can hardly think that he actually believed, like the
ancients, in the supernatural power of the hierophant.
On the contrary, we may fairly suppose that the Poet
(if he had the pagan rites in mind at all when he wrote
*The Tempest*) would come to the only rational conclusion open to any student of the Mysteries—namely,
that the vision presented before the aspirant was in
reality nothing more than a mechanically contrived
affair, and that the hierophant, in order to make a deep
impression upon the candidate, professed to be able
to evoke the gods themselves by means of magical
power. As a matter of fact, this supposition is not
without some warrant in the text of the Play, as I
shall now show.

Before the Masque begins, Ariel is instructed by
Prospero in the following curious terms:

> I must use you
> In such another trick. Go, bring the rabble,
> O'er whom I give thee power, here to this place.
> Incite them to quick motion. . . .

(Ibid.)

I do not propose to rest any argument upon the fact
that Prospero alludes to the impending vision as a
" trick," because this word may quite reasonably be

held to refer to Prospero's magic art.  But the allusion to " the rabble " is arresting.  It is almost inconceivable that Prospero would speak thus contemptuously of the deities themselves; and even Ariel is markedly disrespectful, for in answer to Prospero's instructions he says:

> Each one, tripping on his toe,
> Will be here with mop and mow.

> (*Ibid.*)

" Mop " and " mow " both signify a grimace.  Moreover, Prospero's contempt is heightened by his peremptory command that Ariel shall " incite them to quick motion."  It is clear, therefore, that neither Prospero nor Ariel holds in much esteem those who are to take part in the Masque.  Furthermore, at the end of the Masque we are told concerning the " spirits " that—

> To a strange, hollow, and confused noise, they heavily vanish (*ibid.*).

Why to a " strange, hollow, and confused noise "? And why " heavily "?  Are these alleged deities really spirits, or are they merely figures or actors who subsequently vanish by means of some cumbrous stage machinery?  We certainly cannot believe that real deities, spirits evoked by magic, would vanish heavily and noisily.

It is not easy to see how the literalist can account for these inconsistencies in the text.  They can, however, be fully explained on one supposition (which I leave the reader to make or not, as he chooses)—viz., that the Poet is giving expression to a view of the pagan rites which presumes that a deception was practised upon the initiate, who was led to believe that the hierophant possessed the magical power of evoking the gods.  For, while we are expressly told with notable exactitude that the " rabble " vanishes in a way which strongly suggests stage machinery, Prospero solemnly assures Ferdinand that he had called forth " spirits " by means of his magic art.

And here a word may be said with regard to Ariel. It would seem that in one of its aspects the part played by Ariel is that of a junior minister who assists the hierophant in the conduct of the initiations. Now, Porphyry records that some of the junior ministers of the Ceres Mysteries of Eleusis were called *bees ;** and this may be compared with the fact that Ariel explicitly associates himself with the bee:

> Where the bee sucks, there suck I.
>
> (Act V., Scene 1.)

Moreover, although I know of no evidence for a positive statement on the subject, it is more than likely that the junior ministers were neither required nor even permitted to participate in that phase of the higher initiation in which the gods were supposed to appear; for the fact that the power of magical evocation was universally credited by the ancients to the hierophant himself strongly suggests that he conducted this part of the ceremony entirely unaided by his subordinates. I mention this for what it is worth, because in the Play Ariel is not allowed to be present during the celestial vision. Before the Masque begins he is dismissed by Prospero with the warning:

> Do not approach
> Till thou dost hear me call. . . .
>
> (Act IV., Scene 1.)

and he is not summoned again until the Masque is ended and the " spirits " have vanished. There will be occasion later for a close analysis of the part of Ariel in its esoteric aspects; but the foregoing two points

* *De Antro Nympharum,* c. 8.

# The Play and the Pagan Rites

form an interesting commentary upon the position he occupies in the exoteric design of the Play.

At the conclusion of the Masque, Prospero (as already noted) remarks to Ferdinand:

> You do look, my son, in a moved sort,
> As if you were dismay'd; be cheerful, sir.
>
> (Ibid.)

There is no special reason why Ferdinand (but not Miranda) should be " dismayed," unless he thinks that what he has just seen were the deities themselves; in which case his state of mind must resemble that of the awed initiate after the *epopteia* (vision) which was the climax of the Greater Initiation. We observe, moreover, that here also, as in the case of the Court Party at the end of the Lesser Initiation, there is the exhortation to " be cheerful."

Then follows the great and famous passage spoken by Prospero:

> These our actors,
> As I foretold you, were all spirits, and
> Are melted into air, into thin air;
> And, like the baseless fabric of this vision,
> The cloud-capped towers, the gorgeous palaces,
> The solemn temples, the great globe itself,
> Yea, all which it inherit, shall dissolve,
> And, like this insubstantial pageant faded,
> Leave not a wrack behind.
>
> (Ibid.)

Now, what are the circumstances in which this splendid speech is made? Prospero has just remembered the plot of Stephano and Trinculo against his life, and we read:

> FER. Your father's in some passion
> That works him strongly,
> MIR.                                      Never till this day
> Saw I him touched with anger so distempered.
>
> (Ibid.)

Yet, despite his anger and the fact that (as he says) "the minute of the plot is almost come," Prospero must needs fall to philosophising. Why, then, does he do so at this very moment? Consider what it is he says to Ferdinand. Is not this speech a brief but complete statement of the doctrine of Idealism, which is generally supposed to have been a feature in the Mysteries?* Commentators have remarked, somewhat ineptly, that Prospero's discourse is an anticipation of the philosophy of Bishop Berkeley; but surely the Poet is looking back to the thought of the ancients rather than forestalling that of the moderns? Indeed, it is a simple matter to show that the lines which immediately follow those just quoted furnish a clear answer to this question.

The pagans undoubtedly regarded initiation not only as a revelation, but also as an awakening. In his work on the Mysteries, Taylor writes that, according to the philosophy of the ancients—

> The soul's punishment and subsistence hereafter is nothing more than a continuation of its state at present, and a transmigration, as it were, from sleep to sleep, and from dream to dream (*op. cit.*, p. 6).

This manifestly implies that the earth-life was regarded as a sleep and a dream. Taylor cites Plotinus as saying of the soul that—

> To be plunged in matter (*i.e.*, to be incarnated) is to descend into Hades, and there fall asleep (*Ennead* I. viii.).

Here again an unexceptionable authority implies that the earth-life was held to be a sleep. Taylor also cites Plato as saying of the man whose rational or in-

* Cf. W. F. C. Wigston, *Bacon, Shakespeare, and the Rosicrucians.* Mr. Wigston makes this same point; but his main thesis differs widely from my own, and more especially from the case I shall presently proceed to formulate.

tellectual faculty does not enable him to " define the idea of good " that—

> In the present life he is sunk in sleep, and conversant with the delusions of dreams (*Repub.* vii.).

Ficinus, likewise, is quoted by Taylor (*op. cit.,* pp. 13–14) to the effect that the ancient theologists considered that those who concern themselves with divine things are awake, but that other men are asleep and engaged in the delusions of dreams.

The meaning of all these passages is the same—viz., that the earth-life is a sleep and the material world a dream. And this is precisely what Prospero tells Ferdinand after enunciating the doctrine of Idealism at the close of the Masque:

> We are such stuff
> As dreams are made on, and our little life
> Is rounded with a sleep.*
>
> (Act IV., Scene 1.)

This doctrine was certainly implied in some way in the Mysteries. For full awakening from the sleep of the earth-life is achieved not only by the exercise of the intellectual faculty (as Plato says), and by the contemplation of divine things (as Ficinus says), but also by initiation into the Mysteries. In the Introduction to Thomas Taylor's dissertation it is declared that—

> The earth-life is a dream rather than a reality. In this state, and *previous to the discipline of education and the mystical initiation,* the rational or intellectual element, which Paul denominates the spiritual, is asleep (*op. cit.,* xvii.).†

In other words, the mystical initiation involves an awakening from sleep and from the dream of the earth-life. This, on the hypothesis that *The Tempest* is an

* " Rounded " here means surrounded or encompassed.
† Cited by Wigston.

account of initiation, would explain the entire speech of Prospero at the close of the Masque. For Prospero, in order to complete the initiation of Ferdinand, must " awaken " him. He therefore accords him a vision of the gods, to turn his mind to those divine things which are the only realities, and he disillusions him concerning the things of this world. He tells him that our (earth) life is encompassed with a sleep, and that all the beauties and the glories of the material world are but the delusions of dreams—phantasms that will fade away and vanish like the baseless fabric of an insubstantial pageant of spirits.

Thus, in enunciating the doctrine of Idealism, Prospero is " awakening " Ferdinand and so completing his mystical initiation. And all this occurs at the close of a celestial vision, such as was presented to the initiate in the pagan Greater Mysteries, and while Ferdinand is in a place that is expressly declared to be Paradise.

Nothing in the Play is too small to merit our attention. Let us, therefore, consider how Prospero prefaces his discourse on Idealism:

> Our revels now are ended.
> (Act IV., Scene 1.)

Nowhere else in his works does the Poet use the word " revels " in any but its popular and debased sense, as riotous festivity. He must, therefore, quite consciously have used it on the present occasion with a special and purer meaning; and I suggest that the word is here employed in the sense of the Greek ὄργια (orgies). For not only is the debased meaning of " revels " the same as the debased meaning of " orgies " (viz., riotous festivity), but the pure meaning of both words is the same—viz., the rites of the Mysteries. We frequently find the word " revels " used in this latter sense. For instance, in the Apocryphal *Wisdom of Solomon* there is reference to—

> Slaughtering children in solemn rites, or celebrating secret mysteries, or holding frantic revels of strange ordinances (xiv. 23).*

The frantic abandon displayed during the ὄργια (orgies or revels) in the decadent phase of the ancient Mysteries was the cause of the debasement of the two words; but the strict meaning of both is " mystic rites." It is, therefore, a perfectly sound suggestion that when Prospero says " Our revels now are ended " he means simply what the hierophant might be expected to say to the candidate after the celestial vision with which the higher initiation culminated.

I have shown that, with the close of the Masque and the enunciation of the doctrine of Idealism, the initiation of Ferdinand is completed. He is then, but not till then, invited to enter the Cell of Prospero:

> If you be pleased, retire into my cell.
> (Act IV., Scene 1.)

It is noteworthy that no one else is permitted to enter the Cell throughout the entire action of the Play, while the initiation scheme is being treated. Only at the end of the Play, when the Poet's design has been quite completed and the threads have to be drawn together for a suitable dramatic finale, are the others (including Caliban, Stephano, and Trinculo) permitted to enter. It will be noticed that the Court Party is invited only to " look in " when the entrance of the Cell opens (V. 1).

Nothing is told us in the text concerning the nature of the Cell, save that it is " weather-fended by a line-

---

* This is the version set forth in 1611, so that " revels " was, undoubtedly, used in Shakespeare's day to signify the rites of the Mysteries.

grove" (V. 1. 10); and there is no reason to suppose, nor is it at all likely, that the Cell is anything more than a natural cave.

Now, caves have always been closely associated with the Mysteries. In the Thirteenth Book of the *Odyssey*, Homer describes the Cave of the Nymphs at Ithaca, and he says that a branching olive throws its boughs across the head of this sacred cave—a circumstance of which the "weather-fending line-grove" is somewhat reminiscent. An important and illuminating treatise on this Cave of the Nymphs was written by Porphyry, in the course of which the following passages occur:

> The Persians . . . initiate the mystic (or him who is admitted to the arcane sacred rites) in a place which they denominate a cavern. For, as Eubulus says, Zoroaster was the first who consecrated in the neighbouring mountains of Persia a spontaneously produced cave (c. 2).
>
> After this Zoroaster likewise, it was usual with others to perform the rites pertaining to the Mysteries in caverns and dens, whether spontaneously produced or made by hands (c. 3).
>
> Caves, therefore, in the most remote periods of antiquity were consecrated to the gods (c. 9) (*De Antro Nympharum*).

Caves, then, are associated with the Mysteries; and the intimacy of the association is indicated by the fact that the Latin *arca* means a "cave" or "cell," while *arcana* (literally " the things of the cave ") signifies " the Mysteries."

True, Porphyry says that the Persians actually conducted their mystic ceremonies in a cave, whereas in the Play Prospero does not admit Ferdinand into his Cell (Cave) until his initiation has been completed. But I shall have occasion later on to show, from textual evidence, that Prospero's Cell is rather the *sanctum sanctorum*, which may be entered only after full initiation. In any case, it is clear from the foregoing that caves, such as we must suppose the apartment of

# The Play and the Pagan Rites

Prospero to be, were consecrated to mystic rites, and that the initiate was brought into a cave either during or at the end of his initiation. And in the Play it is "before the Cell of Prospero" that all the principal initiation incidents take place—viz., the celestial spectacle accorded to Ferdinand, the repentance and " self-finding " of the Court Party, and the final confusion of Stephano and Trinculo.

At the end of the Play Ferdinand, speaking of Prospero, says:

> This famous Duke of Milan,
> Of whom so often I have heard renown,
> But never saw before; of whom I have
> Received a second life. . . .
>
> (Act V., Scene 1.)

*Received a second life !* These are surely very curious words, which a literal reading of the Play can in nowise explain. Even a poetical hyperbole should be right in essence, though it be wrong in degree. But, from the standpoint of the present thesis, the words are neither wrong in essence, nor even excessive in degree; for *death and rebirth*, as we gather from Apuleius,* are the distinguishing features of the last stage of initiation—the stage through which Ferdinand passes.

It will be remembered that in the same Scene Gonzalo, speaking for the Court Party, says:

> All of us [found] ourselves,
> When no man was his own.
>
> (*Ibid.*)

In this " self-finding " consists the Lesser Initiation, as the Greater consists in " receiving a second life." Subsequent pages will fully explain this distinction;

---

* *Metam.* xi. Apuleius distinctly states that in the last stage of his initiation into the Isiac Mysteries he was " born again " (*renatus*)

57

but from what has already been said it should be manifest that, while the Lesser Initiation was concerned with life and purgation from sin, the Greater Initiation was concerned with death and rebirth. For, as in the former the aspirant trod the winding paths of an intricate maze that signified our mortal life,* and came at last through repentance to that clarity of intellect which is self-finding and self-mastery, so in the latter he was deemed to go through the grave itself, that thereby he might come face to face with the gods and learn the ultimate mysteries of existence.

It will, I think, be conceded that the proposition I laid down with regard to Ferdinand has been substantially proved; but, before proceeding to examine the part played by Miranda, I wish to point out that I have consistently refrained from committing myself to the opinion that Shakespeare deliberately copied the pagan rites. The foregoing comparisons are made solely for the purpose of establishing that *The Tempest* does indeed correspond very closely to the ancient initiation ritual; and in a subsequent chapter I shall show that this correspondence may quite well be due to some other factor than that of design. No doubt the conclusion is inevitable that there was some measure of conscious design on the Poet's part in the case of Miranda, if the interpretation I am about to put forward in respect of her character and her rôle be accepted. But, so far as the very numerous comparisons I have made with the pagan rites are

* Cf. Stobaeus, already cited. True, I have argued that the Lesser Initiation comprised a passage through Purgatory, generally known as a " Descent into Hell "; but it does not follow that a ritual death was implicit in this Degree. Indeed, an essential feature of the traditional " Descent into Hell " is that it is made by one who is still alive—a point that will be explained in due course.

concerned, I repeat once more—explicitly, and with all the emphasis at my command—that my main theory does not necessarily require the reader to believe that Shakespeare deliberately contrived the resemblances which have been noted, or, indeed, to presume even that he knew anything whatever about the mystic rites of the pagan world.

Now, having regard to the allegorical character I am imputing to the Play, which certainly cannot be adequately explained on any other basis, there is no great initial improbability in the suggestion that Miranda personifies an abstract idea; and I am prepared to submit a large volume of textual evidence in support of the contention that in one of her aspects she personifies Wisdom (Sophia) or Truth—the " bride " of the initiate.

Throughout mythology and tradition there recurs the concept of a Celestial and Immaculate Lady, who is often represented as the beloved and bride of the aspiring human spirit—as the Church is said to be the " bride " of Christ.* The many particular versions of this general concept do not all agree in every respect, nor have they all precisely the same significance. Different men woo different ideals, although to each his own may be the highest and the purest which he can conceive. To the philosopher the " beloved of the spirit " is Wisdom or Truth; to the priest she is the perfect Church; to the statesman she is Service; to the poet she is pure Beauty; and so on. Yet, after all, these are but different aspects of that same archetypal ideal of perfection which I shall hereafter denominate the Celestial Bride.

From certain broad resemblances it may be premised that among the many versions of the Celestial Bride are the Egyptian Isis, the Babylonian Ishtar, the

---

* *Rev.* xxi. 2 and 9; *ibid.* xxii. 17; etc.

Hebrew Shechinah, the Gnostic Sophia, and the Greek Aphrodite Ourania. Another version is found in the Bride of Lebanon, if (as many have thought) the *Song of Songs* be allegorical in character; while in *Proverbs* the Celestial Bride is explicitly called Wisdom. She is the prototype of the German Brunhilde, bride of the mythical hero Siegfried; of the Persian Arduizur, the " beloved " of Zoroaster; and of Dante's idealised Beatrice, the " most gentle Lady " whom he expressly identifies with the Bride of Lebanon and with Wisdom.* In allusion to the remote and seemingly inaccessible perfection which she personifies, she is generally represented as being heavily veiled, as in the case of Isis and Beatrice; and, like Isis and the Bride of Lebanon, she is often held to be black of face, though comely beyond compare and utterly without defect.† She is at once both sister and bride, as we find in the case

---

\* With the Bride of Lebanon in *Purgatorio* xxx., and with Wisdom in his *Convito* frequently. Dante sometimes calls his Lady Wisdom and sometimes Philosophy. In the *Convito* (III. xi.) he says that, like Pythagoras, he is a " Lover of Sophia," and that his Lady is therefore " Philosophy." This is a curious conception, because Sophia is properly Wisdom. Philosophy is love for Sophia, rather than Sophia herself.

I take it that no serious thinker really supposes Dante's Lady to be simply the historical Beatrice Portinari and nothing more. Such a supposition is practically excluded by the prevailing tone of his allusions to her—especially in the *Convito* and in the *Vita Nuova*, in which latter he calls her " the glorious lady of my mind." Other allusions of the same sort will presently be cited.

† That Isis was reputed black is well known. Compare the case of the Bride of Lebanon in the *Song*, i. 5-6. Isis, of course, was utterly immaculate; compare the case of the Bride of Lebanon in the *Song*, iv. 7.

If any reader be unalterably convinced that the *Song of Songs* is merely an extravagant Eastern love song or play, he may ignore the few references I make to it; for, although they are not without interest in the present connection, they are not in any sense vital to my main contention.

# The Play and the Pagan Rites

of Isis, of Dante's Lady, of Wisdom, and of the Bride of Lebanon.*

The case I am about to formulate is that Miranda is a version of the " beloved of the spirit " as Wisdom or Truth; and that, as such, she may be equated with any or all of these other versions I have mentioned. Full initiation, whether ritual or empirical, must always involve a union, implicit or explicit, between the aspirant and the Celestial Bride; and it is this union which is represented by the marriage of Ferdinand and Miranda in the Play. That the pagan candidate was deemed to be wedded to Wisdom or Truth in the Greater Initiation will be argued fully in a later chapter. For the moment, it will suffice to point out that a passage in the *Book of Ecclesiasticus* clearly implies that Wisdom is the " beloved and bride " of the initiate. The passage in question has all the features of a reference to initiation, for it speaks of " straight and crooked paths " (the " forthrights and meanders " of the Play), and of the disciplinary trials and labours which her lover has to undergo before Wisdom reveals her secrets to him.†

In the *Wisdom of Solomon* we read that Solomon determined to take Wisdom as his bride‡—as Ferdinand resolves to take Miranda; that Wisdom is " initiated into the knowledge of God "§—as Miranda must be, for she shares with Ferdinand the supreme privilege of the celestial vision; and that Wisdom " will toil with me "||—as Miranda offers to toil with Ferdinand.

---

* Of Isis this is traditional. Of Dante's Lady, see *Convito* III. xii. Of Wisdom, see *Wisd. Sol.* viii. 2 and 9, and *Prov.* vii. 4. Of the Bride of Lebanon, see *Song* iv. 9-12 and v. 1.

† *Ecclus.* iv. 17-19. I shall presently recur to this passage, giving reasons for regarding the phrase " reveals her secrets " as an essential and significant part of the sexual allegory of the " bride."

‡ viii. 2 and 9.　　　　§ viii. 4.　　　　|| ix. 10.

# Shakespeare's Mystery Play

In the *Song of Songs* we read of a Lover and his Bride, who are generally held to represent Christ and the Church, but who may equally well represent Solomon and Wisdom. In either case, the protagonists are types of the aspirant and of the pure ideal to which he is wedded in initiation. It will be noticed that the Lover is depicted as saying of his Bride:

Who is she that looketh forth as the morning? . . . (vi. 10).

This simile (like others in the *Song*) is not chosen at random, for the Celestial Bride is often associated with Morning. For example, the Egyptian Isis is practically identical with Hathor, who is the Dawn; and it is immemorial that Wisdom, like the Dawn, comes from the East. In the Play Ferdinand distinctly associates Miranda with Morning:

> 'Tis fresh morning with me
> When you are by, at night.
> (Act III., Scene 1.)

It may be demurred that this link with the *Song of Songs* is probably accidental and certainly slender. Then let the critic observe that in the very next speech of Ferdinand there is a singularly frank and quite gratuitous confession concerning numerous other women—a confession made in a context praising Miranda in the most extravagant terms as being utterly without defect, perfect, and peerless:

> Admired Miranda,
> Indeed the top of admiration; worth
> What's dearest to the world! Full many a lady
> I have eyed with best regard, and many a time
> The harmony of their tongues hath into bondage
> Brought my too diligent ear; for several virtues
> Have I liked several women; never any
> With so full soul, but some defect in her

62

Did quarrel with the noblest grace she owed
And put it to the foil; but you, O you,
So perfect, and so peerless, are created
Of every creature's best !

(Ibid.)

Is it not curious that the Lover in the Song of Songs should make precisely the same kind of confession in the course of his extravagant praise of his Bride as being the choice one, the undefiled; and that this should occur immediately before his use of the simile of Morning?   For we read:

There are threescore queens, and fourscore concubines, and virgins without number.

My dove, my undefiled, is but one; she is the only one of her mother, rhe is the choice one of her that bare her. . . .

Who is she that looketh forth as the morning? . . .

(Song vi. 8-10.)

Here is a notable coincidence.   I am contending that Miranda is the Celestial Bride, as Wisdom; and we find that two consecutive speeches by Ferdinand concerning Miranda embody exactly the same curious and unexpected allusions as three consecutive verses relating to the Bride in the Song.   And there are certainly some grounds for regarding the Bride in the Song as the Celestial Bride.   For not only is she identified by the Oxford Bible with the Church, as the " bride " of Christ, but also she is identified by Dante with Beatrice; and moreover, she resembles Dante's " most gentle Lady " (Wisdom) in that both are said to be, like Isis, simultaneously sister and spouse.*

* In fact, Dante explicitly declares (Convito II. xv. fin.) that the Bride in the Song is the Divine Science.   He also declares that the other women in the Song—the queens, concubines, and virgins—represent the lower sciences.   I prefer to interpret these other women more widely as representing all those things which appeal to the lower faculties of man; but, in any case, what Dante says of this passage in the Song confirms the essential principle of the present argument.

63

# Shakespeare's Mystery Play

Any thoughtful person must, I think, be struck by the strangeness of Ferdinand's speech. Why should he exalt Miranda by talking of the defects of other women he has loved? More particularly, why should he emphasise that these other women have been many and he himself a willing slave to their charms? Surely the speech has a powerful flavour of allegory? To these questions my theory offers a full and adequate answer. As in the case of the perfect Bride of Lebanon and the women without number, the contrast between the peerless Miranda and the numerous ladies whose sweet smooth tongues have many a time held Ferdinand a willing captive represents the contrast between the aspirant's lofty white ideal and those countless worldly and sensuous pleasures which too often hold down his winged spirit in the bondage of dalliance.

There is abundant reason for this interpretation, which all the rest of my case supports. For, just as the great white ideal (be it Wisdom, or Truth, or Service) is traditionally depicted as a Celestial and Immaculate Lady, so those false and facile pleasures of the senses which snare and enslave the spirit of the aspirant are traditionally allegorised under the figure of sweet-voiced alluring women. The true initiate is wholly devoted to the purest ideal it is in his power to attain. His spirit has finally escaped from the siren voices and winged its upward way to the Celestial Lady—or, as it is expressed in *Proverbs*, by his devotion to wisdom he is delivered from bondage to that " strange woman " whose snare is a tongue sweet as honey and smooth as oil.* *In the confession*

* *Prov.* ii. 10, 16; v. 1-3; vii. 4, 5 and 22, 23. It needs but little imagination to perceive that these verses refer allegorically to the pleasures of the senses, rather than literally to the actual harlot. This point will be more fully dealt with in a later note.

*of Ferdinand when he first meets Miranda we have an exact parallel to the confession of Dante when he meets his lost Beatrice.* And the context in this latter case clearly indicates that the meaning is precisely that which I am imputing to the speech of Ferdinand in the Play; for, since in the passage in question Beatrice undoubtedly personifies Wisdom, the other women Dante has loved must personify those sensuous pleasures which are the meretricious rivals of Wisdom in the affections of frail mankind. The confession of Ferdinand to Miranda, like that of Dante to Beatrice, represents a phase in the universal psychology of aspiration. It is the recognition of past weakness and dalliance—the confession made by the contrite spirit when, soaring upward from the siren pleasures of the senses, it gazes upon the austerely veiled and immaculate " beloved " who is the ideal to which it is ultimately wedded in initiation.*

Of Wisdom it is frequently said in the Bible that she is above gold and silver and rubies.† And in *Proverbs* we read:

> She is more precious than rubies: and all the things thou canst desire are not to be compared unto her (iii. 15).

---

* Cf. *Purgatorio* xxx. and xxxi., in which the theme is obviously aspiration, conceived as an upward flight to the ideal. In Canto xxxi. the veiled Beatrice, answering Dante's confession, speaks of the fleeting pleasures which young damsels confer, of sirens, and of the weighing down of the wings with which he should have risen up to her. Moreover, she uses the same metaphor of the arrow which occurs in *Proverbs* (vi. 23) in connection with him who yields to the " strange woman "; and this is followed by the very words of *Prov.* i. 17, about the net spread in the eyes of the bird. It is clear, then, that Beatrice is here Wisdom, and that the other women Dante has loved —the sirens who seduced him from his higher and purer devotion— are those fleeting sensuous pleasures of which it may be said, as of the sirens and the " strange woman," that their " lips drop as honey, but their end is bitter " (cf. *Prov.* v. 3-4).

† *Prov.* iii. 14-15, viii. 10-11, and 19; *Job* xxviii. 15-19; etc.

# Shakespeare's Mystery Play

In like manner, Ferdinand calls Miranda "precious creature"; says that she is "worth what's dearest to the world"; and exclaims:

> I,
> Beyond all limit of what else in the world
> Do love, prize, honour you.
>
> (Act III., Scene 1.)

When he vows to take her as his bride, Ferdinand says to Prospero:

> As I hope
> For quiet days, fair issue, and long life. . . .
>
> (Act IV., Scene 1.)

Which may be compared with the blessings that are said to fall upon him who is united to Wisdom:

> 16. Length of days is in her right hand; and in her left hand riches and honour.
> 17. Her ways are ways of pleasantness, and all her paths are peace.
>
> (*Prov.* iii.)

And again: at the moment when Ferdinand first sees Miranda he is bewildered by the magic music around him. We may reasonably suppose that he has a feeling of insecurity in the place to which he is come, for he exclaims: "This is no mortal business." Observe, then, his first words to Miranda:

> Vouchsafe, my prayer
> May know if you remain upon this island,
> And that you will some good instructions give
> How I may bear me here.
>
> (Act I., Scene 2.)

Is this not a remarkable appeal, addressed by a man and a prince to a young girl? Why does Ferdinand ask for guidance from Miranda, rather than from Prospero, who is also present? Now, it is written in *Ecclesiasticus* concerning Wisdom that "he that

66

giveth heed unto her shall dwell securely "; and in *Proverbs*, likewise, Wisdom is represented as saying:

> Whoso hearkeneth unto me shall dwell safely, and shall be quiet from fear of evil (i. 33).

What, then, is more appropriate than that Ferdinand, finding himself in strange incomprehensible surroundings, should ask for " good instructions how to bear himself " from one whose prototype is no other than Wisdom herself?

All these are, to say the least, interesting parallels. True, not one of them would be very striking or suggestive if it stood alone; but the importance of each increases as their number multiplies. Furthermore, the case I have made out with regard to Ferdinand necessitates this view of Miranda before any textual confirmation is sought for at all. Ferdinand, of whom she is the beloved and bride, is (as I have shown) the initiate into the Greater Mysteries; and the " majestic vision " which constitutes his Greater Initiation is in token of his union with her.* That Miranda is a version of the Celestial Bride is, therefore, predetermined by the earlier part of my argument; and this fact must very greatly enhance the value of any evidence based upon direct textual references to her in the Play.

It may be objected that the parallels I have just shown have no special significance, because in each case all that is involved is the universal language of lovers. But the matter is far too complex to be dismissed in this way. For instance, in the very first speech of Ferdinand to Miranda he thus addresses her:

> O you wonder.
>
> (Act I., Scene 2.)

Even if this phrase be no more than a lover's unthinking hyperbole, we cannot overlook a striking coin-

---

* This is three times affirmed during the Masque.

cidence; for the word *miranda* means literally "wonderful woman" (Latin, *mirandus*). Yet Ferdinand is not consciously making play with this fact, for he uses the phrase in question before he knows her name. Clearly, then, Miranda is essentially " wondrous," quite apart from her lover's fervid estimate; and we may inquire why this is her distinctive quality.

Now, a " wonder " is a rarity, something unique —as Shakespeare frequently implies.* The phrase " O you wonder," therefore, means " O you rare unique thing." Moreover, the Latin *mirandus* has also the meaning of " unique "; so that *miranda* means literally " unique woman." Apart, then, from the evidence already adduced, Miranda by her very name is, like the Bride of Lebanon, "but one, the only one, the choice one "; and it is her rareness, emphasised both in her name and in the words of Ferdinand, that makes her, like Wisdom, " more precious than rubies" and above everything else that can be desired in the world.

This is not a piece of special pleading, for the " wondrous " nature of Miranda is stressed to a quite extraordinary degree in the text. When Ferdinand learns her name, he exclaims:

> Admire Miranda,
> Indeed, the top of admiration; worth
> What's dearest to the world.
>
> (Act III., Scene 1.)

The word " admire " refers properly to the emotion of wonder, and is often used by Shakespeare in this sense.† There is a clear instance in *The Tempest*; for,

* E.g., *Much Ado*, V. 4. 70; *Shrew*, III. 2. 96-8; 1 *Hen. IV.*, III. 2. 46-7; *Tempest*, V. 1. 181-4; etc. Ferdinand himself implies that rareness is the essence of a wonder when he calls Prospero " so rare a wonder'd father " (IV. 1).

† E.g., *Hen. VIII.*, V. 5. 40-3; *Winter's Tale*, V. 2. 11-8; *All's Well*, II. 1. 91-2; *Hamlet*, I. 2. 192-5; etc.

when the members of the Court Party are struck with wonder at meeting the lost Duke of Milan, he remarks:

> I perceive these lords
> At this encounter do so much admire. . . .
>
> (Act V., Scene 1.)

In view, therefore, of the other considerations I have just advanced, it would seem that the exclamation of Ferdinand on learning Miranda's name is intended to emphasise yet again her essential quality (viz., wonder-provoking); for it means—

> Wondrous woman, wondered at, you are the height of wonder. . . .

And, since a " wonder " is a rarity, Miranda is the height of rarity. She is the rarest of all rare things. Thus again she is, like Wisdom, above gold and silver and rubies—in Ferdinand's words she is " worth what's dearest to the world." Furthermore, as Plato points out:

> (The emotion of) wonder is the special affection of the philosopher, for philosophy has no other starting-point than this (*Theaetetus*, 155 D).*

That is to say, Love for Wisdom (" philosophy ") always begins with the emotion of wonder, precisely as Ferdinand's love for Miranda begins with the wonder he expresses at first sight of her, and which he expresses again so strongly at their second encounter.

From the foregoing we perceive that there is a marked resemblance between Miranda and the Wisdom (Sophia) whom Dante's Beatrice personifies. Let us

---

* Cf. R. M. Theobald, M.A., *Shakespeare Studies in Baconian Light*, VI. Mr. Theobald argues that there is identity between the views of Shakespeare and Bacon on the subject of Wonder; but, whilst admitting that he proves this point (for what it is worth), I am especially anxious to dissociate this present study from the controversy as to the authorship of Shakespeare's works.

next see whether there is any direct resemblance between Miranda and Beatrice, the " glorious lady of the mind."

I have shown that Ferdinand's confession to Miranda is the exact counterpart of Dante's confession to Beatrice; and this is perhaps the most important piece of evidence—if not, indeed, all that is required. Nevertheless, there are other points worthy of notice. For example, according to the *Convito*, the Lady of Dante—

lives in Heaven (II. viii.), and her aspect brings us the joys of Paradise (II. viii., xv.).

This may be compared with the fact that (as in the case of Beatrice and Dante) Miranda is with Ferdinand during the celestial vision, when he declares " this place Paradise."  At an earlier stage I gave his words as they appear in the 1623 Folio;* but the comparison I am now making is accentuated if the later and more popular reading be accepted:

> So rare a wonder'd father and *a wife*
> Makes this place Paradise.
>
> (Act IV., Scene 1.)

Of his Lady, Dante makes the exceedingly curious declaration that she—

is of " marvellous aspect " and is " visibly miraculous " (III. vii.). He is " content to call her face a Miracle " (III. xiv.).

Now, a marvel or a miracle is a wonder—something rare or unique, which provokes the emotion of wonder; and Shakespeare distinctly implies as much in *Hamlet*, I. 2. 192–5.  Dante's Lady is, therefore, what Shake-

---

* So rare a wonder'd father and *a wise*
  Makes this place Paradise.
>
> (Act IV., Scene 1.)

The difference between *s* and *f* in the old type is so small that confusion easily arises between them.

speare would call " a wonder "; and in this very strange respect she resembles the " wondrous " Miranda. Furthermore, when Dante seeks to express the worth of his Lady, he says that—

he " considered himself lower than that Lady " (III. i.); that " the exalted nature of my Lady surpasses all " (III. iv.); that his " words are far below the dignity of this Lady " (*ibid.*), and that " not only is this Lady the most perfect in the human race, but more than the most perfect " (III. vi.).

In much the same extravagance of language does Ferdinand speak of Miranda. She is " precious creature "; he prizes her " beyond all limit of what else in the world "; she is " perfect and peerless "; unlike all other women, she is utterly without defect; she is " worth what's dearest to the world "; she is " created of every creature's best." Moreover, she resembles the Lady of Dante (*gentilissima Donna*) in respect of her exceeding gentleness;

> O, she is
> Ten times more gentle than her father's crabbed.
> (Act III., Scene I.)

Again, Dante speaks of the peace his Lady brings (III. xiii.); and Ferdinand, as already noted, implies that Miranda, like Wisdom, will bring him long life and peaceful days. It may be added that Miranda, making a forced and quite gratuitous allusion to her modesty, exclaims:

> But, by my modesty
> (The jewel in my dower) . . .
> (*Ibid.*)

And Dante, using the same metaphor, likewise remarks that his Lady is " adorned with modesty " (III. xiii.).

In a later section I shall consider other aspects of Miranda, but for the present it is enough to regard her in the light of the foregoing evidence. Whatever may be held to be the inner meaning of the *Divina Commedia,* something of the same sort seems to be implied in *The Tempest.* It may be said that I have somewhat exceeded the limits originally prescribed for this chapter in entering upon this analysis of Miranda without first establishing quite definitely—(*a*) that the candidate in the pagan Greater Initiation was deemed to be united to Wisdom or Truth, and (*b*) that there is some connection, some fundamental similarity, between the *Divina Commedia* and the pagan rites. Strictly speaking, the objection is valid; and a word should be said, therefore, in explanation of the position I have taken up.

The whole drift of the later part of this study is that the successive experiences undergone during formal admission to the ancient Mysteries were exactly analogous at every point with those successive psychological experiences which constitute what may be called empirical initiation. This latter consists simply in the successful quest and wooing of Wisdom or Truth by the philosopher. Hence it follows—(*a*) that the pagan aspirant was by ritual representation a philosopher, or "Lover of Wisdom," and (*b*) that the *Divina Commedia,* in so far as it is an account of empirical initiation, must inevitably have some essential similarity, whether intended by Dante or not, with the pagan rites. For the sake of clarity and sequence, I refrain from any attempt to prove these several propositions here and now. I could do so only by anticipating large and important parts of the esoteric argument, and this would have the effect of confusing the presentation of the case. But the broad indication I have just given as to the lines on which my case will presently run suffices to explain why I have looked to find Miranda a personification of Wisdom and a counterpart to the idealised Beatrice of Dante.

# The Play and the Pagan Rites

With this view of Miranda, let us now consider the method adopted by Prospero for testing Ferdinand's love. Commentators have all (so far as I am aware) been quite satisfied that the imposition upon Ferdinand of log-piling labours is a perfectly reasonable method of testing his devotion to Miranda; yet a critical and non-sentimental analysis of the text soon reveals a number of peculiarities that stand in need of explanation.

In the first place, it will be noticed that Prospero expressly disclaims any surprise at the immediate mutual love of Ferdinand and Miranda, for he remarks:

> So glad of this as they I cannot be,
> Who are surprised withal.
>
> (Act III., Scene 1.)

Evidently Prospero quite expected this to happen. Moreover, it was Ariel who contrived it:

> It goes on, I see,
> As my soul prompts it.   Spirit, fine spirit, I'll free thee
> Within two days for this.
>
> (Act I., Scene 2.)

> At the first sight
> They have changed eyes; delicate Ariel,
> I'll set thee free for this.
>
> (*Ibid.*)

> Thou hast done well, fine Ariel!
>
> (*Ibid.*)

It seems reasonably clear that Ferdinand and Miranda promptly fell in love as the result of a definite plan prearranged by Prospero and carried into effect by his agent Ariel. Nevertheless, although Prospero is responsible for what has happened, its further development is to be impeded:

> This swift business
> I must uneasy make, lest too light winning
> Make the prize light.
>
> (*Ibid.*)

73

# Shakespeare's Mystery Play

Prospero therefore makes Ferdinand pile up logs, eat withered roots, and drink sea water; though what, precisely, all this has to do with his love for Miranda is not intimated at the time to Ferdinand, nor is the point very clear to the reader. That it was indeed a love-test is not explained by Prospero until it is over:

> All thy vexations
> Were but my trials of thy love, and thou
> Hast strangely stood the test.
>
> (Act IV., Scene 1.)

Now, quite apart from the fact that Ferdinand can hardly be held to prove his love for Miranda by facing hardships which he has no reason to suppose have any reference to her, we must observe (what all commentators conveniently ignore) that he strove to resist these " vexations " and that they were forced upon him by Prospero (I. 2. 465 ff.). But what sort of a love-test is this? Surely the very essence of any test is that the person tested should retain complete liberty of choice? First Ferdinand is caused to fall in love with Miranda, and then his love is " tested " by trials which have no manifest relation to her and in which he is entirely deprived of all liberty of choice. True, he remarks to Miranda, " for your sake am I this patient log-man " (III. 1. 66–7); but he says this after he has been coerced by Prospero, so that he seems here to be making a virtue of necessity. Furthermore, notwithstanding that he resisted these trials until he was overcome by the powerful authority of Prospero, he is subsequently told that he has " strangely stood the test."

Everyone must, on a moment's reflection, admit that this portion of the story of Ferdinand and Miranda appears to be exceedingly sententious and confused. It seems to be true neither to sound sentiment nor to sound practical reason. Its several parts do not seem

74

to be true even to each other. It has, in fact, precisely those defects of artificiality which can so often be observed in the outward forms of purely allegorical works, where the author's freedom of creation is restricted by the exigencies of a paramount purpose. How far, then, can the faults I have emphasised be explained on the present hypothesis—namely, that the Play deals allegorically with the same ideas as those upon which the ancient rites of initiation were based?

Let us consider the matter in the light of the supposition that the relations of Ferdinand with Prospero correspond (intentionally or otherwise) to those of the pagan novitiate with the hierophant. What does this supposition imply? It implies that Ferdinand must be compelled by Prospero, as the ritual aspirant was compelled by the hierophant, to undergo certain labours and hardships symbolical of (though not necessarily identical with) those which every genuine philosopher must undergo before he can win Wisdom or Truth; and it further implies that, when these perfunctory and quite arbitrary " trials " are ended, Ferdinand must receive from Prospero a perfect and peerless bride who has been preordained for him, and between whom and himself a mutual attachment has been contrived and stimulated—as in the case of the ritual initiate and his " bride " (Wisdom or Truth).

All this is exactly what we find in the Play. From the story of Ferdinand and Miranda, therefore, some considerable presumption accrues in favour of the main theory which I shall presently seek to establish— namely, that Shakespeare, if he had not consciously in mind the pagan initiatory rites, must have had in mind some prototypical conception to which those rites conformed. Is there any other view of the Play which explains equally well the superficial defects to which I have called attention?

75

# Shakespeare's Mystery Play

It may be added that the words used by Prospero in bestowing Miranda upon Ferdinand seem to acquire an added significance when they are considered from a similar standpoint:

> If I have too austerely punished you,
> Your compensation makes amends, for I
> Have given you here a thread of mine own life,
> Or that for which I live; whom once again
> I tender to thy hand.   All thy vexations
> Were but my trials of thy love, and thou
> Hast strangely stood the test: here, afore Heaven,
> I ratify this my rich gift.   O Ferdinand,
> Do not smile at me that I boast her off,
> For thou shalt find she will outstrip all praise
> And make it halt behind her.
>
> (Ibid.)

Here, again, those superlative terms in which Wisdom is so often spoken of are applied to Miranda; and this time it is certainly not a case of amorous extravagance of language, for it is Miranda's father who is speaking. Observe, too, that even for Prospero she is " that for which I live."

There has already been occasion to mention the passage in *Ecclesiasticus* (iv. 17–19) wherein Wisdom is represented as the beloved of the aspirant, whom she encourages in his trials, and to whom she finally unveils herself, revealing her secrets. The same allegory occurs in the *Zohar*, which describes how a deeply veiled lady attracts her lover by signs and hints, and how she finally unveils herself and entrusts him with her secrets.* This Veiled Lady is evidently a personification of Truth, in its particular aspect as the Secret Doctrine which the tradition of Jewish mysticism postulates for the Bible. Now, there is no reason to suppose that an allegory of this kind would be only partially developed. On the contrary, it

* Cf. Isaac Myer's *Quabbalah.*

76

# The Play and the Pagan Rites

would almost certainly be carried to its natural and obvious end. In other words, if every phase of the relation between the aspirant and the Hidden Truth (or Wisdom) be expressed in these allegorical terms of a lover and his beloved, then the last stage of initiation—which involves the fulfilment of the aspirant's desire—must necessarily be represented as involving a consummated marriage, figurative of the complete union of the aspirant with Truth. This conclusion not only accounts for the " mystical marriage " of the ancient ritual initiation, but it also imparts a certain special meaning (which I need not define in words) to the statement in the *Zohar* that the beloved woman removes her veil and " reveals her secrets." That the removal of the veil may be understood to have this intimate sexual significance seems to be implied by Dante, who says that the sin of Eve in the Garden of Eden consisted in her refusal to remain under a veil.*

For obvious reasons, the union of Ferdinand and Miranda is not represented as being actually consummated within the period covered by the Play; and in this respect the Poet's allegory does not completely accord with the mystical tradition. Nevertheless, while the consummation is necessarily omitted from the action of the Play, Miranda makes her desire for it clear beyond all doubt. Indeed, she takes a strong initiative in the matter, for she approaches Ferdinand with modest but unequivocal overtures:

> Hence, bashful cunning,
> And prompt me, plain and holy innocence!
> I am your wife, if you will marry me;
> If not, I'll die your maid.
>
> (Act III., Scene 1.)

---

* *Purg.* xxix. 25-7. Compare also Mr. A. E. Waite's *Secret Doctrine in Israel*, which deals very fully with this sexual allegory as it appears in the Zoharic tradition.

# Shakespeare's Mystery Play

Her attitude is thus precisely that of Wisdom in *Ecclesiasticus* and of the Veiled Lady in the *Zohar*; for in both of these other versions it is not the aspirant, but the Lady herself, who takes the initiative and makes the overtures leading to a full and consummated union.

From the standpoint of the literalist, it is not at all clear how the Masque is related to the union of Ferdinand and Miranda; but that some definite relation does exist is several times implied in the text. For instance, after intimating to the lovers his approval of their union, Prospero declares to Ariel with regard to the Masque which immediately follows:

> It is my promise,
> And they expect it of me.
>
> (Act IV., Scene 1.)

Moreover, the " spirits " whom Prospero then evokes three times affirm that they are come " to celebrate a contract of true love." No one will pretend that it is conspicuously apparent why Ferdinand and Miranda should expect their union to be marked in this peculiar manner by Prospero; and, if a reason have to be assigned, it is difficult to see what is to take the place of the present theory. For if the Masque correspond broadly to the celestial vision of the pagan Greater Initiation, it must be understood to be (like the glimpse of Paradise accorded to Dante) apocalyptic in character; and, as such, it has a direct and definite relation to the union of the aspirant with Wisdom or the Hidden Truth.

Among the ritual practices of the ancients was that of crowning the candidate at the close of his initiation. This fact is well known. Stobaeus confirms it in the passage cited by Warburton, who quotes also from Aristophanes to the effect that the initiated were crowned with a wreath of myrtle. Dupuis likewise, in his *Origine de Tous les Cultes*, says that the initiated were crowned with flowers. We may therefore look to find Ferdinand receiving a crown; and, although this does not occur as an incident in the Play, the idea of crowning is expressly referred to by Gonzalo, who exclaims in the last Scene:

> Look down, you gods,
> And on this couple drop a blessed crown.
>                                  (Act V., Scene 1.)

These words may, of course, quite reasonably be held to refer to the temporal crown which Ferdinand will inherit from his father; yet the fact remains that they suffice to complete the evidence required for the case I am presenting. True, Gonzalo implies that Miranda is to share the crown with Ferdinand; but this is as it should be in an allegory of this kind, for it is solely by virtue of his union with Miranda (Wisdom) that Ferdinand receives the " blessed crown " of the fully initiated.*

Aristides, writing of the Mysteries of Eleusis, describes them as " that most appalling and at the same time most entrancing spectacle." This description doubtless alludes to the fact that the rites comprised representations both of Purgatory and of Paradise. The former would belong to the Lesser Mysteries, and the latter to the Greater Mysteries, as I shall have further occasion to demonstrate. And, truly, the Court Party passes through Purgatory, whilst Ferdinand attains to Paradise. To the members of the Court Party the place to which they are brought

* Cf. *Prov.* iv. 8-9, concerning Wisdom: " Exalt her, and she shall promote thee: she shall bring thee to honour, when thou dost embrace her. She shall give to thine head an ornament of grace: a crown of glory shall she deliver to thee."

79

is a " most desolate isle," wherein nothing but repentance and a new resolve can save them from
" lingering perdition "; but to Ferdinand the winning
of Miranda and the spectacle of the gods make " this
place Paradise." The contrast is clear and striking;
and it is of precisely the same nature as the contrast
between the Lesser Initiation and the Greater.

# PART II

F

# CHAPTER I

## *THE MEANING OF INITIATION*

IT is not only natural and legitimate, but also desirable, that some attempt should be made to explain the occurrence of resemblances as numerous and as striking as those which I have shown to exist between *The Tempest* and the mystic rites of initiation. There are only three possible hypotheses; for such resemblances must be due—(i) to deliberate design, (ii) to sheer coincidence, or (iii) to inherent necessity.

The theory that Shakespeare, at the height of his creative power, deliberately collected a number of fragmentary records whose meaning he did not very clearly understand, and ingeniously fitted them together for the simple purpose of illustrating the outward forms of the ancient initiation ceremonies, is not one that is likely to commend itself to any thoughtful mind, however strong may be the appearance in its favour. Yet a very remarkable similarity does undoubtedly exist between the Play and the pagan rites; and this similarity is of a kind and a degree which practically exclude the suggestion that it occurred quite fortuitously and has no special significance. It must, therefore, be mainly (though perhaps not wholly) due to some factor of inherent necessity; and the question arises—Why and to what extent are these resemblances inevitable?

The answer to this question is implied in the propositions I shall now seek to establish—namely, (*a*) that what the ritual initiate cherishes as a recondite secret

83

is, in fact, simply the figurative representation of truths which are known, even if they are not always appreciated, by all mankind; and (*b*) that *The Tempest* is one of the many works of art in which these same truths are expressed. In other words, I shall argue that every authentic initiation ritual is based upon certain permanent realities which are familiar to all the world in art, mythology, and experience; and that any work of art which, like *The Tempest*, deals with these unchanging realities in the appropriate language sanctioned by universal tradition must, therefore, of necessity correspond broadly to the outward forms of ritual initiation.

It is immediately evident, then, that the ensuing pages will serve to explain not only the case of *The Tempest*, but also the case of every other work which has been found to resemble the rites of initiation. Indeed, the ultimate purpose of this study is to show that the inner theme of *The Tempest* is one which is expressed not only in the pagan initiatory rites, but also in such works as Dante's *Divina Commedia*, Virgil's *Aeneid VI.*, Milton's *Paradise Regained*, and Bunyan's *Pilgrim's Progress ;* in such stories as the Wanderings of Israel and the Temptation of Christ in the Wilderness; in the Zoharic tradition; in the Greek, Persian, and Norse mythological cycles; and even in the popular and enduring fairy-tales. In short, I shall show that *The Tempest* is a version of the one epic theme which has appealed irresistibly to the human imagination through all the ages.

Now, there can be no doubt, unless the testimony of the ancients themselves be rejected, that the initiatory rites of the pagan Mysteries were an enigmatical representation of certain religious truths;*

* Cf. remarks towards end of second section (" The Court Party ") in the previous chapter.

and I shall endeavour first to bring those truths to light, and then to show that they form the dominant theme of *The Tempest*. The relation between this argument and what has already been written in the previous chapter is obvious. If it can be demonstrated (*a*) that the pagan rites were an allegory presenting an important moral philosophy, and (*b*) that *The Tempest* presents precisely the same philosophy in the same allegorical medium, then no further explanation is required in respect of many (if not all) of the resemblances which have been noted; for the existence of a sustained similarity between the main features of the Play and the incidents which occurred during ceremonial admission to the Mysteries becomes a matter of inherent necessity—the automatic result of a fundamental identity of thought and expression. Whether at any given point or points this inevitable similarity was consciously accentuated by Shakespeare is entirely a question of evidential values, with regard to which opinions will perhaps differ.

In the attempt to interpret the meaning of what is called Initiation, I shall deal first with the symbolism used alike in the ancient rites and in the Play; and a considerable excursion into matters not commonly associated with the name of Shakespeare is, therefore, unavoidable.

It should be added that, so far as the pagan ceremonies are concerned, I shall confine myself to an examination of their general framework, basing the argument only upon such facts as are positively known on the authority of the ancients themselves. No reference will be made to the opinions expressed by modern commentators, such as Rohde, Wobbermin, Reitzenstein, and others. These relatively recent writers have dealt very thoroughly with the Greek mystery-cults, and have undoubtedly added a large and important mass of conjectural detail to the few definitely known facts; but, in so far as they have any interpretation to offer, they place the whole subject upon a more abstruse plane of thought than the circumstances seem to warrant. According to the view I shall put forward, there is nothing very difficult to understand in the essential ideas underlying the Greek initiatory rites; it is the enigmatical manner in which those ideas are expressed that has invested the rites with an appearance of profound metaphysical obscurity.

## 1. NATURAL SYMBOLISM.

Natural symbolism is the result of man's imperative need for some convenient and appropriate mode of expressing the facts of his own inner experience, and it consists in describing the subjective world in terms peculiar to the objective world. It differs fundamentally from what may be called artificial symbolism; for, whereas the latter presupposes a knowledge of particular systems of thought or belief (as the use of a cross to represent the sacrifice of self in the service of others presupposes a knowledge of the elements of Christian theology), the former presupposes only a familiarity with the permanent conditions in which all men live and move and have their being. A piece of artificial symbolism that is commonly understood in one age may be quite unintelligible in another; but the chief forms of natural symbolism have been used in some measure throughout all the ages. Indeed, the impulse to describe the world within by analogy with the external world is universal and irresistible. It has been an important factor in the complex organic development of human expression; and its effects are deeply ingrained in art and literature, in religious concepts and ceremonies, in popular tradition, and in the common speech of the peoples.

No doubt it is true that every mystery-cult, pagan or non-pagan, contains a certain amount of artificial symbolism derived from the particular myth or history with which its rites are associated—as the Eleusinian cultus, for instance, contained its own peculiar symbols derived from the Persephone myth. But the first step towards an understanding of the pagan and other mystic rituals must be taken by the light of the natural symbolism common to them all.

Now, from the earliest times the physical body of man has been described as being earthly, the emotional part of him as being watery, the rational part as being airy, and the divine part as being fiery (or aethereal). This, of course, is one of the simplest and most obvious forms of natural symbolism, and its great antiquity is proved by the fact that it is involved in the almost immemorial art of astrology. Furthermore, that Shakespeare himself was consciously familiar with this same symbolical figure is quite evident from *Sonnets* XLIV. and XLV., wherein he declares that his " life's composition " is made up of " four elements," which he expressly calls *Earth, Water, Air*, and *Fire*.*

Scarcely less ancient and widespread than the symbolical figure just noted is the belief that the human constitution comprises not only the physical body, but also a series of superphysical bodies or vehicles. The chief of these latter were called by the Egyptians *Ka, Bi*, and *Khou ;* by the Greeks *Psyche, Pneuma*, and *Nous ;* and by the old Jewish mystics *Nephesh, Ruach*, and *Neshamah*. They are respectively the sensitive, the rational, and the divine parts of man.

* Cf. *Ant. and Cleo.* IV. 2. 292; *Jul. Caes.* V. 5. 73. Also *Hen. V.* III. 7. 21, where the " four elements " are mentioned in reference to the constitution of a horse.

If these four " bodies " be now equated with the four " elements," the following definitions result:

EARTH   is a symbolical term suggested by the solid state of matter in the objective universe. It connotes the physical element in the human composition—that is, it represents the physical body.

WATER   is a symbolical term suggested by the liquid state of matter, and particularly the sea (*i.e.*, the "water below the firmament" referred to in the *Genesis* account of the creation of the world). It connotes the sensuous or passional or impressional element in the human composition. It is the " natural " or psychic body ($\sigma\hat{\omega}\mu\alpha$ $\psi\upsilon\chi\iota\kappa\acute{o}\nu$) of which St. Paul speaks in 1 *Corinthians* xv. 44. It is the Egyptian *Ka*, the Greek *Psyche*, and the Zoharic *Nephesh*.

AIR   is a symbolical term suggested by the gaseous state of matter. It connotes the rational or intellectual or spiritual element in the human composition. It is the "spiritual" or pneumatic body ($\sigma\hat{\omega}\mu\alpha$ $\pi\nu\epsilon\upsilon\mu\alpha\tau\iota\kappa\acute{o}\nu$) of which St. Paul speaks. It is the Egyptian *Bi*, the Greek *Pneuma*, and the Zoharic *Ruach*.

FIRE   is a symbolical term suggested by the hypothetical supergaseous state of matter (*i.e.*, the "water above the firmament" referred to in the *Genesis* account of the creation of the world). This FIRE or WATER ABOVE, often called AETHER, connotes the divine or intuitional element in the human composition. It is the " heavenly " body ($\sigma\hat{\omega}\mu\alpha$ $\dot{\epsilon}\pi o\upsilon\rho\alpha\nu\iota\acute{o}\nu$) of which St. Paul speaks. It is the Egyptian *Khou*, the Greek *Nous*, and the Zoharic *Neshamah*.

The Zoharic theosophy is explicit that *Nephesh* is the sensitive part of man, *Ruach* the rational part, and *Neshamah* the divine part.* As such, they must be respectively the WATER, the AIR, and the FIRE in the human composition, as declared above. Observe that the "spiritual" is not the highest; it is the rational or intellectual part of man (AIR)—an exact definition of a term that is often very loosely and vaguely used.†

Here let me say that, so far as I know, Mr. Arthur Edward Gray was the first to point out the results accruing from a systematic development of the simple and universal symbolical figure now under consideration. In a manuscript commentary upon one of the Dialogues of Plato (a commentary which, it should be added, was prepared simultaneously with the present work) he has dealt very fully with the subject; and, while I cannot agree with some of his conclusions, I wish to acknowledge explicitly and without reserve my indebtedness to him in respect of the essential principle involved in this symbolism of the elements.

Now, according to all mystical philosophies, the several " bodies " comprised in the human constitution —(*a*) are the planes through which the consciousness rises and falls in the changing phases of subjective experience, and (*b*) are successively discarded at death. The " elements " with which they are equated above may, therefore, be used for the purpose of expressing —(*a*) subjective states during life, and (*b*) states of existence after death. For example, an immersion in water may be employed as a piece of natural symbolism to represent—(*a*) an upward movement of the consciousness from the physical plane to the plane

* Cf. Mr. A. E. Waite, *Secret Doctrine in Israel*, 1913, chap. xiii. " *Nephesh* is the fallible part, for sin is suggested neither by *Ruach* nor *Neshamah* " (*ibid.*, p. 157). " When *Neshamah* is pre-eminent in man he is called holy " (*ibid.*, p. 161).

† The Latin word *spiritus* means literally "that which is breathed"; and the Greek word *pneuma* and the Hebrew word *ruach* both mean "spirit" or "breath" or "air."

of sensuous emotion, and (*b*) the shedding of the physical body at death.*

As a successive discarding of the several " bodies," the process which the mystic supposes to ensue at death must correspond to an ascent of the consciousness through those same " bodies " in the course of subjective experience. We may say, therefore, that at death the Soul rises out of EARTH, through WATER, to AIR, and finally mounts (when perfectly purified) to AETHER or FIRE.† And indeed, the Greek mythology declared that at death the Soul, quitting the life on *Earth*, crossed the Stygian *Water* into a Lower Paradise or Elysium that was always described as a place of clear *Air*, and finally mounted (when perfectly purified) into a Celestial Paradise or Empyrean that was essentially a place of *Fire*. Hence it would appear that the mythical River Styx is WATER, the mythical Elysium is AIR, and the mythical Empyrean is FIRE.‡

* The Christian ceremony of Baptism is a case in point. This ceremony is expressly concerned with a rising above the grosser lusts of the flesh (" carnal affections "), and it implies, in a sense, the death of the physical body. Note that, while the going into water in Baptism represents a rising above the carnal plane, the subsequent coming out of the water represents in its turn a rising above the sensuous plane.

† Discussing the doctrines of the Stoic philosophers, Professor J. A. Stewart writes: " The Soul, when perfectly purified, rises out of the Air into the Aether, returning to its original home " (*Myths of Plato*, p. 440).

In order to avoid misconceptions arising out of terminology, I may here explain that throughout the present work the familiar term " soul " will be employed in its generally accepted sense as the Ego or incarnating Essence. But it may be added that, strictly speaking, the " soul " is *Psyche* (WATER), as the " spirit " is *Pneuma* (AIR).

‡ Specific instances of the Lower Paradise as a place of pure air will be cited presently. The word " Empyrean " means literally " the sphere of fire." The Christian Kingdom of Heaven is, of course, the Celestial Paradise. It is the " Heaven of Heavens " which, in

# The Meaning of Initiation

This popular Greek concept is a particular version of an almost universal tradition. The belief that at death the Soul crosses water is found on every hand. For example, the Soul crosses the sea to the Garden of the Hesperides and to the Pindaric Isles of the Blessed—just as King Arthur is fabled to have crossed water to Avalon when he received a mortal hurt. The belief in two Paradises is hardly less widespread; and, as we shall presently see more fully, the Lower is always associated in some marked manner with AIR, and the Celestial with FIRE. From the Lower Paradise (AIR) the Soul must return in due time, being reincarnated in the physical body (EARTH).* But if it attains to the Celestial Paradise (AETHER or FIRE), the Soul need not return at all†—that is to say, the cycle of birth and death and reincarnation takes place between the elements of EARTH and AIR; and, in order to escape from the cycle, the Soul must achieve that perfect purification which is requisite for its ascent out of AIR into FIRE. This, of course, corresponds to the Indian doctrine of Nirvana; and the value of its

---

Ps. cxlviii., is spoken of in apposition with the "water above" (AETHER or FIRE).

Note that no mention is made above of Purgatory, as the place of *post-mortem* expiation. Its position in the symbolical scheme will be indicated presently.

* Cf. *Aen. vi.*, speech of Anchises, who says that the Souls dwelling in Elysium are reincarnated after a lapse of time. The emphasis laid in the myth of King Arthur upon the fact that he will return in due time confirms that Avalon, which lies beyond water, is a Lower Paradise or Elysium (AIR).

† Professor Stewart, as cited above, says: "The Soul, when perfectly purified, rises out of the Air into the Aether, returning to its original home, and there lives for ever and ever. Its perfect purification . . . guarantees its immortality."

According to Indian doctrine, the Soul can reincarnate at will from FIRE, and when it does so a great religious teacher, such as Buddha, is born into the world.

91

# Shakespeare's Mystery Play

presentation in terms of the elements will appear when the pagan Mysteries come under consideration.

From the foregoing argument it would seem that the several regions described in mythological and religious tradition are within us—as Christ said, " The Kingdom of Heaven is within you." They are allegorical figures which represent not only states of existence after death, but also *states of consciousness to which we can attain during life.** Thus a crossing of the River Styx (WATER) to Elysium (AIR) represents not only the shedding of the EARTHLY and WATERY bodies at death, but also an ascent of the consciousness through the plane of sensuous emotion to the plane of reason. In other words, a purely subjective experience may be depicted as a journey of the living through the mythical abodes of the dead.

In his *Divina Commedia* Dante describes what is ostensibly a journey through the realms of the dead. The regions visited include a Celestial Paradise which is a place of *fire in the likeness of water*,† and a Lower Paradise which is *in the pure air*.‡ This journey is made by Dante while he is still alive and in the physical body.§ According to the principle just

* Olympiodorus, in MS. commentary on *Georgias* of Plato, says of the Elysian fields, or Fortunate Isles: "He who in the present state vanquishes as much as possible a corporeal life, through the exercise of the cathartic virtues, passes in reality into the fortunate isles of the soul."

† *Parad.* xxx. This fire, like water, is clearly the FIRE or AETHER which is the WATER ABOVE. In the Epistle to Can Grande, which is authoritatively held to be the work of Dante himself, this Heaven of Heavens is thus described: " It is called the Empyrean (*i.e.*, the sphere of fire), which is to say that it is a heaven blazing with fire. . . ."

‡ Not only is Dante's Lower Paradise a place of sweet and pleasant air (*Purg.* xxviii. 7); it is " all free in the pure air " (*ibid.* 106, 107); it is " above the earth and water " (*ibid.* 97, 98); elsewhere it is said to be " most high above the waters " (*Parad.* xxvi. *fin.*).

§ This is repeatedly emphasised. See *Inf.* viii.; *ibid.* xii.; *Purg.* iii.; *ibid.* xxvi.

92

enunciated, therefore, it should be interpreted as a pilgrimage through the successive planes or states of consciousness—the Lower Paradise being the plane of pure reason (AIR), and the Celestial Paradise being the plane of intuition (FIRE). That such an interpretation actually is intended will hereafter be shown in more detail. But it is immediately evident that Dante, notwithstanding that he depicts these places as regions beyond the grave, conceives them in what may be called an *ante-mortem* sense. For he identifies the Lower Paradise with Eden and with the Golden Age, as the guiltless and happy state of mortal man before the Fall; and the context especially commends this identification, of which Dante imagines the ancient poets to smile approval.*

This latter point warrants a brief digression. If Dante's Lower Paradise, which he identifies with the Lost Estate of Man, be the subjective plane of reason, then he regards the Fall as a particular psychological experience. He regards it as a forfeiting of the Elysian serenity of the rational state for the tumults and stresses of the emotional state—as a lapse of the consciousness from the AIR of pure reason, whence it is lured down to the passional WATER by that insidious serpent which is desire. Conceived in this way, the myth of the Fall does not refer exclusively (or even at all) to an historico-legendary past. It is true to the recurrent psychological experience, actual or potential, of every man.† And, in as much as this view of the

---

* *Purg.* xxviii. 91-96, 136-147.

† Since the above passage was written, I observe that the Very Rev. W. R. Inge, Dean of St. Paul's, London, has declared that " the time has now come when we must give up the idea of the ancient parable of the Garden of Eden and the Fall of Man as a chapter of actual history. The narrative of the Fall will always be valuable as a kind of mystery play of the psychology of man " (at Kingsway Hall, London, December 12, 1920).

Fall involves the assumption that the Garden of Eden represents the plane of reason, such assumption is confirmed by the general resemblance between the Lost Estate and the typical Lower Paradise of tradition.\* Observe also that in the descent of the consciousness from the Lost Estate (AIR) in the Fall we have a subjective parallel to the descent of the Soul from Elysium (AIR) in the process of incarnation.

Now, if Dante's journey is to be understood as a psychological pilgrimage, it is akin to the pilgrimage of Christian in Bunyan's transparent allegory. No one can fail to perceive that the regions through which Christian passes—such as the Slough of Despond and the Valley of Humiliation—are figurative of subjective states; and they certainly bear a striking resemblance to the regions visited by Dante. For instance, after many trials Christian comes to a place called the Land of Beulah, *whose air was very sweet and pleasant*, and where there was " no want of corn and wine, for here they met with abundance "; and thereafter he attains to the Heavenly Jerusalem, which is a place *blazing with fiery light*. Clearly, then, these two places are particular versions of the Lower Paradise (AIR) and the Celestial Paradise (FIRE); and if the earlier regions through which Christian passes have a purely subjective significance, so also must these latter.

It is difficult to see how the persistent resemblances

---

\* Cf. Ovid's *Metam.* i. 107, 108. Like Elysium, the Golden Age was characterised by the sweet and pleasant air. It was an age of perpetual spring, when flowers and fruit grew in abundance without the labour of cultivation. Then man lived without toil, as in the Garden of Eden. Note the resemblance not only to Elysium, but also to the Garden of the Hesperides, the Isles of the Blessed (or " Fortunate Isles "), etc.

Likening England to Eden, Shakespeare calls it a " demi-Paradise "; which seems to imply that he regards Eden as the Lower Paradise (see *Rich. II.*, II. 1. 42).

which may be observed in a survey of mythological and religious concepts can be explained, save on the hypothesis that these concepts are determined by some human standard that is unchanging from age to age. And the conclusion which the foregoing argument suggests, and which further analysis will amply confirm, is that the standard with which the concepts in question accord is to be found in certain permanent realities of psychological experience.

One example may here be cited to illustrate my meaning. Virgil and his follower Dante locate the mythical River Lethe, somewhat vaguely, in or near Elysium. But in his Aridaeus-Thespesius myth Plutarch indicates very exactly that the Place of Lethe is the region through which the Soul passes in its descent from AIR to EARTH; in other words, it is WATER. Now, if the Place of Lethe be WATER, it represents the passional plane; and indeed, the tradition concerning the former expresses an enduring truth concerning the latter. For, as in the process of incarnation the Soul, descending from Elysium to the Place of Lethe, there " drinks oblivion " of the region whence it has come— so likewise it is true in the universal psychology that the consciousness, falling from the plane of pure reason to the passional plane, there " drinks oblivion " of the higher things which it has forsaken.

It may be objected that this argument implies that Lethe is precisely the same as Styx, since both have been identified with WATER. The answer to this is that these two rivers, which are different in character, represent two different aspects of the passional element. Note how they are distinguished in the mythological account of the cycle of incarnation. According to Plutarch, Lethe (" forgetfulness ") is a river to which the Soul comes in its descent from Elysium; whereas the river which the Soul leaves behind in its reascent to Elysium is represented as Styx ("the hateful"). This curious distinction between the two rivers seems to determine, or to be determined by, the different characters assigned to them; and the whole conception has its precise analogy in psychological experience. For, whereas the passional WATER confers a not unwelcome forgetfulness in a downward movement of the consciousness thither from the AIR of pure reason, it assumes a hateful aspect when the consciousness is rising thence again to AIR. In short, the passional WATER desired in the Fall is Lethe; whereas the passional WATER renounced in the Ascent is Styx.

Such was the correlation between pagan myth and pagan ceremonial that what is true of the former is probably true of the latter; and, in so far as the ritual of the Mysteries was based upon mythical concepts (as undoubtedly it was to a very large extent), this ritual should likewise conform to the permanent realities of subjective experience, in accordance with the principle adumbrated in the foregoing pages. This principle will now be assumed as a working hypothesis. Its validity can be finally determined when all the evidence in its favour has been stated, and when we have seen how much it is competent to explain alike in the myths and in the Mysteries.

But first it must be observed that, if the whole series of mythical regions is to be identified with the whole series of subjective states, then the theory thus far developed is inadequate; for there remain other regions and states which have not yet been dealt with.

Thus far only four "bodies" have been considered in association with symbols drawn from the external world; but, as every student of such matters is aware, mystical and theosophical doctrines almost invariably involve the assumption that the human constitution comprises in all seven "bodies"—four cardinal and

# The Meaning of Initiation

three intermediate. Hence, if such doctrines are to be fully expressed in terms of the " elements," three more symbols of the same kind are required; and these are obtained by a very simple extension of the hypothesis that the world within is analogous with the external world. For, as between the physical and the sensuous elements in man there is the sensual (which is a mixture of the two), so between EARTH and WATER there is MIRE. Similarly, between WATER and AIR there is MIST, which connotes the plane of false and confused thinking—the plane upon which the reason is (so to speak) " clouded " by sensuous or emotional influences. And between AIR and AETHER (FIRE) there is an intermediate which, for reasons that will be apparent later, is generally represented as a RING OF FIRE (or of LIGHT).

We now have seven symbolical terms wherewith to designate the traditional Seven Principles of Man. They are, it should be observed, terms which are to a very large extent used instinctively by all mankind to describe subjective facts, quite apart from any question of mystical and theosophical doctrines.* But what I wish for the moment to emphasise more particularly is the fact that by the aid of these seven symbolical terms we can express—(a) the whole range of the Soul's supposed experience after physical death, and (b) the whole range of subjective experience during life. For by an ascent through all the " elements " from EARTH

* We talk, for instance, of an utterly dispassionate reasoner as being " above the clouds," which must imply that he is in the clear air. We talk of a " wave " or a " flood " of emotion, and of a " flash " of intuition. We describe the sensualist as " sinking in the mire "; and we speak of the desire for sensuous or passional satisfactions as a " thirst "—which it is, symbolically, for it is a drawing of the consciousness towards the plane of WATER. All these common figures of speech have their origin in man's instinctive impulse to describe the world within by analogy with the external world.

TO FIRE can be represented—(*a*) the successive shedding by the Soul of all the " bodies " with which it is vested, and (*b*) a movement of the consciousness through all the planes upon which it can function.

The respective connotations of the three intermediate " elements " can be inferred at once from the connotations of the four cardinal elements. Thus the sensual MIRE must connote the mythical Cocytus—the river of boiling mud which Aeneas passes after quitting the place or state of mortal existence (EARTH), and before reaching the River Styx (WATER).* Similarly, the MIST of erroneous thinking must connote that dark purgatorial region traversed by Aeneas after he has crossed the River Styx (WATER) and before he reaches Elysium (AIR).† The RING OF FIRE is not included in the scope of Virgil's narrative, for Aeneas does not go beyond Elysium; but Dante describes great circles of fire or light which he saw while ascending out of the Lower Paradise into the Empyrean.‡

That MIST connotes the purgatorial region is confirmed by the *Divina Commedia*. Dante represents

* Cf. *Aen. vi.* According to Plato (*Phaedo, prope finem*), Cocytus and Styx are identical, and the river of boiling mire is Phlegethon. My concern is with the principle, rather than with the names; and I here follow Virgil's version because I shall have occasion to refer frequently to *Aeneid vi.*

† The purgatorial region is described by Virgil as " the place of night " (*Aen. vi.* 390). Note that the Anglo-Saxon word " mist " means darkness. Cf. 2 *Pet.* ii. 17, which speaks of " the mist of darkness."

‡ *Parad.* xxviii. *sub initio.* Dante speaks of nine fiery circles of different magnitude. This is a characteristic elaboration of the essential idea. In like manner he depicts ten stages in the Celestial Paradise, seven stages in Purgatory, and so on. Cf. *Zech.* ii. 5: " For I, saith the Lord, will be unto her [Jerusalem] a wall of fire round about, and will be the glory in the midst of her." Here Jerusalem, as the dwelling-place of the Lord, is the Celestial Paradise (AETHER), with the RING OF FIRE around it. Other instances will be cited in appropriate context.

# The Meaning of Initiation

Purgatory as being on a mountain-side. The base of the mountain is water-lapped.* On the top of the mountain is the Lower Paradise, which is in the pure air, *above the vapours exhaled by the water that lies below.*† This figure clearly implies that Dante's Purgatory is a place of mist, above and beyond water. Dante crosses water, climbs the misty slopes of the Mount of Purgatory, and attains to the clear air of the Lower Paradise—as Aeneas crosses the River Styx (WATER), passes through the purgatorial region (MIST), and attains to Elysium (AIR).

One important point remains to be dealt with before a detailed application of these principles is attempted. It concerns the AIR and AETHER; and it is, in fact, one of the pivotal points upon which a large part of the subsequent argument will turn.

Every genuine philosopher aspires to learn the divine mystery which is Truth. To achieve this, he must rise above the MIST of error, prejudice, and sentiment. Yet it is not in the AIR of reason, but in the AETHER of intuition, that his purpose is wholly attained. For whereas on the plane of intuition there is a direct and complete perception of Truth, on the lower plane of reason there are only partial intimations thereof. In terms of the elements, Truth received through the intuition is received through the medium of AETHER, which is the medium of light and vision; whereas Truth received through the reason is received through the medium of AIR, which is the medium of sound or the voice. The symbolical figure which this suggests is obvious. In relation to the divine mystery, the

* Cf. *Purg.* xxi., line 36 in Carey's translation. " Wave-wash'd foot" is, perhaps, a very free rendering of the Italian *piè molli ;* but there is no doubt that Dante conceives the mountain as having water at its foot.

† *Purg.* xxviii. 97-102.

operation of intuition was likened to the seeing by the eye, and the operation of pure reason was likened to the hearing by the ear.*

" I have heard of Thee by the hearing of the ear," says Job to the Lord, after suffering many grievous trials; " but now mine eye seeth Thee." Job does not say " mine eyes see Thee," nor is there any indication that physical vision is referred to. The passage is to be understood subjectively. Job closes his eyes, as the true mystic does, to the things of the outside world, and sees God with the eye of intuitive certitude.†

In this symbolical distinction between *seeing* and *hearing*, as the distinction between knowledge gained through intuition and knowledge gained through reason, we have the distinction between Revelation and Inspiration. That Revelation consists in a direct presentation to the eye, as to the faculty of intuitive perception, needs no proof. And what is Inspiration? Literally, it is a " breathing into." Now, Truth transmitted by the breath is Truth transmitted orally. Inspiration, therefore, is symbolically represented as a breathing of the Word of Truth into the ear of reason; and hence the phrase " the voice of inspiration." According to one of the Greek concepts, inspiration is received from an aerial daemon (or genius); and hence it is " the breath of genius." Among the pagan deities

* The word "intuition" involves the idea of " a seeing into " (from *tueor* = I see).

Interpreting the Greek mythology in his *Wisdom of the Ancients*, Bacon declares, in a somewhat cryptic phrase, that the ear represents the rational judgment. He writes: " Now to the ears of mortals, that is, to human judgment, . . ." (On Pan).

† See *Job* xlii. 1-5. The word "mystic" is derived from the Greek *myo* = to close the eyes. Oscar Wilde has well expressed this idea in his *Salome*. Speaking to Jokanaan (John the Baptist), Salome exclaims: " Thou didst put upon thine eyes the covering of him who would see his God."

the airy Hermes was the winged messenger of Zeus; and it is significant that he was held to be the god of speech and was often associated directly with the Word.*

There are many variations of this symbolical figure. For example, when Adam was in Eden (AIR), he heard the Voice, but did not see the Face, of God. That is, on the plane of pure reason (AIR), he heard the " voice of inspiration " which is the Word of God, but full revelation was not accorded to him.† In this same subjective manner we must interpret the wellnigh universal tradition concerning a Voice that speaks from behind a Veil which is lifted only in supreme revelation. The drawing aside of the Veil is the ascent of the consciousness from reason to intuition; and we may equate the Veil itself with the RING OF FIRE which divides the AIR from the AETHER. Indeed, in *Exodus* (iii.) it is related that Moses, being upon the Mount of God (*i.e.*, in the upper air), heard the Voice proceeding from behind the burning bush. So Siegfried, being upon the mountain-top, had yet to pass through the fiery ring before he could gain the bride Brunhilde—another version of the myth of the Veiled Lady who is the Bride of the initiate. The Veil corresponds to the " wall of fire " around the heavenly Jerusalem, protecting the Shechinah who is the " glory in the midst thereof."‡ It is the Veil of Sanctuary, concealing the mystery of that Holy of Holies whose archetype is Heaven, and into which none save the High Priest

---

* Cf. Bacon's *Wisdom of Ancients*, Essay on Pan.

† *Gen.* iii. 8: " And they heard the voice of the Lord God walking in the garden in the cool [Hebrew, wind] of the day. . . ." According to the Hebrew, the voice was in the wind; and, according to the Vulgate, it was in a breath of air (*aura*). The " voice that breathed o'er Eden " is the voice of inspiration that is heard in the serenity of pure reason.

‡ Cf. *Zech.* ii. 5, already cited.

may enter. It is the Veil worn by the sacred Isis and by the Veiled Lady of the Kabbalah. It is the Veil which Wisdom draws aside when she " reveals her secrets " to her tried and proved lover.* And, in like manner, it is the Veil which Beatrice wears when she speaks to Dante in Eden and which she subsequently removes.

Implicit in all such symbolical concepts is the distinction between Inspiration and Revelation—between Truth as " heard " on the plane of pure reason (AIR), and Truth as " seen " on the plane of intuition (AETHER). This point will be further dealt with and developed in the course of the argument upon which I shall presently embark.

At the conclusion of this brief outline, it may be remarked that the difficulty has been to present in something like *a priori* form a series of principles which are entirely the result of *a posteriori* reasoning. These principles are based upon a very large mass of detail, the bulk of which I have as yet withheld; and, for the moment, I ask only that they be provisionally accepted as a working hypothesis, in the light of which the formal or ritual initiation, and more particularly that of the pagan Mysteries, may be examined.

## 2. THE WAY TO SALVATION.

Now, a moral purpose was undoubtedly intended by the pagan initiation. So far as it goes, it may be true to say that the candidate was induced to rightdoing by a series of impressive experiences which contrasted the punishments of Purgatory with the rewards of Paradise. But behind that series of experiences lay a complete philosophy, of which each of the incidents of the ceremony allegorised a salient

* Cf. *Ecclus.* iv. 17, 18, already cited.

feature. Thus (to use Prospero's phrasing), each of the " happened accidents " of the ritual initiation could be " resolved " so as to " seem probable " to the candidate.

What, then, was the philosophy which shaped the ritual proceedings in the ancient Mysteries? Broadly, it may be called a philosophy of Salvation, based upon a clear conception of what Salvation consists in. The ritual initiation showed enigmatically (" through a glass darkly ") how Man may restore himself to the state from which he fell. It was a ceremony designed as a reversal of the process implied in the Fall. If the myth of the Fall of Man is the story of Paradise lost, initiation was the story of Paradise regained.

But, according to almost universal tradition, there are two Paradises, the Lower and the Celestial. There were, therefore, two successive objectives in initiation—viz., (i) the recovery of the Lost Estate or Lower Paradise, and (ii) the attainment of the Celestial Paradise. In the realisation of these two objectives consisted (i) the Lesser Initiation, and (ii) the Greater Initiation.

Now, in the scale of the " elements " the Lower Paradise is AIR and the Celestial Paradise is AETHER. The full initiation consisted, therefore, in an ascent through all the elements. In this connection we may note that in certain of the Indian Mysteries a Seven-Step Ladder was used to allegorise the manner of approach to perfection.* The Seven Steps represent the seven elements, and the Ladder stretches from EARTH TO AETHER. In other words, it stretches from Earth to Heaven, like the Ladder of which Jacob dreamed.†

* Cf. John Fellows, *Myst. of Freem.*, p. 321.
† *Gen.* xxviii. 12. Mr. A. E. Waite (*Sec. Doct. Isr.*, p. 116), says that, according to the *Zohar*, Abram mounted the " Ladder of

# Shakespeare's Mystery Play

Apuleius tells us that in the final stage of his initiation into the Mysteries of Isis he received " a new life." He does not, of course, describe the ceremony; but he remarks that he returned to his original state, *being carried back through all the elements.** This singular phrase has certainly not received the measure of attention it deserves. For example, dealing with the pagan Mysteries in the Hulsean Lectures, Dr. S. Cheetham cited the context somewhat extensively, but actually omitted these— the crucial—words, nor did he give the slightest intimation that the passage, as he quoted it, was incomplete.†

Dupuis, whose scholarship is unquestionable, declares quite positively that the doctrine of the Fall and Ascent through the elements was involved in the pagan Mysteries. He writes:

" They disclosed the origin of the soul, its fall to earth through the spheres and the elements, and its return to the place of its origin. . . . Here was the most metaphysical part, which most of the initiates could hardly understand, but of which they were given indications by figures and allegorical spectres " (*Origine de Tous les Cultes*, " Traité des Mystères," 2e partie, pp. 391-2).‡

---

Sanctity " step by step, until he reached the highest state of holiness. This Zoharic concept is a mystical interpretation of *Gen.* xii. and xiii. In *Gen.* xii. 8 it is said that Abram built an altar to the east of Beth-el, having Beth-el on the west. In *Gen.* xiii. 1-4 it is said that he went into the South, thence to Beth-el, and thence to the place of the altar (which was east of Beth-el). It is this journey to the South, thence to the West, and thence to the East, which the *Zohar* conceives as a mounting of the Ladder of Sanctity. The point has a significance upon which, for various reasons, I do not at present enlarge.

* *Metam.* xi.: " per omnia vectus elementa remeavi."

† *The Mysteries, Pagan and Christian*, Being Hulsean Lectures for 1896-97, by S. Cheetham, D.D., F.S.A. (Macmillan and Co., Ltd., 1897), pp. 107, 108.

‡ The " spheres " to which Dupuis alludes are the spheres of the planets. With this aspect of the ancient doctrine I do not deal in the present study.

# The Meaning of Initiation

And Plato, although he does not mention the elements, clearly implies that the initiatory rites constituted a ceremonial reversal of the Fall; for he says that "it was the aim and drift of initiation to restore the soul to that state from which it fell."* These testimonies, taken together, not only confirm the broad proposition with which I began, but also furnish a reasonable warrant for treating the pagan initiation as a ritual ascent through the elements.

Now, it is quite likely that in some of the Mysteries —as, for example, in those of Eleusis—the rites of the Lesser Initiation assumed the ostensible form of a journey, like that of Aeneas in *Aeneid VI.*, through Purgatory (MIST) to Elysium (AIR);† and that those of the Greater Initiation ostensibly represented the escape of the Soul from the cycle of incarnation by an ascent to the Celestial Paradise (AETHER). But, as I have already argued at length in the preceding section, these successive regions beyond the grave correspond to the successive states or planes of consciousness. From this it follows that ritual initiation, as an ascent through the elements, may quite properly be regarded as symbolising a series of purely psychological changes; and it is upon these lines that I am about to reconstruct and interpret it.

In the first place, observe that the ascent through the sevenfold scale of the elements has three main stages; and here we have the prototypical "Three Degrees" which figure not only in the pagan rites but throughout the entire tradition concerning initiation. Of these Three Degrees—

---

* *Phaedo;* cited by Warburton.

† Note that, as Aeneas rises only to the Lower Paradise or Lost Estate, he takes only the Lesser Initiation. Warburton argues (incorrectly, as I think) that Aeneas takes also the Greater Initiation.

# Shakespeare's Mystery Play

THE FIRST DEGREE is the ascent to WATER. Its implications are, therefore, passional. In this Degree the aspirant reaches the third step of the Mystic Ladder.

THE SECOND DEGREE is the ascent to AIR. Its implications are, therefore, rational or intellectual. In this Degree the aspirant reaches the fifth step of the Mystic Ladder, and achieves inspiration.

THE THIRD DEGREE is the ascent to AETHER (FIRE). Its implications are, therefore, intuitional. In this Degree the aspirant reaches the seventh step of the Mystic Ladder. He " closes his eyes " in a death to this world, and attains to supreme revelation.

" I baptise you with water," says John the Baptist; " but he that cometh after me shall baptise you with the Holy Ghost, and with fire."* In the Greek text, Ghost is *Pneuma*, which means also Air. To be baptised with the Holy Ghost (Spirit) is to mount to the rational plane of AIR and receive the " divine afflatus "—that divine breathing into which is the voice of inspiration. Thus the three baptisms of which St. John speaks imply "immersion" (i) in WATER, (ii) in AIR, and (iii) in FIRE; and they correspond, therefore, to the Three Degrees of Initiation, as outlined above.

Although in certain monastic orders there is a Third Degree on the lines I have indicated, the ordinary member of the present-day Christian Church takes only the Lesser Initiation, comprising the First and Second Degrees (WATER and AIR). These two Degrees are represented respectively by Baptism and Confirmation, upon completion of both of which

* *St. Matt.* iii. 11. Compare the words of Christ in *St. John* iii. 5: " Except a man be born of water and of the Spirit, he cannot enter the Kingdom of God." That is to say, except a man pass through WATER and AIR he cannot attain to the Celestial Paradise which is FIRE (AETHER).

106

the candidate may partake of the Eucharist, exactly as the " drinking and tasting " in the Eleusinian rites was permitted only to those who had taken the Lesser Initiation. The Christian ceremony of Baptism is clearly passional in its implications; for the candidate is dipped in Water, and it is supplicated that " all carnal affections may die in him." Similarly, the ceremony of Confirmation is clearly rational or intellectual in its implications; for it takes place when he has " come to years of discretion " and is capable of thinking for himself.* And we might add that he takes the Third Degree empirically; for in due time he dies, and thereby gains access to the supreme mystery.

That there were Three Degrees in the pagan ritual hardly requires proof: it is commonly acknowledged. Clement of Alexandria implies that there were three main stages; and he calls them Cleansings (*Katharsia*), the Lesser Mysteries, and the Greater Mysteries.† Theon of Smyrna says that there were five stages; but, as Dr. Cheetham pointed out in his Lectures,‡ his version amounts to only three distinctive grades—viz., *Katharsia*, *Paradosis*, and *Epopteia*. As a working guide, the following table may now be set out:

| | | | | |
|---|---|---|---|---|
| I = WATER | = passional | = Katharsia | = Baptism. |
| 2 = AIR | = rational | = Paradosis | = Confirmation. |
| 3 = AETHER | = intuitional | = Epopteia | = (after death). |

---

* As a matter of fact, the original tradition is slightly confused in the present-day ritual. In the first ceremony the candidate is baptised " with Water and with the Holy Ghost "; but the appeal for divine inspiration in the succeeding ceremony (cf. first prayer therein) suggests that it is rather the *second* part of the first ceremony which is " confirmed " at a suitable age. For the sake of clarity I have made a distinction accordingly, treating Baptism as the First Degree (WATER) and Confirmation as the Second Degree (AIR). John the Baptist, as we have seen, makes a clear distinction between baptism with water and baptism with the Holy Ghost.

† *Stromata* v.; cited by several authorities.

‡ *Op. cit.*, Lect. iv.

The three intermediate " elements " (as I shall show) determine the ordeals of the three degrees. Thus the ordeal of the First Degree is referable to MIRE; that of the Second Degree to MIST; and that of the Third Degree to the RING OF FIRE.

From this table it ought to be possible to deduce at least the salient features of the esoteric scheme which underlies ritual initiation. In the ensuing pages I shall first indicate quite briefly what is implied in each of the Three Degrees, with especial reference to the rites of Eleusis; and thereafter the entire scheme will be reconstructed and interpreted in detail, concurrently with an examination of the text of *The Tempest*.

THE FIRST DEGREE is a preliminary purification. It consists in the ascent to WATER, involving the ordeal of MIRE. At Eleusis the candidate was smeared with mud or clay before the purifying immersion in water.* This smearing and the subsequent Cleansings (*Katharsia*) clearly represent the passage through MIRE into WATER. It denotes the mounting of the consciousness through the sensual plane to the sensuous or passional plane; and it implies a repudiation by the aspirant of those grosser and carnal lusts to which the Christian ceremony of Baptism makes specific allusion.

THE SECOND DEGREE is the Degree of Self-conflict and of the Ear. It consists in the ascent to AIR, involving the ordeal of MIST. To determine its import and the nature of the ordeal, we must consider both the mythological and the subjective connotations of these two elements. Mythologically, MIST is Purgatory; hence the ordeal is one of expiation. Moreover, AIR is the Lower Paradise from which Man fell; hence that which must be expiated, as a condition precedent to the recovery of the Lost Estate, is what

* This is well known. Cf. *Ency. Brit.*, 9th ed., vol. xvii., pp. 151-2.

we call " the original sin," and the mode of expiating it is by a triumph over the very temptation by which the Fall was compassed. Subjectively, MIST is the plane or state of error; hence the ordeal is one of wanderings, figurative of those discursive intellectual speculations in search of Truth which take place before the plane or state of inspired reason (AIR) is attained. Thus we may infer—what I shall presently prove—that the Second Degree comprises long wanderings and a triumph over temptation, and that it culminates in a discourse upon the particular Mystery cherished by the cultus. In this manner is figured the long quest for Truth, the struggle for self-mastery as the means to divine favour, and the hearing at last of the Voice which utters the Word of Truth into the ear of reason. It may be added that, since the plane of AIR (upon which alone the inspired Word is received) is the prototype of the mythical Lost Estate, the Second Degree of Initiation involves a search for the Lost Word.

In the Eleusinian Mysteries the candidate, after bathing in the sea (WATER), wandered in darkness upon the seashore, ostensibly making a ritual search for the lost Persephone. He then passed into the vestibule of the temple, where temptations were simulated.* Thereafter came what Theon of Smyrna calls *Paradosis* (transmission). What, then, was transmitted to the candidate at this stage? Lobeck, in a downright assertion which a lesser and more cautious authority on the subject would wisely have avoided, declares that we shall never know. It might (he says) have been sacred objects, or precepts and admonitions relating to the conduct of life or the observance of ceremonies. In any case (he concludes), " latet

* This will be demonstrated inferentially at a later stage in my case.

aeternumque latebit "—it is hidden and will remain hidden for ever.*

But, notwithstanding Lobeck's opinion, we have ample material for a reasoned conjecture. According to Liddell and Scott, the word παράδοσις means more particularly oral transmission. Using the word in connection with this stage of initiation, Theon of Smyrna speaks of " the transmission of the mystery ";† and Clement of Alexandria declares that in the second stage the candidate received " some groundwork of teaching and preparation for what was to follow." ‡ That which followed in the next stage was the sublime spectacle in which the gods appeared. From these several facts I surmise—confidently, in view of the coherence of my whole case—that παράδοσις consisted in a spoken discourse whereby the aspirant *heard* of those same gods whom in the next stage he *saw*—as in the case of Job and the Lord (xlii. 1–5). Thus, between παράδοσις (transmission) in the Second Degree and ἐποπτεία (full vision) in the Third Degree we have again that distinction between *hearing* and *seeing* which is precisely the difference between receiving inspiration on the plane of AIR and receiving revelation on the plane of AETHER. In short, *Paradosis* was the mystery audible. It symbolised the process of inspiration; and it was accordingly the culminating feature of the Lesser Initiation.

THE THIRD DEGREE is the Degree of Death and of the Eye. It consists in the ascent to AETHER, involving the ordeal of the RING OF FIRE. I have already argued somewhat fully that AETHER is the Celestial Paradise;

---

* *Aglaoph.*, p. 188; cited by Cheetham, Lect. iv.

† Cf. Cheetham, *op. cit.*, Lect. iv. Theon's words are ἡ τῆς τελετῆς παράδοσις.

‡ Cf. Cheetham, *op. cit.*, Lect. iv.; Taylor, *Eleus. and Bacch. Myst.;* Warburton, *Divine Legation.*

# The Meaning of Initiation

so that the ascent thither is a passing behind the Veil into the very Presence of God (or the gods). Interpreted subjectively, it is the ascent of the consciousness to the plane of intuition, which is the plane of Revelation. Here the aspirant is completely united (as it were, married) with the Truth he seeks. The divine mystery is now seen with the eye of intuitive certitude; and, in the ecstasy of this direct and full inward perception, the aspirant is temporarily dead to the external world.\* Hence the ritual ordeal of the Third Degree is a simulated death, to represent that " closing of the eyes " to all the things of this world which is a condition precedent to divine revelation. And, indeed, there is a mythological connection between death and the RING OF FIRE, although for the moment I prefer to withhold the evidence.†

The records concerning the pagan Third Degree are necessarily meagre, for the utmost secrecy was required

\* Cf. *Ency. Brit.*, 9th ed., vol. xvii., p. 129: " Mysticism demands a faculty above reason, by which the subject shall be placed in immediate and complete union with the object of its desire—a union in which the consciousness of self has disappeared, and in which subject and object are one. This is the intuition or ecstasy or mystical swoon which appears alike among the Hindus, the Neo-Platonists, and the mediaeval saints " (*sub voce* " Mysticism ").

This passage clearly involves the whole principle I am ascribing to the Third Degree; but, to be quite precise, the ecstatic swoon is not, as the passage suggests, the intuition itself; it is rather the psychological condition precedent to the intuitive seeing. The Greek word *ekstasis* means a standing aside, and connotes also a trance. The ecstatic swoon corresponds, of course, to that state of consciousness which Indian doctrine calls Nirvana. It is the experience described at the close of Rudyard Kipling's *Kim*, by Teshoo Lama, who gives what may be regarded as an account of the Third Degree of Initiation.

The idea of revelation taking place while the recipient of it is in a death-like trance occurs frequently in the Bible. See *2 Cor.* xii. 2-4; *Rev.* i. 17; *Acts* x. 10; xi. 5; xxii. 17; and compare also *Num.* xxiv. 4, and *Dan.* viii. 18.

† It is given in the next chapter, in the section dealing with Ferdinand.

of the initiate. But we have the testimony of Apuleius that in the last stage of his initiation into the Isiac Mysteries he received " a new life " and was " born again ";* which suggests quite clearly that he suffered what amounted to a ritual death. In the Eleusinian rites the Third Degree was called *Epopteia*, which means " seeing "; and it included a spectacle wherein the aspirant was supposed actually to behold the gods. This apocalypse was the mystery visible. The aspirant now *saw* that of which in the Second Degree he had *heard ;* and henceforward he bore the title of *epoptes*, which means " a seer." In short, *Epopteia* symbolised the process of revelation, and it was accordingly the culminating feature of the Greater Initiation.

Such, then, is the framework of the traditional Three Degrees of formal or ritual initiation; and by the aid of this general plan we can reconstruct and interpret the initatory rites of the pagan Mysteries. It is evident, from what has already been said, that those rites were designed in accordance with the realities of religious experience, and that they had a purely psychological significance. Their purpose was to teach the aspirant, by means of illustrative ceremonies, the intimate self-knowledge which is the key to self-mastery, and thereby to assist him to achieve " salvation " in actual experience. In their practical effect, therefore, they may be described as a system of intensive introspection. This view of the pagan rites is certainly not contrary to the spirit of Greek thought. Indeed, it is strongly confirmed in a passage cited by Professor Max Müller from the writings of Proclus, who says:

As the Mystae in the holiest of their initiations meet first with a multiform and manifold race of gods, but when entered into the sanctuary and surrounded by holy ceremonies receive at once divine

---

* *Metam.* xi., as already cited.

# The Meaning of Initiation

illumination in their bosom and like lightly armed warriors take quick possession of the Divine, the same thing happens at the intuition of the One and All. If the soul looks to what is behind, it sees the shadows and illusion only of what is. If it turns into its own essence and discovers its own relations, it sees itself only; but, if penetrating more deeply into the knowledge of itself, it discovers the spirit in itself and in all orders of things. And, if it reaches into its inmost recess, as it were into the Adyton (sanctuary) of the soul, it can see the race of gods and the unities of all things even with closed eyes. (See Lect. xiii. in Müller's *Theosophy and Psychological Religion,* The Gifford Lectures for 1892, published by Longmans, Green and Co.)

Here it is expressly affirmed by Proclus that what occurred in the holiest of the pagan initiatory rites was analogous to the psychological experience of perceiving intuitionally "the One and All." Continuing this parallel between ritual initiation and psychological experience, he speaks of the self-knowledge acquired by inward examination, and refers to three degrees of introspection of increasing intensity which culminate in full subjective revelation. Moreover, Proclus implies that the external world is but the shadow and illusion of reality—which is practically what Prospero tells Ferdinand in awakening him from the dream of the earth-life. It may be added that Professor Max Müller remarks of Proclus that he is—

The connecting-link between Greek philosophy and the scholastic philosophy of the Middle Ages, and with Dionysius, one of the chief authorities of the Mediaeval Mystics. Through Proclus the best thoughts of the Stoics, of Aristotle, Plato, nay, of the still more ancient philosophers of Greece, such as Anaxagoras and Heraclitus, were handed on to the greatest scholastic and mystic Doctors in the Mediaeval Church (*ibid.*).

In so far as a "mystical marriage" occurred in the Third Degree of the ancient Mysteries, it represented the same psychological allusions, rendered in a sexual allegory. The Bride is Wisdom—the Veiled Lady of the Kabbalah. She is married to the initiate himself; who, being ritually depicted as a seeker after,

113    H

# Shakespeare's Mystery Play

Truth, is ritually a philosopher (*i.e.*, a lover of wisdom). In the Second Degree Wisdom is sought and found by the initiate; and in the Third Degree she removes her Veil to "reveal her secrets" to her tried and proved lover.*

It is generally declared that the hierogamy in the Eleusinian Mysteries was a union of the deities. Taylor supposes that it was the marriage of Persephone with Pluto; others that it was the marriage of Zeus with Demeter. Here the difficulty is that of disentangling the esoteric scheme that underlies the concept of Initiation from the particular mythological references with which it may be complicated in any given cultus. In all authentic initiation rites certain features may be expected to appear, such as long wanderings in the Second Degree in search of that which is lost, and a ritual death in the Third Degree. What these common features really signify I have attempted to indicate; but the form they may take in a given cultus is another matter. For instance, the candidate's search for Truth (the Lost Word) assumed at Eleusis, by an obvious adaptation, the ostensible form of an imitation of Demeter's quest for the lost Persephone. In like manner, the death of one of its mythical persons or deities might quite well be imitated in a particular cultus, and thus furnish the ostensible pretext for the ritual death of the initiate. In short, although the rites refer to the candidate himself, their significance is concealed by their apparent reference to purely mythical characters.

* Cf. *Ecclus.* iv. 17-18; also Kabbalah, as cited in Part I. hereof. In the *Divin. Comm.*, Dante seeks Beatrice. He finds her, veiled, after he has ascended through Purgatory (MIST) to Eden (AIR). Contrary to the tradition, Dante depicts Beatrice as unveiling herself to him before the ascent to the Celestial Paradise (AETHER); but observe that it is only her face that she reveals, so that here the meaning is not the same as in the ritual allegory (*i.e.*, complete unveiling in revelation).

# The Meaning of Initiation

As a matter of fact, this device of substitution is well authenticated; and if the principle, to which there will be occasion to recur, be valid in the case of the hierogamy, the " mystic marriage " would likewise involve and concern the aspirant himself. Observe what follows. Initiation is a search for and a marriage with Wisdom. At Eleusis the aspirant was represented as searching for Persephone; hence the subsequent " marriage " should be between Persephone and the aspirant.

This conclusion is, no doubt, novel and incapable of direct proof by the aid of a number of reliable records. But it may be noted that Persephone, who in the Lesser Mysteries was called *Pherrephatta*, was called in the Third Degree *Kore*, which means not only the maid but also the bride. Moreover, Thomas Taylor quotes from a Greek MS. of Psellus to the effect that in the Eleusinian Mysteries sexual relations were simulated and that the initiated sang: " I have born the mystic cup; *I have entered into the bed*."* This clearly implies that it was the initiate himself who was figuratively " married "—a conclusion to which the whole of my case will tend.

Before proceeding to a more detailed analysis, I may with advantage briefly summarise the results of the foregoing argument. Formal or ritual initiation was a ceremony designed as a reversal of the process implied in the Fall of Man. It consisted, therefore, in an Ascent through the Elements. As such, it could— and probably did to some extent—comprise an ostensible crossing of the River Styx (WATER), a passage through Purgatory (MIST) to Elysium (AIR), and finally an ascent into the Empyrean (AETHER). But, since these mythical abodes of the dead have their

* Psellus, *On Daemons*; cited by Taylor, *Eleus. and Bacch. Myst.*, edit. J. Weitstein, Amsterdam, p. 179.

counterparts in the planes or states of consciousness, ritual initiation may be interpreted as a purely psychological experience. It figures the ascent of the consciousness from the material or physical plane of EARTH, through the passional WATER and the MIST of error, to the AIR of pure reason, which is the plane of inspiration; and finally the ascent—during a death to this world—to the intuitional AETHER, which is the plane of revelation.

Interpreted in this manner, the ancient ritual initiation corresponds exactly with what may be called empirical initiation. For this detachment of the consciousness from material and passional concerns is precisely what every philosopher must achieve before the Truth he seeks can be heard in inspiration—as he must, further, rise beyond reason before Truth can be fully revealed to him through intuition, making him an (empirical) initiate, or *a seer*.

As an Ascent through the Elements, therefore, the ancient ritual initiation was neither an arbitrary nor a fantastic ceremony. It was a symbolical counterpart of empirical initiation—that is, of the renouncing of " the world, the flesh, and the devil " in the pursuit of divine illumination. In other words, the initiatory rites which the pagan aspirant had to undergo before he might learn the secrets of the Mysteries and become *epoptes* (a seer) were a faithful allegory of the subjective changes which are a condition precedent to every revelation of Truth in experience. Furthermore (as I shall show), the testing ordeals of the pagan rites were an equally faithful allegory of the difficulties and temptations encountered by every man who seeks salvation in the quest for Truth.

Now, this conception of the ancient ceremonies has implications of really high importance. For example, it sheds a new light upon the problems arising

# The Meaning of Initiation

from the resemblance between Christian institutions and the pagan Mysteries. Many students have attempted to account for that resemblance; but even so unexceptionable a scholar as Isaac Casaubon could explain it only on the hypothesis that the early Christian Fathers deliberately adopted the terms and rites of the pagan Mysteries as a concession, not entirely disinterested, to the deep-rooted conservatism of most men in regard to religious forms and ceremonies.*

But if (as I shall presently argue exhaustively) the rites of the pagans were an accurate account in symbols of the subjective experience by which alone a man acquires divine illumination and achieves " salvation," then those rites may well have found a place in the Christian Church by virtue of their own intrinsic merits. For that which they expressed was the very essence of all religious experience. They were true for every aspirant, quite irrespective of his particular religious beliefs. And their appearance in the Christian Church requires no other warrant or explanation than this—that no better ritual could be devised, because it was at every point a true and a relevant ritual.

I have already had occasion to refer to Bunyan's *Pilgrim's Progress*. This work is an allegory of the renunciation of material and passional things and the attainment of salvation; so that, according to the argument I have been formulating, we are perfectly justified on *a priori* grounds in expecting to find a general resemblance between the experiences of Christian and those of the initiate into the Mysteries.

Nor is this expectation falsified. Certain features of the story will be fully dealt with later; but the most

* Is. Casaubon, *Exercit. in Baronium*, No. 16; cited by several authorities, including Warburton and Cheetham.

cursory examination suffices to show that Christian's "journey" corresponds in character and in sequence to the Ascent through the Elements. For, after quitting the gross materialistic City of Destruction (EARTH), Christian passes through the miry Slough of Despond (MIRE). He is tempted and tried by long and bitter self-conflict in that Valley of Humiliation which is demonstrably the subjective Purgatory (MIST); and in due time he reaches the pleasant Land of Beulah, which manifestly corresponds to the mythical Lower Paradise (AIR). Finally, in a death to this world, he mounts to the Heavenly Jerusalem, which is the supreme Celestial Paradise (AETHER or FIRE).*

In this broad resemblance the answer to the riddle of the ancient initiation rites is intimated, and the principle of my argument is confirmed. The Ascent through the Elements, like the pilgrimage of Christian, was an allegory of what may be called the psychology of salvation. Its chief value lay, therefore, in its intimate relation to the permanent facts which are the basis of all religion. Theological systems may differ widely, according to time and race and cultural circumstance; but the inner religious experience, actual or potential, of all mankind is unchanging from age to age. It was this experience that was allegorised in the pagan rites of initiation. Of every aspirant, ritual or empirical, it is inexorably required that he renounce material and passional things; no otherwise can he attain to divine Truth. This renunciation is the "straight and steep and narrow way" which is the only Way to Salvation. It was the path trodden by Christian in his pilgrimage and by his pagan brother in the Mysteries;

* Note that no reference is made to WATER in the above summary. Bunyan seems to have confounded the passage through Water with the death that precedes revelation in the Celestial Paradise (AETHER).

and from the trials of the one we can reconstruct the ritual ordeals of the other.*

Speaking of the pagan initiation as an Ascent through the Elements, Dupuis (in the passage already cited) remarks that this was " the most metaphysical part, which most of the initiates could hardly understand." But, with all deference to Dupuis as an authority, I think he somewhat exaggerates the difficulty of the subject. In the course of the ensuing chapters I shall offer a detailed interpretation which, whatever may be its merits, is neither abstruse nor fantastic. And, in so far as the reader has himself been a seeker after Truth, he can verify my case by comparing it with his own psychological experience.

* Since the above argument was formulated, the following has come to my notice: " The inspired prisoner who wove the *Pilgrim's Progress* (as he tells us) out of the substance of his dreams, has reproduced with marvellous fidelity the very incidents of the initiation ceremonies of ancient Egypt, almost in the language of the Book of the Dead " (Mr. Allen Upward, *The Divine Mystery*, p. 222).

# CHAPTER II

## *THE ASCENT*

I COME now to the task of analysing in detail the meaning of Initiation as outlined in the foregoing pages, and of proving concurrently that the same ideas are embodied—with, it would seem, some measure of deliberate purpose on Shakespeare's part—in *The Tempest*.

The argument falls naturally into two parts; and I shall accordingly treat (1) the Lesser Initiation, with especial reference to the case of the Court Party in the Play, and (2) the Greater Initiation, with especial reference to the case of Ferdinand.

It will, perhaps, serve to prevent any misconception if I first indicate briefly what I believe to be implied, consciously or otherwise, in *The Tempest*. I contend that the Play deals primarily with certain permanent realities of spiritual experience; that it expresses the universal psychology of upward endeavour in the same allegorical terms as are employed in all authentic myth and ritual; and that it may be regarded as an account of Initiation in so far as Initiation (whether ceremonial or empirical) is understood to signify the renouncing of " the world, the flesh, and the devil" in the upward struggle " out of darkness into light." Furthermore, I maintain that actually the Poet has reproduced with extraordinary fidelity both the substance and the form of the Christian and of the non-Christian traditions; that if this fact be not due to deliberate design, it must be due to some necessity inherent in the essential theme of the Play; and that this same fact not only supports my interpretation of the Play, but also renders any other interpretation inadequate or inadmissible.

There are some lines in Shakespeare's *Richard III.* which may here be cited as a curious and illuminating little commentary upon the title of the Play with which this present study is concerned. They are uttered by the conscience-tormented Clarence, who dreamed that he fell from a ship into the raging sea, and that he passed thereafter through the mythical abodes of the dead. Describing the dream, Clarence exclaims:

> O, then began the tempest to my soul,
> Who pass'd, methought, the melancholy flood,
> With that grim ferryman which poets write of,
> Unto the kingdom of perpetual night.
>
> (*Richard III.*, I. 4. 44–47.)

It is enough for the moment to remark that I am about to treat *The Tempest* as an account of a purely psychological pilgrimage described (after the manner of the pagan rites) as a journey through Purgatory to Elysium and beyond—that same pilgrimage which, according to Clarence, involves a " tempest to the soul."

## 1. The Court Party

In the New Testament account of the Baptism of Christ we read how, coming up out of the water, He went straightway up into the Wilderness, where He remained fasting for forty days; and, being hungry and thirsty, He was tempted by the Devil, whom He resisted; whereupon angels came and ministered unto Him.

This myth, for such we may call it with no irreverence, is by no means peculiar to the life-story of

Christ. It is related in some form of all the great religious teachers. It is to be understood, I think, not in the literal sense, but as an allegory in objective or environmental terms of a purely subjective experience. It is, in fact, an account of the Lesser Initiation; and, indeed, it has manifestly all the essential features of an Ascent through WATER and MIST to AIR.

In the first place, the Wilderness is clearly that subjective Purgatory which is the plane of MIST. Note the phrasing in the Gospels: " And straightway coming up out of the water, He went up into the Wilderness." This distinctly implies not only an ascent, but also that the Wilderness is superjacent to the baptismal Water—just as Purgatory is superjacent to the River Styx, and as MIST is superjacent to WATER. Moreover, the traditional nature of the Wilderness corresponds to the nature of the plane of MIST, as I shall now show.

What does the Lesser Initiation, in its psychological aspect, comprise? It comprises the renunciation of worldly and passional things and the achievement of that state of divine inspiration which is the prototype of the mythical Lost Estate of Man. Rising from the plane of EARTH, through and beyond the plane of WATER, the consciousness reaches the plane of MIST. That is to say, the aspirant renounces material and passional things and concerns himself with intellectual speculation. But MIST is the plane of error and illusion. Being partly emotional and partly rational, it is the plane of imperfect thinking; for here the influences which rise from the passional plane (as Mist rises from Water) darken and obscure the reason, causing the aspirant to follow many false paths in his search for Truth. After a long period (" forty days ") of these fruitless wanderings, the seeker grows weary. The passional inhibition and the sense of isolation from

122

the ordinary life of men are now realised in all their bitterness, while the compensating rewards are yet withheld. The seeker is desolate and disappointed: his long abstinence from normal worldly satisfactions seems to have been endured in vain. He hungers for the bread of fellowship and he thirsts for passional indulgence.* He is assailed by Desire, tempting him to abandon his quest. This is the testing time for the seeker after Truth. He must hold fast to his purpose. Desire, if it be resolutely resisted, will depart from him, leaving him to pursue his way in peace.† When at last this triumph over Desire has been accomplished and all the darkening clouds of prejudice, sentiment, custom, and the like have been surmounted, the consciousness reaches the next plane. It passes out of MIST into the pure dry AIR—out of error and doubt and temptation into serene and dispassionate reason. The aspirant now learns in some measure the Truth he seeks. This partial apprehension in the AIR of reason of the Truth whose complete apprehension is possible only in the AETHER of intuition is (as I have explained) represented in tradition as a hearing by the ear of a distinctly speaking Voice that bears witness of the mystery which is not yet seen by the eye.

All this is undoubtedly implied in the myth of

* That the " thirst " which the aspirant suffers is a thirst for the passional WATER, is obvious enough. As for the " hunger," I need only refer to the universal practice of breaking bread together as the outward symbol of worldy fellowship. This fellowship is one of the worldly pleasures which must be renounced by the aspirant to initiation.

† Cf. *Jas.* iv. 7: " Resist the Devil, and he will flee from you." Similarly, Apollyon left Christian when the latter resisted him in the Vale of Humiliation. Both the Devil and Apollyon are figures for Desire—that same insidious Serpent which caused (and causes) the Fall from the Elysian AIR of reason, and which must be overcome as a condition precedent to a return thither in the Second Degree of Initiation.

# Shakespeare's Mystery Play

Christ's Sojourn and Temptation in the Wilderness. I have just shown that the Wilderness is the plane of MIST, and in the previous chapter I gave reasons for regarding the baptismal Water as symbolical of the WATER, which is the passional plane. For the rest, the Gospel story follows the tradition quite accurately. Christ passed up out of the WATER into the MIST, where He was in solitude, "fasting for forty days." Thereafter, being hungry and thirsty, He was sorely tempted, being assailed by desire for worldly and passional things. Nor was it until He had resisted all the persuasions of the Tempter (Desire) that He was left in peace upon the mountain-top, where "angels came and ministered unto Him." This association with the angels, which ensues upon the triumph over Desire, clearly marks His ascent out of MIST into AIR. And although the nature of the ministrations is not defined in any of the Gospels, it can be confidently predicated. Tradition certainly ascribes to these winged messengers of the Most High, to the angels whose proper element is the Air, a distinguishing quality of speech or the voice.* This ascription is assuredly neither haphazard nor meaningless. It is symbolical, and its purport is

* The angel who appeared to Dante as he passed from Purgatory to Eden had a voice more clear and piercing than ours (*Purg.* xxvii. 6, 7: "I' angel . . . cantava . . . in voce assai più che la nostra viva"). Compare *Macbeth* I. 7. 19:

> His virtues
> Will plead like angels, trumpet-tongued. . . .

One of the appellations of the Archangel Gabriel, the winged messenger of God, is "The Distinctly speaking Spirit." So, too, the airy Hermes, winged messenger of Zeus, was held to be the god of speech and is often associated directly with the Word.

The tongue of angels is, of course, proverbial, as in the phrase "the tongues of men and angels."

In the angelology of Philo Judaeus, the angels are practically identified with the Word or Words of God, and are called *logoi* (words).

124

unmistakable. Clearly the function of the angels—as of the aerial daemons of the Greeks, to which in this respect they correspond—is that of inspiration. In terms of the full symbolical figure which has already been explained, the clear-voiced angels are the messengers of God who utter the Word of Truth into the ear of reason. There is not the slightest reason to suppose—indeed, to do so were contrary to the essential spirit of all symbolism—that the angels who came to Christ upon the mountain-top performed any other than this their traditional function. Their ministration may, therefore, be said to have consisted in communicating orally the Truth for which He was seeking. That is to say, Christ had now achieved that state of being " inspired " which is the concluding phase of the Lesser or " Auricular " Initiation.

Thus, in respect of what it signifies, the angelic ministration corresponds to the pagan *paradosis* (oral transmission). Indeed, in every respect the Gospel myth bears a curious and instructive resemblance to the Eleusinian Lesser Initiation as briefly outlined in the previous chapter. Christ was immersed in the River Jordan, ascended thence to wander in the lonely Wilderness, and finally received the Word of Truth from the aerial agents of inspiration. Similarly, the pagan aspirant was immersed in the sea, ascended thence to wander on the dark and deserted seashore,* and finally received the mystery in an oral communication called *paradosis*, which was symbolical of inspiration. In like manner, Aeneas crossed the River Styx, passed through the purgatorial region, and finally came to a pleasant place (Elysium) where he received a spoken discourse from his father Anchises—

---

* It may, of course, be said that the seashore is superjacent to the sea, as the wilderness is to Jordan, Purgatory to Styx, and MIST to WATER.

precisely as the Children of Israel crossed the Red Sea, wandered in the Wilderness, and came at last to the Promised Land. Of the same kind is the pilgrimage of Dante up the Mount of Purgatory to Eden, and that of Christian through the Valley of Humiliation to the Land of Beulah.

All these stories employ the same allegorical medium to express the same subjective experience—namely, the rising of the consciousness above sensuous or passional things, the long wanderings in the lonely wilderness of speculation in quest of Truth, and the coming at last to that serenity of pure reason in which the voice of inspiration is heard. And, since the psychological state thus finally attained is the proto-type of the mythical Lower Paradise, or Eden, the Gospel myth—like these other stories it resembles—is an account of self-redemption conceived as the re-covery of the Lost Estate of Man. It deals with a reversal of the process implied in the myth of the Fall. In other words, the Gospel myth contains all the essential features of the Lesser Initiation. Nor need we wonder that Christ, the Way-shower, should tread the same path as the pagan seeker in the Mysteries, since for all mankind, whether pagan or Christian, there is but one Way to Salvation.

It is the object of this present section to prove that the same ideas are embodied, and the same allegorical medium is employed, in that part of *The Tempest* which deals with the Court Party, whose experiences have already been shown to bear a sustained resem-blance to those involved in the earlier stages of the pagan initiatory rites.

First let me call attention to a passage in one of the Essays of Francis Bacon. Again disclaiming any desire to suggest that *The Tempest* is the work of Bacon's pen, I quote the passage because it serves as a curious link between the Play and the traditional allegory I have been treating. Citing the poet Lucretius and interpolating a noteworthy phrase of his own, Bacon writes:

> No pleasure is comparable to the standing upon the vantage-ground of Truth (a Hill not to be commanded, and where the Air is always clear and serene) and to see the errors and wanderings, and mists, and tempests, in the vale below (Essay *Of Truth*).

A state of consciousness is manifestly alluded to, and Bacon goes on to describe it as " heaven upon earth." Can anyone fail to perceive that this Hill of Truth corresponds to the Mount of Purgatory which Dante describes? Like that of Dante's Mount, the summit of this Hill is high above the mists of the slopes and vales below—an " earthly paradise " where the air is clear and serene. And that Bacon intends the whole passage (including the " mists and tempests ") in a purely psychological sense is quite evident from the paraphrase he gives elsewhere. Again citing Lucretius, he writes:

> But it is a pleasure incomparable for the mind of man to be settled, landed, and fortified in the certainty of Truth; and from thence to descry and behold the errors, perturbations, labours, and wanderings up and down of other men (*Advance. Learn.* I. viii., 5).

Here the " errors and wanderings," of which we read so much in accounts of initiation, are again referred to as such; but, instead of " mists and tempests " looked down upon from the serene air of a hill-top, this version speaks of " labours and perturbations " contemplated from a calm state of assurance concerning Truth. Further comment is needless. Those who argue that Bacon wrote the works of Shakespeare may make what use they care to of the fact; but there is no shadow of a doubt that the meaning of these passages is exactly what I have imputed to the Gospel myth and to the pagan rites, and what I suggest is to be found in the story of the Court Party in the Play.

There is certainly ample warrant in the text for the assumption that the plunging of the Court Party into the sea has some symbolical significance. As I have already pointed out, the fact is emphasised no less than five times in the dialogue that the men's garments are in nowise impaired by the water. It is not enough to argue that the Poet is at pains to intimate—with curious insistence—that the experience of the immersion in the sea was an illusion, for this does not explain why the garments are said to be " fresher than before," and to be " rather new-dyed than stained with salt-water." What is implied in the extraordinary fact of this improvement? In what sense has the Court Party (to use Ariel's words in reference to Alonso) " suffered a sea-change into something rich and strange"?

To these questions, which can hardly be ignored, my theory supplies a perfectly adequate answer. Just as the Eleusinian aspirant was immersed in the sea and thereafter wandered on the deserted shore, and just as Christ was immersed in the River Jordan and thereafter wandered in the lonely Wilderness—so the Court Party is immersed in the sea and thereafter wanders on the shore of the " most desolate isle." In other words, the immersion of the Court Party corresponds in significance to the pagan *Katharsia* (cleansing) and to the Christian ceremony of Baptism.*

* Cf. 1 *Cor.* x. 1-2, where St. Paul distinctly implies that a passage through the sea corresponds to the ceremony of Baptism. The story of the passage of the Israelites through the Red Sea and of their long wanderings in the Wilderness to the Promised Land is an account, expressed in the same traditional allegory, of the religious endeavour and self-discipline (*i.e.*, the initiation) of a whole people. Note that the Promised Land is a place " flowing with milk and honey "—a place of abundance, like Dante's Eden, Bunyan's Beulah, Ovid's

# The Ascent

It therefore represents the upward passage of the consciousness through the emotional WATER. And the arrival of the Court Party upon the island in a better condition than before represents that mounting of the consciousness from WATER to MIST which is involved in the change from emotional to intellectual activity, and which is mythologically described as an ascent into the Wilderness. It marks the end of the First Degree of Initiation and the beginning of the Second Degree.

If this view be correct, the Court Party must now be in the subjective state of MIST; and indeed, Gonzalo seems quite plainly to declare that this is so:

> It is foul weather in us all, good sir,
> When you are cloudy.
>
> (Act II., Scene 1.)

Moreover, the King and his company now commence those long wanderings in a desolate place which traditionally ensue upon a crossing of water, and which represent the long effort of the aspirant to rise out of this state of MIST into the AIR of pure reason.

It is generally affirmed by commentators that the wanderings upon the shore at Eleusis were a reproduction of the mythical search for the lost Persephone; and, as I have said, this is no doubt true as far as it goes. It is quite likely that at the time the neophyte himself received this ostensible explanation of the wanderings, and that at the corresponding stage in the Isiac Mysteries the candidate was said to be seeking the lost Osiris, exactly as the wanderings of the Court Party have for their ostensible purpose the finding of

---

Golden Age, the mythical Elysium, and so on. To arrive there is to achieve plenty after privation, recompense after endeavour, inspiration after long and steadfast seeking.

the lost Ferdinand. But if we look from the outward form of the pagan rites to their inner significance, we can hardly doubt that what was intended by the ritual wanderings was the search for Truth. This is not mere assumption. I have argued that every authentic initiation embodies the same essential principle; and, since every cultus professed what may be called its own traditional history, it is obvious that each initiation ritual—certainly the Eleusinian, and probably also the Isiac and the Orphic—was the complex result of uniting the common principle with the essentials of the particular story on which the cultus rested. Hence we should expect to find the salient points of the common principle expressed in each cultus in its own peculiar mythical terms, and we must make discriminating allowance for such superficial inconsistencies as are obviously due to this process of arbitrary fusion. There is, therefore, nothing inherently improbable in the suggestion that the search for the lost Persephone was the ritual expression, in terms peculiar to the Eleusinian cultus, of the search for Truth.

But there are other considerations to be noticed in this connection. For the quest for Truth in the Lesser Initiation is (as I have shown) a quest for " the lost Word " of inspiration; and, as every student of mystical systems is aware, there is a close symbolical relation between the Word (*Logos*) and the Son—as Christ, the archetypal Son, is actually identified in the New Testament with the Word (*St. John* i. 14). Upon the ultimate origin of this mystical association between the Word and the Son, or between " the lost Word " and " the lost Son," I need not here digress to speculate. But, clearly, there are other reasons besides the one I have just given why the search for " the lost Word " assumed at Eleusis the outward or ritual form of a search for *the lost Child* Persephone, as in the Play it assumes the outward form of a search for *the lost Son* Ferdinand.*

While the analogy between the case of the Eleusinian neophyte and the case of the Court Party is thus far exact, I do not, of course, press it to the extreme limit of arguing that Ferdinand is actually and directly a personification either of Persephone or of Truth. My point is simply that the quest for Truth, which commences when the consciousness rises above the WATER of emotion to the plane of MIST, is represented in the Play, as at Eleusis, by wanderings upon the shore after a symbolical immersion in the sea, and that in both cases the ostensible or outward purpose assigned for these wanderings is, not without reason, the finding of *a lost Child* (Son or Daughter).

Let us consider further the story which I contend is the basis of the ancient initiation rites and of *The Tempest*—namely, the story of the psychological experience, narrated symbolically as an Ascent through the Elements, of every man who seeks for Truth as the means to Salvation.

Now, it is one thing to rise above material and passional preoccupations to a state of intellectual inquiry. But to rise still higher to a state of complete

---

* The fact that at Eleusis " the lost Word " was represented by a lost Daughter, rather than by a lost Son, is one of the superficial inconsistencies to which I referred as resulting from the fusion of the common principle with the essentials of a particular myth. Later pages will shed further light upon the relation suggested in the ritual of the Mysteries between Persephone and Truth.

In view of the frequency with which in the Bible the Word of Truth is represented as a death-dealing and destroying sword that proceeds out of the mouth (*Eph.* vi. 17; *Heb.* iv. 12; *Rev.* i. 16; ii. 12, 16; vi. 8; xix. 15, 21), it is curious to note that, according to Liddell and Scott's Lexicon, the name of Persephone—whom the above argument associates with the Word of Truth—means literally " Bringer of Death."

mental clarity, to a state in which the judgment is not in the smallest measure clouded and confused by the intrusion of the emotional element into the reason (as Water intrudes into the Air in the form of Mist or Cloud)—to accomplish this is quite another matter, and requires prolonged and arduous discipline.* Until the judgment has been thus purged of every trace of passional and sensuous influence, the thinker wanders vainly in a wilderness of barren speculation. He is (as it were) in an intricate labyrinth, wherein he strays long and painfully amid countless winding paths that lead nowhither. Upon every seeker after Truth the same remorseless intellectual discipline is imposed. There is no royal road to divine inspiration. Rising from the passional WATER, every seeker must pass through this Labyrinth or Wilderness (MIST), and mount thence into the clear AIR of reason. No otherwise can he succeed in his quest and hear at last the Word of Truth spoken by the aerial agents of Inspiration.†

This passage through the Labyrinth or purgatorial Wilderness is, then, the main ordeal of the Lesser

---

* Spinoza defines erroneous ideas as opinions suggested to the mind by the senses. In other words, they are opinions formed while the consciousness is neither in the rational AIR nor in the sensuous WATER, but between the two—that is, in MIST.

† Omar Khayyam sings (xxvii.) of this labyrinth of intellectual speculation:

> Myself when young did eagerly frequent
> Doctor and Saint, and heard great argument
> About it and about: but evermore
> *Came out by the same door as in I went.*

But Omar failed in the initiation ordeal. He did not persevere through the Labyrinth until he found the way to Truth. He never rose out of the MIST of error into the clear AIR of inspired reason, but rather turned back to the sensuous WATER. He did not achieve even the Lesser Initiation.

# The Ascent

Initiation. Without doubt, in some of the ancient ritual initiations the neophyte was required to pick his way, actually or by representation, through a labyrinth or maze.* In any case, the ritual wanderings in darkness—which were an allusion to the period of intellectual discipline during life, no less than to the period of the soul's discipline after death—certainly bore some marked resemblance to wanderings in a maze. For Lucian describes them as a "blind march";† and moreover, some verses in *Ecclesiasticus* which I have already had occasion to quote‡—verses which obviously have a purely subjective significance, and which at the same time have the strong stamp of an allusion to the ordeals of initiation (whether of ritual or of empirical initiation makes no difference)—declare that the aspirant walks in "crooked ways," wherein he is tormented by the laws and discipline of Wisdom, before he finally wins her by the "straight way."

To this traditional allegory, which we find in both mythology and ritual, the story of the Court Party thus far conforms unfailingly. For, after a symbolical immersion in the sea (WATER), the King and his company pass into a desolate place that is also a place of expiation—in short, a purgatorial wilderness (MIST).

* In his *Phaedo* (lvii. E.108) Plato, speaking of a road traversed after death, says: "This road is not a plain united road . . . but there are several *by-ways and cross-ways*, as I conjecture from the method of our sacrifices and religious ceremonies." This distinctly implies that in the ancient religious ceremonies a journey through a labyrinth was simulated.

† Warburton cites from Lucian's *Dialogue of the Tyrant* as follows: "You are initiated in the Eleusinian mysteries. Tell me now, do you not think this very like the blind march they make there? Oh, extremely. . . ." The speakers of these words are at the moment lost in a thick darkness.

‡ *Ecclus.* iv. 17-19.

# Shakespeare's Mystery Play

Here they wander in search of "the lost son," and, after prolonged and fruitless seeking, they realise that they are wandering in a maze of straight and crooked paths:

GON.                    I can go no further, Sir,
        My old bones ache: here's a maze trod, indeed,
        Through forth-rights and meanders!
                            (Act III., Scene 3.

Every genuine philosopher knows from his own experience what follows upon this realisation. Confused in the maze of speculation, discouraged by failure, his spirit dulled and depressed by weariness, the seeker passes through doubt to a sense of the hopelessness of his quest for the "lost Word" of Truth. So in the Play:

GON.                    Here's a maze trod, indeed,
        Through forth-rights and meanders! By your patience,
        I needs must rest me.
ALON.                    Old lord, I cannot blame thee,
        Who am myself attached with weariness
        To the dulling of my spirits.  Sit down and rest.
        Even here I will put off my hope, and keep it
        No longer for my flatterer: he is drowned
        Whom thus we stray to find. . . .
                            (*Ibid.*)

The constancy of the seeker after Truth is now severely tested.  His unavailing search is mocked by his own passional nature, by the WATER whence he has risen.  As Alonso says of the Court Party:

                    The sea mocks
        Our frustrate search on land. . . .
                            (*Ibid.*)

Relaxing his efforts in weariness and failure, the seeker becomes a prey to desire.  He is haunted by doubts and fears and unclean thoughts, which crowd upon him like evil creatures in the darkness.  He is troubled

134

by memories of sensuous delights, memories that make a sweet appeal and beckon him back to forbidden things. He is tempted to abandon his purpose and return to the commoner and easier concerns of mankind. And upon the issue of this temptation depends the issue of his high endeavour.

As this experience is part of the discipline imposed upon the philosopher in the course of empirical initiation, so likewise it was represented as befalling him who sought for Truth by the way of formal or ritual initiation into the pagan Mysteries. I contend that it was ceremonially depicted by the candidate's encounter with " monstrous apparitions," and that in the Play it is figured by the Court Party's encounter with the " strange shapes." In default of adequate data concerning the monsters of the pagan rites, it is possible to give direct evidence only of the latter part of this double proposition; but such evidence as can be adduced in support of the former part is greatly enhanced by the consistent similarity which my argument establishes between the ancient rites and the Play.

First let it be observed that the temptation of the aspirant may be described in at least three different ways. We may say—(i) that he is assailed by desire, or (ii) that he becomes obsessed by unclean thoughts, or (iii) that he hears the sweet compelling summons to sensuous indulgence. There is, of course, little essential difference between these three conceptions, for they all refer to the same phase of psychological experience. Nevertheless, in the process of allegorical elaboration the three produce somewhat divergent results. Temptation myths fall, in fact, into three main classes, typical of which are—(i) the struggle with the Dragon, (ii) the encounter with horrid Monsters, and (iii) the hearing of the Sirens' Song.

# Shakespeare's Mystery Play

Stories of a struggle with the Dragon or suchlike creature are myths of temptation by Desire. Note the nature of the Dragon, which is generally hybrid in form and native to water; also the point of encounter, which is invariably out of and above water. St. George slew the Dragon and thereby saved the "king's daughter" (his own soul). Perseus also saved the "king's daughter" by slaying the monstrous serpent that rose out of the sea. Cadmus, likewise, fought with and slew the serpent or dragon that rose out of water.* Christian fought in the Valley of Humiliation with the hybrid tempter Apollyon, who was a dragon with "scales like a fish." And it was after He had ascended into the Wilderness that Christ was assailed by the Tempter, who is described in *Revelation* both as a serpent and as a dragon.† All these myths have manifestly a common significance; and their prototype is the struggle which takes place when the aspirant, wearied and despondent after long seeking in the Wilderness of error, is assailed by the evil Desire whose native element is the passional WATER.

The mythical Monsters which figure in other versions of the tradition represent the doubts and fears and unclean thoughts which obsess the tired seeker. They differ from the mythical Dragon precisely as evil thoughts differ from evil desire; for the Monsters

---

* Cf. Ovid, *Metam.* iii. 26 *et seq.* Note that Ovid uses the words "serpent" and "dragon" interchangeably (cf. *ibid.* iv. 599 *circ.*).

† *Rev.* xii. 9; xx. 2: "The great dragon, that old serpent, which is the Devil, and Satan . . ." For obvious reasons, Christ is not depicted in the Gospels as struggling desperately with the Tempter. But a subjective struggle is implied in the series of offers made to Him by the Tempter (Desire), each offer representing something desirable of which, in His loneliness, He thought half regretfully, but which in the pursuit of His high purpose He resolutely rejected. That He was indeed half-regretful is implied by the very fact that Desire came to Him.

(like thoughts) are many and can be passively resisted, whereas the Dragon (like desire) is one and must be actively fought and vanquished. In all other respects, the Monsters resemble the Dragon. They are evil in nature and generally hybrid in form; and the point of encounter is out of and above the water with which they are often associated. Chaldean mythology (to which I shall recur) tells of evil hybrids born of water and inhabiting the darkness. The exact station of the hybrids which Aeneas encounters during his " Descent into Hell," and of which several are explicitly water-monsters, is not easy to determine; but in Aristophanes' *Frogs* it is quite clearly indicated that such horrid monsters are met with in the purgatorial region after the crossing of the River Styx. In Persian mythology we read how Zarathustra, going into a desolate place to meditate in solitude, was presently haunted in the darkness by a swarm of vile creatures;* and St. Mark declares that Christ, after emerging from the River Jordan, and wandering in the lonely Wilderness, was "tempted of Satan and was with the wild beasts,"† exactly as the Eleusinian neophyte, after emerging from the sea and wandering on the deserted seashore, encountered certain "monstrous apparitions" in the dark vestibule of the temple. Having regard to all the circumstances, it needs but little imagination to perceive that these evil creatures figure the unworthy

* In a later section ("Miranda") the myth of the temptation of Zarathustra is fully summarised.

† *St. Mark* i. 13. In the Greek Testament (*in loc.*) the phrase " with the wild beasts " is ἦν μετὰ τῶν θηρίων. Note that the Greek θήρ is cognate with the Latin *fera*, by which Virgil designates the monstrous shapes seen by Aeneas, and that it has the special meaning of " a mythical monster or hybrid." If Satan be understood in a subjective sense as desire, these wild beasts of which St. Mark speaks in apposition to him must surely have a subjective significance also.

137

thoughts which come to the aspirant in the stress of his severe discipline and of which he must purge himself as a condition precedent to the fulfilment of his purpose.

Cognate with the Monsters are the mythical Sirens. The term "siren" has, of course, a very wide usage; but it always connotes the idea of seduction by means of sensuous appeal. A siren is literally a binder or entangler (from *seira*, a cord). In many allegories, as in the reproof of Dante by Beatrice, sirens are conceived as alluring women who entangle the victim by honeyed speech and sweet enticements—like the ladies who have often brought Ferdinand into "bondage" by the "harmony of their tongues." But the Sirens of the pagan mythology clearly belong to another category. They are generally associated with water, although they are always out of and above water when encountered; they are baleful and voracious creatures; and they are depicted as being hybrid in form. In these respects they are of the same kind as the Dragon and the Monsters, and should therefore be understood in the same subjective manner. They differ, however, from these other evil creatures in that they are said to draw the wanderer to ruin by music of compelling sweetness. From these several facts we may conclude that the mythical Sirens represent the sweet alluring thoughts (or memories) which trouble the seeker in his weariness and which draw him from his purpose by their sensuous appeal.

It is evident, therefore, that the struggle with the Dragon, the encounter with horrid Monsters, and the hearing of the Sirens' music all refer to the same phase of psychological experience, and that in the ultimate analysis they all have the same significance as the Temptation in the Wilderness.

Reverting now to *The Tempest*, we find therein a remarkable synthesis of the several conceptions with which I have been dealing. For the Court Party, being despondent after prolonged and fruitless search for " the lost son," is beset by certain strange creatures which resemble those of ancient myth and ritual in that they are " of monstrous shape "; and, moreover, these creatures act the part of the Tempter. Making their appearance when the King and his company are wearied by their wanderings in the desolate isle, the " strange shapes " present a banquet and "invite the King, etc., to eat." So, in the symbolical myth of the Gospels, Christ wandered in the Wilderness; and, being hungry, He was accosted by the Tempter, who sought to turn Him from His purpose by *inviting him to eat:*

If thou be the Son of God, command these stones that they be made bread.

To which Christ made the obvious reply of a steadfast seeker after that divine inspiration which is the word of God:

Man shall not live by bread alone, but by every word that proceedeth out of the mouth of God.

In the Poet's version of this temptation, Ariel intervenes. He causes the banquet to disappear when the Court Party approaches it. There is, of course, a seeming inconsistency in the suggestion that the King and his company, who would have eaten of the banquet had they not been deprived of it by Ariel, have now successfully withstood (as every initiate must) the symbolical temptation to eat. This difficulty is dispelled by a correct appreciation of the part of Ariel, with which I shall deal fully later on. But, broadly, he may be said to play at this point the restraining part of Conscience, which upholds the initiate against temptation. It will be noticed that it is at this very moment that he lashes the Court Party with scornful accusation, and declares himself to be the instrument of moral retribution; and, moreover, that the Court Party (or, at least, Alonso), stung by Ariel's condemnation, straightway resumes the search for Ferdinand:

> I'll seek him deeper than e'er plummet sounded. . . .
> (Act III., Scene 3 *fin.*)

The allegory is quite clear and is perfectly consistent with the interpretation I am formulating. Just as Christ, being submitted in the Wilderness to the symbolical temptation to eat, chose instead to pursue His quest for " the lost Word," so Alonso, being similarly tempted in like circumstances, is prevented from eating by Conscience, whose accusing voice drives him to continue his search for " the lost son."

When Ariel intervenes, he appears in the form of *a harpy*. Comment has already been made upon this point, and further suggestions will be made in the later section dealing exclusively with Ariel. But it is certainly not inappropriate at this juncture to call attention to a passage in the work of Milton, whose knowledge in matters of myth and legend was unquestionably profound. From what has already been said, it is clear that, while *Paradise Lost* is an account of the Fall, *Paradise Regained* is an account of Initiation within the meaning assigned to the word in this study. The theme of the latter work is, therefore, of the same kind as the one I am imputing to *The Tempest*. Now, in *Paradise Regained* Milton depicts Christ as being tested by means of a banquet set before Him in the Wilderness by the Tempter; and this banquet is said to disappear—

> With sound of harpies' wings and talons heard.
> (Book II., line 403.)

# The Ascent

I need not labour the point. The conclusion seems irresistible that the story of the Court Party contains the same ideas as the Gospel myth, and that Milton's poem corresponds to both of them.

In the Wilderness the aspirant not only hungers; he also thirsts. After long abstinence, he craves for those sensuous satisfactions of which the pursuit of his purpose has deprived him. In symbolical terms, he " thirsts " for the sensuous WATER. It is this experience that is represented in the pagan mythology by the hearing of the music of the Sirens; and in the Gospel myth it is implied in the statement that the Tempter offered Christ all the glories of kingship.* The story of the Court Party corresponds to the former of these two versions of the same essential idea, although the latter is also suggested by the plotting of Sebastian and Antonio. Like the mythical Sirens, the Strange Shapes in, the Play make " gentle acts of salutation " to the accompaniment of " marvellous sweet music." They are monstrous and unnatural in form; yet they seem at the first encounter to be pleasing and attractive in their manners, a curious combination of qualities peculiar to the mythical Sirens:

> Though they are of monstrous shape, yet note
> Their manners are more gentle-kind than of
> Our human generation you shall find
> Many, nay, almost any.                    (*Ibid.*)

---

* Temporal power and glory gratify man's love of display. Desire for them (ambition) is desire for sensuous satisfactions, and may be symbolically described as a " thirst " for the sensuous WATER. Thus Prospero, speaking of his brother, remarks:

> So *dry* was he for sway. . . .
> (Act I., Scene 2, line 112.)

Ambition lures men to spiritual death or bondage, like the music of the Sirens. Every true initiate must resist it. By rigid self-

# Shakespeare's Mystery Play

Their seductive appeal being frustrated by the intervention of Conscience (Ariel), these Strange Shapes do not become fierce and violent, as the mythical Dragon (Desire) is often and quite properly said to do: they only " dance with mocks and mows," wherein they aptly resemble siren memories which one strives to ignore.

The third temptation to which Christ was submitted has no parallel in the Play; but a word may be said here with regard to it. According to the Gospels, the Tempter invited Christ to cast Himself down from a high pinnacle, saying, " It is written, He shall give his angels charge concerning thee; and in their hands they shall bear thee up, lest at any time thou dash thy foot against a stone." This seems to be an allusion to the " loneliness " suffered by the seeker in the Wilderness. What is implied is the temptation —which every philosopher feels when, in moments of weariness and disappointment, his " loneliness " becomes wellnigh intolerable—to escape from the lofty isolation of recondite inquiry by flinging himself down into the common affairs of the world. Observe the Tempter's subtle suggestion that Christ will not come to disaster by abandoning His attempt to solve the great mystery, for the divine messengers will protect and support Him. In other words, man has knowledge enough for his needs, without spending his days in search of the whole truth. Many a tired seeker has asked himself, " What does it matter ?" and, urged by Desire, has flung himself down.*

---

discipline he must become utterly indifferent to the sweet satisfactions of temporal power and glory. No otherwise can he be successful in his quest for Truth.

* It is said in the Gospels that it was the Tempter himself who set Christ upon the high pinnacle. This is because the seeker after Truth is not necessarily conscious of " lofty isolation " until the desire for lower things has made him acutely aware of it.

# The Ascent

Thus the three specific temptations which Christ underwent allude to the three typical hardships which must be endured in the Wilderness—viz., " hunger " and " thirst " and " loneliness." The value of the Gospel myth lies entirely in its relevance to the case of every seeker after Truth; and to deny that Christ, the Way-shower, felt desire strong within Him is to destroy the chief merit of the myth by claiming that He was by nature free from the ordinary susceptibilities of mankind.  If this be claimed on behalf of Him who is expressly stated to have been " made a little lower than the angels " (Heb. ii. 7–9), how can it be said that He suffered the symbolical " hunger " and " thirst " and " loneliness," or that the Tempter (Desire) came to Him at all?  The myth is true to the experience, actual or potential, of every man.  It deals with that phase in the universal psychology of renunciation in which the aspirant, looking back, muses wistfully and not a little regretfully upon the pleasant things he has forsworn.  As Alonso says, when in like circumstances the " monstrous shapes " appear before the Court Party:

> I cannot too much muse,
> Such shapes, such gesture, and such sound, expressing
> (Although they want the use of tongue) a kind
> Of excellent dumb discourse.

*(Ibid.)*

But this, of course, is before the intervention of the accusing and restraining Conscience.

I have already pointed out that the Dragon, the horrid Monsters, and the mythical Sirens are all associated in some way with water, although they are encountered out of and above water, and that they are all monstrous in the sense that they are hybrid creatures.  These characteristics persist throughout the many versions of the tradition dealing

143

with the agent (or agents) of temptation. Chaldean mythology, for example, tells of hybrid monsters which rose from water and inhabited the darkness. They are described, in the Berosus fragment preserved through Polyhistor by Eusebius and George Syncellus, as being—

monstrous animals of mixed forms and species. For there were men with two wings, others with four, and some again with double faces. . . . There were bulls with human heads. . . . A woman ruled over the whole, whose name was Omoroca, in the Chaldee tongue Thalath, which signifies the sea. . . .*

These creatures formed the army with which Thalath waged war against the gods. Thalath, as the sea, may be regarded as corresponding to the emotional WATER. In his *Oannes according to Berosus*, the Rev. J. J. Garth Wilkinson remarks of Thalath that "her rule is the empire of lusts by persuasions." He mentions, moreover, the curious fact that the Armenian translator in the Latin includes in Berosus' list of the monsters of the deep "manifold animals in the shape of *dragons*, and also *fish like sirens*." All this confirms the present argument that the Dragon, the Monsters, and the Sirens have a common significance —viz., the desire or evil thoughts and memories which have their origin in the sensuous or passional WATER.

Now, the monstrosity of the Chaldean hybrids is of the very kind ascribed to the Strange Shapes in the Play; for Gonzalo, speaking of the Shapes, expresses astonishment that men should exist—

Dew-lapped like bulls, whose throats had hanging at them
Wallets of flesh; or that there were such men
Whose heads stood in their breasts; which now we find. . . .
(Act III., Scene 3.)

---

* This passage is cited *in extenso* by Warburton, who gives the Greek text of Syncellus. Warburton is of opinion that the myth has some recondite significance; but he has no interpretation to offer, nor does he give any hint of the principles involved in this present study.

# The Ascent

These extraordinary creatures described by Gonzalo are clearly of the same nature as the " bulls with human heads " and the " men with double faces " which figure among the Chaldean monsters. Many other sorts are referred to in the Berosus fragment which do not appear in the Play. But, in mentioning expressly the mixture of man and bull, Shakespeare may quite possibly have had in mind the mythical Minotaur of Crete, a hybrid creature half man and half bull, *which devours those who lose their way in the Labyrinth;* for the idea underlying this myth is manifestly the very one with which the Poet was dealing. The Minotaur, of course, is explicitly associated with evil lust.

The Berosus record declares quite definitely that the Chaldean monsters, which the Strange Shapes in the Play resemble, were supposed to be born of water and to inhabit the darkness. Thus, in respect of their hybrid nature, their origin, and the point of encounter, they correspond to all the other mythical monsters I have mentioned—all of which, like desire and sensuous or passional thoughts, have their origin in water (WATER) but are met with in the darkness (MIST).* It must be admitted that one definite and direct link is wanting in the case of the Strange Shapes in the Play. There is no specific intimation in the

---

* The equating of MIST with darkness is justified repeatedly throughout this study. In a previous footnote I quoted from 2 *Pet.* ii. 15-17, wherein the purgatorial place or state is alluded to as *the mist of darkness.* Compare also *Odys.* xi., *sub initio,* which describes the Cimmerian darkness. Odysseus crosses the sea to the City of the Cimmerians, *a city of darkness, enveloped in mist and cloud,* and here encounters the shades of the dead. This city, beyond the water, is thus a place of darkness and a place of mist; and it may be likened to the purgatorial region, beyond the River Styx. There will presently be occasion to show that the same association of mist (cloud) and darkness is actually implied in the text of *The Tempest.*

text that they are water-creatures; but they are certainly met with in the Wilderness (MIST), and in every respect they conform to the general tradition as exemplified in the various myths.

One other word about the point of encounter. The Monstrous Shapes are met with during the ascent through Purgatory (MIST) to Elysium (AIR). In terms of two particular allegories to which the story of the Court Party corresponds, we may say that the Monsters rise up out of the subjacent water to overtake and accost the tired pilgrim while he is—(*a*) climbing the misty slopes of the Dantean Mount of Purgatory into the pure air of Eden, or (*b*) climbing the Baconian Hill of Truth into the " heaven upon earth " where " the air is clear and serene." In either case, the Monsters may be described, in an allegorical sense, as mountain-climbers; and this fact gives a peculiar aptness to the term applied to the Strange Shapes in the Play:

> Who would believe that there were *mountaineers*
> Dew-lapped like bulls. . . .
>
> (*Ibid.*)

The ordinary opinion is that Gonzalo here uses the word " mountaineers " with the meaning of " savages " or " barbarians "—*i.e.*, wild men of the mountains. This is not quite consistent with the fact that Gonzalo has just declared the creatures to be remarkable for their kind and gentle manners, and has expressly implied that they are not of " our human generation." But, if the present view of the Play be correct, no better word could have been chosen to emphasise the allegory.

Turning now to the " Monstrous Apparitions " of the pagan rites, we must confess that the records are very meagre. I am not aware that there exists, for instance, any direct evidence that the monsters seen during ritual initiation were hybrid in form, or that they were native to water. Nevertheless, in respect of the point of encounter, they conform to the tradition; for the records indicate that the candidate saw them after he had emerged from the sea and wandered in darkness seeking " the lost child " Persephone. That is to say, in terms of the tradition with which I have been dealing, the ritual monsters were seen by the candidate after he had " come up out of the water " and wandered in the darkness of the purgatorial Wilderness in search of " the lost Word," which is divine inspiration. In so far, therefore, as the present thesis establishes that the pagan rites and the Play are alike in their general framework and in their inner significance, we are justified in concluding that the ritual monsters were figurative of evil thoughts and memories, and that the encounter with them in the dark vestibule of the temple represented the traditional temptation of the aspirant.

Now, since in accordance with the foregoing argument the Strange Shapes in the Play must be understood to figure the sensuous or passional thoughts or memories which trouble the weary seeker after Truth, they must be regarded as being purely subjective afflictions; and, as such, they should be seen by the Court Party as ghosts or phantoms, rather than as creatures having material or objective reality. This point, if not explicitly dealt with, is strongly suggested by a side-stroke in the text: for, when the Shapes depart, Francisco exclaims:

> They vanished strangely.
>
> (*Ibid.*)

What, precisely, was the idea in the Poet's mind when he inserted this remark, which is quite gratuitous and can hardly be without purpose? The word " vanish " suggests a sudden fading away—a " strangeness " in their mode of going which is peculiar to immaterial phantoms. It is worth mention that the monsters which Aeneas meets in the purgatorial region are expressly stated to be insubstantial shades; but this, of course, may possibly be accounted for on the grounds that Aeneas is represented as being in the realms of the dead.

So far as the pagan rites are concerned, it is generally supposed that the Monstrous Shapes which the neophyte encountered were introduced by mechanical means. There is nothing in this view to controvert my main thesis, for such mechanical monsters would simply be images employed to give ceremonial expression to a subjective experience.*

Alonso's resumption of the search for " the lost Son," following the bitter accusing speech of Ariel, is the closing feature of the third Scene of the third Act; and the Court Party does not reappear for some time, although we are given to understand that in the interval these men, stung by the lash of Conscience, suffer remorse and sorrow in full measure. In the final Scene (V. 1) we witness the completion of their Lesser Initiation; for we see them pass from this purgatorial subjective state to the happy state of purity and self-mastery which is the Lower Paradise or Elysium.

The Scene opens with Ariel reporting to Prospero on the state of mind of the King and his friends. Being sent to fetch them, Ariel presently returns with the Court Party.

In the first part of this work I closely compared with Themistius' account of the ancient rites the fact that

* There is, however, an alternative hypothesis; but to discuss it here would involve a long digression from my principal theme, which is *The Tempest*.

# The Ascent

the Court Party here makes a " frantic gesture," loses control of its footsteps, and sees Prospero throw open the entrance to the cell, as the hierophant threw open the doors of the temple after the candidate's wanderings. It may now be added that the entry of the neophyte into the brilliantly lighted temple from the gloom of the seashore and the darkness of the vestibule where the " Monstrous Shapes " were encountered obviously expresses that passage *out of darkness into light* which constitutes initiation. It figures the mounting of the consciousness out of the dark mists of error and illusion and desire into the clarity of pure reason, traditionally represented as an ascent from Purgatory (MIST) to Elysium (AIR). And indeed, Themistius, describing this stage of the ceremony, says that when the doors of the temple were thrown open—

> The mist and thick cloud were dispersed, and the mind (of the aspirant) emerged from the depth, full of brightness and light in place of the previous darkness (*Orat. in Patrem*).*

Here Themistius undoubtedly suggests the very interpretation for which I am contending.

Now, in the last Scene of *The Tempest*, we find not only a similarity (already dealt with) between the Play and the external features of the pagan rites as recorded by Themistius; we find also the same psychological allusion, expressed in the same terms of darkness and light. And, what is more, the Poet makes a clear and unequivocal use of the symbolism upon which (as I maintain) the pagan initiatory rites were based. Let me repeat that the Court Party is now passing from the subjective Purgatory to the subjective Elysium—that

* Cited by Warburton, thus: . . . ἥ τε ὀμίχλη ἐκείνη, καὶ τὸ νέφος ἀθρόον ὑπερρήγνυτο καὶ ἐξεφαίνετο ὁ νοῦς ἐκ τοῦ βάθους, φέγγους ἀνάπλεως καὶ ἀγλαΐας, ἀντὶ τοῦ πρότερου σκότου.

the consciousness is now rising from the MIST of error and illusion to the AIR of clear reason:

> And as the morning steals upon the night,
> Melting the darkness, so their rising senses
> Begin to chase the ignorant fumes that mantle
> Their clearer reason.
>
> (Act V., Scene 1.)

The psychological change here referred to is explicitly an upward movement of the consciousness out of the " fumes " of error into the clear and unclouded reason.* In terms of the symbolism, it is an ascent out of MIST into AIR; in terms of the allegorical tradition, it is an ascent out of Purgatory into Elysium. It is directly likened by the Poet to a change from a state of darkness to a state of light, precisely as Themistius, describing the entry of the neophyte into the lighted temple from the dark vestibule after the wanderings upon the shore, speaks of the mist and cloud being dispersed and of the mind ascending out of darkness into light. It is unnecessary to labour the point. I need only ask, What are the probabilities that this remarkable correspondence between the Play and Themistius' account of the pagan initiation is purely fortuitous?

Immediately after the speech I have just dealt with, Prospero sends for his hat and rapier, in order that he may present himself to the Court Party " as he was sometime Milan." And while helping to attire his master in these, Ariel sings a song.

Now, it cannot be too strongly emphasised that the irruption of Ariel at this juncture involves a considerable sacrifice of dramatic effect for which

* " Fumes " are, of course, mist or cloud. Bacon, of whose familiarity with the symbolism I have already given presumptive evidence, describes an error as a " fume." He writes: " . . . For that is the *fume* of those that conceive the Celestial Bodies have more accurate influences upon these things below than indeed they have . . . " (Essay on *Viciss. of Things*).

the literalist can hardly point to any necessity. If *The Tempest* is to be judged solely on the basis of its ostensible plot and without reference to any ulterior purpose of paramount importance, then the present juncture must be regarded as the very climax of the Play. Prospero, the exiled Duke of Milan, has already begun to make the startling revelation as to his identity. He is at this moment the centre of the dramatic action, and interest should be focussed upon him with the utmost intensity. Yet the Poet, contrary to the standards of good construction, shatters the whole effect of Prospero's revelation by making Ariel sing—at the crucial moment—a song that seems to be quite without the slightest relevance. What is the explanation of this apparent inconsequence?

Consider the nature of Ariel's song. At the moment when the King and his friends, rising from the MIST of error and illusion which is Purgatory, attain to the AIR of clear reason which is Elysium, they hear Ariel singing a song that likens him to the bee:

> Where the bee sucks, there suck I,
> In a cowslip's bell I lie. . . .

In like manner, Virgil says that Aeneas, passing from Purgatory to Elysium, sees there a number of spirits who are making the whole plain resound with a humming like that *of bees* which sit upon the blossoms on a summer's day.*

---

* Some English versions being ambiguous, it may be well to emphasise that the humming noise heard by Aeneas is actually made by the spirits. The words *strepit omnis murmure campus* are preceded by a semicolon; they form the apodosis, and refer to the spirits, and not to the bees.

Virgil says that these spirits are seen near the River Lethe. This, I think, is an erroneous conception, which Dante follows to some extent. Lethe (as I have shown) corresponds to the passional WATER. Hence it cannot be placed in Elysium, which corresponds to the

The parallel is suggestive. And here I offer a conjecture in respect of this curious allusion, which occurs at the very same point in two works that both reflect the ritual of the Mysteries. I have already mentioned, on the authority of Porphyry (*De Antro Nymph.*, c. 8), that the junior ministers of Ceres were called Bees. Is it not, in any case, an irresistible supposition that at the climax of the Lesser Initiation ceremony the Eleusinian neophyte, passing from the deserted seashore and the dark vestibule (*Purgatory*) into the lighted temple (*Elysium*), was greeted by a celebrating chorus of the assembled ministers of the cultus (*Bees*)? Such a supposition not only accords with the figure used by Virgil in his allegory of the outward forms of the Mysteries, but it also adequately accounts for Shakespeare's extraordinary dramatic solecism, which undoubtedly calls for explanation.

The first main object of the Lesser Initiation has now been achieved. The Court Party has undergone that subjective change which is allegorised in ancient myth and ritual as a passage through the Wilderness or Purgatory to Eden or Elysium. In their own psychological experience these men have brought back the Golden Age of happy innocence—to which, indeed, we find Gonzalo expressly aspiring at an earlier stage in the Play:

> Had I plantation of this isle, my lord, . . .
> I would with such perfection govern, sir,
> To excel the golden age.
>
> (Act II., Scene 1.)

---

rational AIR. Tradition certainly assigns a river of some sort to the Lower Paradise, as there was a river in Eden (*Gen.* ii. 10). But whatever it was, it was not Lethe. Here we may note that, of the river which flowed through Eden, it is said that "from thence it was parted, and became into four heads" (*Gen.* ii. 10); and in this idea we recognise the pagan concept of four rivers.

# The Ascent

Like Dante, at the close of the *Purgatorio*, they have recovered from the consequences of the Fall, and have regained the Lost Estate of Man.

Shakespeare, of course, does not actually say all this. Not one of these familiar allusions occurs in the last Scene of *The Tempest*. But the psychological change which the Court Party undergoes is precisely that which Dante describes in terms of the age-old allegorical tradition. For as Dante, having returned through Purgatory (MIST) to the Lost Estate (AIR), which he expressly associates with the Golden Age,* becomes " sovereign of himself,"† so the Court Party, when their " rising senses " have mounted out of " the ignorant fumes "(MIST) into clear reason (AIR), achieves *self-mastery and self-finding* :

> . . . all of us [found] ourselves
> When no man [of us] was his own.
>
> (Act V., Scene I.)

Observe also that Dante, being now on the top of the Mount of Purgatory, is in the subjective Lower Paradise or Eden, which (he says) is " in the pure air, above the mists and tempests of the earth and water below."‡ So likewise the Court Party, being come into the Elysian AIR of reason and looking back thence upon their experiences, may be said in the symbolical words of Francis Bacon to be in " heaven upon earth,"

---

* *Purg.* xxviii. 139-141.

† *Ibid.* xxvii. 139-142; " Free, upright, and whole, is thy will," says his guide, who now leaves him; " . . . wherefore I do crown and mitre thee over thyself." In other words, having attained to clear unclouded reason, Dante no longer requires temporal or ecclesiastical guidance.

As far as the pagan rites are concerned, the evidence indicates that the crowning of the candidate took place at a later stage—viz., on completion of the Greater Initiation. Cf. the case of Ferdinand in the Play.

‡ *Purg.* xxviii. 97-103, 106-7.

and to " stand upon the top of the Hill of Truth (where the Air is clear and serene) and to look down upon the errors and wanderings, the mists, and tempests, in the vale below."*

The identity between the inner meanings of the *Purgatorio* on the one hand, and of this part of *The Tempest* on the other, seems hardly contestable; and in this connection a point I have already mentioned is worth repeating. I refer to the fact that both poets took Virgil as their guide. If Dante did so explicitly, Shakespeare did so implicitly, in the sense that the Play exactly reproduces many features of *Aeneid VI*. Nor is this fact surprising, since each of these three works is an allegory of that psychological pilgrimage which is called Initiation.

Now, while the Court Party is in the subjective Wilderness or Purgatory, the Island assumes (for these men) a corresponding character; it is " this most desolate isle." Similarly, when Ferdinand is in the appropriate subjective state, he finds " this place Paradise." If a definite principle be here involved, the Island should present an entirely different aspect to the Court Party, when they attain to the subjective Elysium. It should then assume (for them) a gracious character; it should no longer be the " most desolate isle," but rather it should become a pleasant place of soft clear air and of serene and temperate climate, a place of " perpetual spring."†

There is, it is true, no specific intimation that such a change is observed by the Court Party at the end of the Play. Nevertheless, a distinct suggestion is

* Essay *Of Truth* and *Advance. Learn.*, cited in full at the opening of this section.

† Such is, as I have thown, the traditional character of Elysium. Cf. *Purg.* xxviii. *sub initio ; ibid.* xxviii. *prope fin. ;* Ovid, *Metam.* i. 107-8; Homer, *Odyss.* iv. *prope med.*, etc.

made in respect of the Elysian aspect of the Island, and it occurs in a very curious context. It is made in one of the earlier scenes, and *is straightway denied*. Moreover, the suggestion is made by the best of the men (Gonzalo and Adrian) and is denied by the worst (Sebastian and Antonio). What is thus implied is clear. The Island presents the aspect of Purgatory, of Elysium, or of Paradise, according to the subjective state of the percipient. And the members of the Court Party, being in the subjective Purgatory when they first emerge from the water, cannot yet perceive the Elysian aspect of the Island, exception being made in the case of Gonzalo and Adrian, for reasons which I shall presently indicate. I refer to the following extraordinary passage:

ADR. It [the Island] must needs be of a subtle, tender, and delicate temperance.
ANT. Temperance was a delicate wench.
SEB. Ay, and a subtle, as he most learnedly delivered.
ADR. The air breathes upon us here most sweetly.
SEB. As if it had lungs, and rotten ones.
ANT. Or as 't were perfumed by a fen.
GON. Here is everything advantageous to life.
ANT. True, save means to live.
SEB. Of that there's none, or little.

(Act II., Scene I.)

This is surely a most remarkable disagreement upon a simple matter of fact. How, then, is it to be explained, save on the lines I am suggesting? The description given of the Island by Gonzalo and Adrian, who are not evil men, is precisely the description given of Eden by Dante and invariably given of Elysium. On the other hand, Sebastian and Antonio, who have much to be purged of before they can even faintly realise the Elysian state, see the Island as a dreary place, arid and desolate, and foul of climate, as if it were some Wilderness or Purgatory. Does not this fact explain the whole passage in the sense I suggest?

Observe that the atmosphere of the Island is said by Adrian to be " subtle," a point indirectly commended as being " most learnedly delivered." The word seems here to be used with its proper meaning of " tenuous " or " rarefied," possibly in allusion to the state of the Air high above the Mists and Clouds. Similarly, Virgil says of Elysium that " a more extended (rarefied) atmosphere " is its conspicuous characteristic.*

A feature of the Lower Paradise is the rich verdure produced by the " tender and delicate " climate. Eden, says Dante, is a place of perpetual spring, where fresh flowers abound. So, too, in the Golden Age.† And Elysium, says Virgil, is a place of " delightful green retreats."‡ Compare:

> GON. How lush and lusty the grass looks! how green!
> ANT. The ground, indeed, is tawny.
> SEB. With an eye of green in 't.
> ANT. He misses not much.
> SEB. No; he doth but mistake the truth totally.
>
> (*Ibid.*)

Here, again, is flat contradiction in a matter of direct observation. Yet the meaning is clear. To Gonzalo (" Holy Gonzalo, honourable man "), who a moment later is aspiring to the Golden Age, an anticipatory glimpse of the Elysian state is vouchsafed; wherein these others, still in the darkness of the purgatorial state, deem him to " mistake the truth totally."

* *Aen.* vi. 640.
† Ovid, *Metam.* i. 107-8: " Then Spring was everlasting, and gentle zephyrs with warm breath played upon the flowers that sprang unplanted. . . ." Note the tender climate, as in Elysium.
‡ *Aen.* vi. 638.

# The Ascent

Apples are curiously associated with the Lower Paradise. Eden is the Apple-garden; so, too, is the Garden of the Hesperides, where there are golden apples, guarded by a dragon. The name of the Arthurian Avalon is said to be derived from *aval* (apple) and *yn* (island).* Compare:

ANT. His [Gonzalo's] word is more than the miraculous harp.
SEB. He hath raised the walls, and houses too.
ANT. What impossible matter will he make easy next?
SEB. I think he will carry this island home in his pocket, and give it his son for *an apple*.

(*Ibid.*)

Here Sebastian, still in a tone of mocking disbelief, makes allusions that are seemingly as inconsequent as they are extraordinary. Why should the Island be likened, even mockingly, to an apple, of all things? Eden is associated with apples; and the Arthurian Avalon is, as I have said, explicitly the Apple Island. Note also Sebastian's other reference. According to Tennyson, on what authority I am unable to say, the walls of Camelot were built by the music of the harp.† If this be a genuine feature of the Arthurian legend, there is a direct association of ideas in Sebastian's two speeches. In any case, that he is making (as my main point implies) authentic mythological allusions is evident; for Amphion is mythically reputed to

* Mr. Wigston, arguing (*Bac. Shak. and Rosi.*) for a thesis that differs widely from my own, but commenting in a somewhat similar vein (as I gladly acknowledge) upon these passages, cites Baring-Gould to the effect that Avalon means " The Island of Apples." To this I add a further testimony. Baring-Gould (*Curious Myths*, xx.) says: " The Slavs believe in a paradise for souls wherein is a large apple-orchard." He refers as his authority to Mannhardt's *Germanische Mythen*, p. 330.
  Dealing with the Zoharic tradition in *Sec. Doc. in Isr.*, Mr. A. E. Waite speaks of Eden as the " Apple-garden " (*op. cit.*, p. 129).
  † *Gareth and Lynette.*

157

have built the walls of Thebes by the music of his
lyre.

If the explanation I have given of the purpose of
the foregoing passages be rejected, then some other
explanation must surely be forthcoming. Otherwise,
we must conclude that the Poet has here indulged
in mere freakishness, and that the lines in question
are simply purposeless nonsense. I leave it at that,
and now revert to the final Scene of the Play.

Now, when the initiate has come at last to Elysium,
he finds that for which he seeks during his "wanderings." And indeed, it is only when the King
and his company have risen out of the darkness of
error (Purgatory) into clear and unclouded reason
(Elysium) that the ostensible purpose of their wanderings is fulfilled by the finding of "the lost son"
Ferdinand, who is discovered when Prospero throws
open the entrance of the cell.

But my whole argument throughout this section
has been to the effect that what is really implied in
the wanderings of the Court Party, as in the ritual
wanderings of the pagan aspirant, is the quest for Truth.
How, then, is Truth found in Elysium? The *Divina
Commedia*, which adheres consistently to the allegory
of the Celestial Bride, depicts the pilgrim Dante as
finding in Eden the lost Beatrice for whom he has
laboriously sought. (As already noted, she is veiled
when he meets her in Eden; for full revelation is not
yet.) But the same essential idea is often expressed
in another and quite different allegorical conception.
According to this latter version, what the aspirant
seeks for in his wanderings is Truth, in the form of that
inspired Word which man lost (and *always* loses) in
the Fall. Having returned through Purgatory to the
Lost Estate of pure and serene reason, the aspirant
achieves his purpose, for he now hears " the voice of

inspiration " which utters the Word of Truth.* Such (as I have shown) is the idea underlying the *Paradosis* of the pagan rites—the " oral transmission " which the candidate heard when, purified by the purgatorial ordeals, he passed by ritual representation into Elysium. If, therefore, the Play correspond to the pagan rites, we should find the King and his company receiving a spoken discourse at the close of their experiences.

This, indeed, is precisely what we do find, for Prospero promises the Court Party a discourse " at picked leisure." For obvious reasons, it is not actually delivered within the period covered by the Play; but we know quite definitely that it is of an explanatory nature. And, since *Paradosis* in the pagan rites must also have been an explanatory discourse, we are quite justified in saying that up to this point, if no farther, the resemblance between the case of the Court Party and that of the pagan aspirant is maintained.

As a matter of fact, we may go still farther with the aid of a reasoned conjecture. The view I have formulated of the Eleusinian ritual presents it as a psychological allegory which set forth enigmatically how man can achieve self-mastery as the means to salvation; and this clearly implies that one of its chief objects was to instruct the candidate in that most important subject, the knowledge of himself. There can be little doubt, therefore, that at some time the inner meaning of the initiation ceremony was expounded to him, for without such exposition it would defeat its own purpose. Did the requisite explanation form part of

---

* I mentioned earlier that in Elysium Aeneas learned what he desired to know in a discourse spoken by the shade of his father Anchises.

In Elysium man " hears," but does not " see." He receives inspiration, but not full revelation. He hears the Voice speaking from behind the Veil—that Veil which reason cannot penetrate.

the " oral transmission " with which the lesser rites concluded ?  We cannot say with complete assurance that it did; but the whole of the earlier portion of my argument gives some grounds for a surmise.  For if *Paradosis* was " the transmission of the mystery " in the sense that it was an oral account of the deities and a recondite interpretation of the particular myth upon which the cultus was based, it probably (though not necessarily) dealt with the subject from a psychological standpoint.  It would thus furnish an opportunity for the speaker to intimate that the ritual search for the lost Persephone was figurative of the quest for Truth; and this would lead naturally to the further explanations which—like the discourse promised by Prospero to the Court Party—would " resolve " to the listener all the " happened accidents " of the initiation ceremony, making each and every feature of the ritual " seem probable " as part of a coherent and intelligible allegory.

These last considerations are stated for what they may be worth; and I do not wish to press them, because they involve so much that is conjectural. But, in concluding the case with regard to the Court Party, I cannot too strongly emphasise the fact that the terms in which Prospero promises the discourse are tantamount to a direct affirmation of the entire principle for which I have been contending—namely, that the extraordinary experiences that befall the Court Party can be, and ought to be, " resolved " into a coherent allegory.  In short, the text of the Play furnishes *an explicit and complete justification, through the mouth of Prospero himself, for the present undertaking;* and how far I may claim to have constructed in the foregoing pages the full and comprehensive explanation which Prospero admits to be necessary, is a question I now leave the reader to determine.

# The Ascent

## 2. FERDINAND.

There is little to add to what has already been said concerning the Greater Initiation. In the ancient rites it comprised a simulated death and a seeing of the gods and their mystery, by virtue of which revelation the aspirant became *epoptes* (a seer). Mythologically, as in Dante's *Divina Commedia*, the Greater Initiation consists in an ascent from Elysium (AIR) to the Celestial Paradise (AETHER), where a glimpse of divine things is obtained—precisely as in psychological experience Truth is fully revealed only when the seeker, "closing his eyes" to the external world, has mounted from the plane of reason (AIR) to the plane of intuitional perception (AETHER).

I contend that the story of Ferdinand in the Play is an account of this Greater or "Ocular" Initiation; and that, although it is told concurrently, it continues and completes the allegory presented in the story of the Court Party.

When we first see Ferdinand, his passion and the wild waters have already been simultaneously allayed by the sweet music of Ariel:

> Sitting on a bank,
> Weeping again the king my father's wreck,
> This music crept by me upon the waters,
> Allaying both their fury, and my passion,
> With its sweet air.
>
> (Act I., Scene 2.)

In other words, Ferdinand has already passed through emotional tumult to that tranquillity which is the subjective Elysium. That he has passed through "Hell" is implied in the special and seemingly gra-

tuitous reference contained in Ariel's initial report to
Prospero:

> The king's son, Ferdinand,
> With hair up-staring (then like reeds, not hair),
> Was the first man that leapt; cried, " Hell is empty,
> And all the devils are here."

(Ibid.)

But this Hell-like scene has been wholly transformed
when Ferdinand first appears. He is now following
after Ariel, who is singing a song that we may fairly
take as describing the pleasant place to which Ferdinand is led when the wild waves of his passion have been
stilled:

> Come unto these yellow sands,
>     And then take hands;
> Court'sied when you have, and kissed
>     The wild waves whist:
> Foot it featly here and there;
> And, sweet sprites, the burden bear.

(Ibid.)

The transformation of his environment is thus as
complete as that of his mood. Moreover, it closely
resembles the change Aeneas experienced when he
passed up from Purgatory to Elysium; for Virgil
expressly says that the mythical Elysium is a pleasant
place where " happy spirits dance and sing upon the
yellow sands."*

In the mythological as well as in the subjective
sense, then, Ferdinand is in Elysium. Here he meets
Miranda, as Dante meets Beatrice in Eden. Both
Miranda and Beatrice represent (as I have shown)
that Immaculate Woman who, as the beloved of the
aspirant, is a personification of Wisdom. Like the
Woman Wisdom, Miranda is " wondrous " and unique

---

* Cf. *Aen.* vi. 643-4:

Contendunt ludo, et fulva luctantur arena,
Pars pedibus plaudunt choreas, et carmina dicunt

peerless and perfect, precious beyond compare. Like Wisdom, she comes to toil with her lover in his trials, and ultimately becomes his bride. She is the Veiled Lady of tradition; and, like her counterpart in the Kabbalah version, she openly takes the initiative with her lover, modestly encouraging him and even making frank overtures of union with him. These points have already been dealt with, and further evidence in regard to Miranda will be given later. For the present, I confine myself entirely to the case of Ferdinand.

Like the pagan candidate for the Greater Initiation (who had already made a ritual ascent to Elysium in the preceding ceremony), Ferdinand has to accept the discipline of ascetic diet and arduous labours. His labours, it is interesting to note, consist in carrying a heavy burden of wood—as Christ, before His crucifixion and death, was made to carry the Cross.* These preliminaries having been completed, Ferdinand then undergoes the experience which constitutes the supreme initiation.

Now, I have explained that the ordeal of the Third Degree consists—(a) mythologically or symbolically, in a passage through the RING OF FIRE, and (b) ritually, in a simulated death. Not only are both these versions present in the Play, but they are actually united under a single figure.

Hitherto, I have said little with regard to the RING OF FIRE, save to assert that it ranks in the cosmic symbolism as the intermediate between the " elements " of AIR and AETHER, and that mythologically it is the

---

* *St. John* xix. 17. Nevertheless, the other Gospels affirm that the Cross was carried by one Simon, a Cyrenian. I do not press the comparison between the case of Ferdinand and that of Christ according to St. John. But I may here point out that as Christ's Baptism and Sojourn in the Wilderness represent respectively the First and Second Degrees of Initiation, so His Death and Resurrection represent the Third Degree.

fiery wall around the Celestial Paradise. Let us now consider the matter more closely. We have seen that not only the four cardinal " elements " but also the first two intermediates—viz., MIRE (between EARTH and WATER) and MIST (between WATER and AIR)—correspond to something with which everyone is familiar in the external universe. Is there, then, any familiar feature in the external universe that could furnish a convenient symbol for the third and highest intermediate (between AIR and AETHER) ? There is nothing that would serve—except the Rainbow, which, hanging high in the heavens, seems to divide the air from the aether of space.

True, such a conception of the Rainbow does not accord with the prosaic conclusions of later physical science. But the symbolical system I am dealing with need not necessarily conform to all the teachings of science. It is as poetical and imaginative in character as mythology, and as ancient. It is based upon what is given to all mankind in direct observation of the world wherein he lives; and the use it makes of the Rainbow for the purpose just referred to needs no other warrant than a moment's inquiry as to what could take its place in the following sevenfold scale relating to the objective universe: (1) *Earth*, (2) *Mire*, (3) *Water*, (4) *Mist*, (5) *Air*, (6) *the Rainbow*, (7) *Aether*.

Thus, in default of another and a better, the Rainbow is the natural and obvious prototype of the sixth of the seven cosmic symbols, which is accordingly conceived as a RING OF FIRE (LIGHT) placed between the fifth symbol AIR and the seventh symbol AETHER. And hence the mythological concept of the fiery ring around the Celestial Paradise (AETHER), a parallel to which is found in the Veil that shrouds the Sanctuary.*

---

* *Exod.* xxvi. 33. Cf. *Heb.* ix. 1-8. In the construction of the Temple, the " holy place," or worldly sanctuary, corresponds to

# The Ascent

Dealing in the previous chapter with the symbolical framework of the initiation scheme, I argued that the ordeals of the three degrees are determined by the nature of the three intermediate symbols. Thus in the First Degree the ordeal of MIRE precedes the ascent to WATER; in the Second Degree the ordeal of MIST precedes the ascent to AIR; and in the Third Degree the ordeal of the RING OF FIRE precedes the ascent to AETHER. But I have also argued that the ordeal of the Third Degree is death. Is there, then, some direct connection in tradition between the RING OF FIRE and death? There certainly is; for to the mythical Iris, who personifies the Rainbow, is ascribed the function of cutting the thread of life in the dying.*

These considerations clearly foreshadow what I have to say with regard to Ferdinand in the Play. His ascent through the RING OF FIRE is signified by the coming of *Iris, the Rainbow,* to whom, indeed, Dante refers in association with the fiery circle around the

---

the Lower Paradise (AIR); the " most holy place," or inner sanctuary, corresponds to the Celestial Paradise (AETHER); and the Veil between them corresponds to the RING OF FIRE which separates the AIR from the AETHER.

Note, however, that *Heb.* ix. 3 speaks of the " second veil." Here the first veil, through which one must pass to reach the " holy place " (AIR), corresponds to MIST, and the second veil, through which one must pass to reach the " holy of holies " (AETHER), corresponds to the RING OF FIRE.

I pointed out in the previous footnote that, when Christ died upon the Cross, He took empirically the Third Degree in Initiation. In terms of the cosmic symbolism, He passed up from AIR, through the veiling RING OF FIRE, to AETHER. Hence, the allegorical statement in the first three Gospels that, at the moment of His death, *the veil of the Temple was rent asunder.*

* Cf. *Aen.* iv. 693 *et seq.* See also Davidson's note on this passage. In the Homeric and Hesiodic versions it was Atropos who cut the thread, which was prepared by Clotho and spun by Lachesis.

Celestial Paradise.* And his " death " (he certainly " dies " at some time in the Play, for he speaks of receiving " a second life "; and this cannot refer to the shipwreck, for he never fancied he had been drowned) is likewise signified by the coming of *Iris, the cutter of the thread of life.*

Thus Ferdinand undergoes the ordeal of the Third Degree in (*a*) its mythological aspect and (*b*) its ritual aspect. Moreover, the fact that the two aspects can be presented simultaneously, by the use of a figure (Iris) which involves them both, confirms that the ordeal of the RING OF FIRE is an ordeal of " death "; which is what my earlier argument with regard to the framework of the initiation scheme implied.

Beyond the RING OF FIRE (Rainbow) lies the AETHER, symbol of the intuitional plane and of the Celestial Paradise. For the sake of clarity, I may repeat yet once more that just as, in the supreme psychological experience, the ecstatic " closing of the eyes " (or mystical swoon) in a temporary death to this world precedes the arrival of the consciousness upon the plane of complete and instantaneous knowledge, which is the plane of revelation, so, in mythology, the passage through the fiery circle precedes the aspirant's arrival in the Celestial Paradise, where a glimpse of divine things is obtained. In like manner, the simulated death in the ritual Third Degree was followed by a seeing of the gods of the cultus.

Such is the case with Ferdinand. For, immediately after the advent of Iris, Ceres (deity of Eleusis) appears,

---

* *Parad.* xxviii. *sub initio.* Observe that the RING through which one must pass to enter the presence of the Most High in the Celestial Paradise and so achieve revelation is *expressly described as the Rainbow* in *Rev.* iv. 3. Cf. *Ezek.* i. 28, which also deals with an apocalypse and mentions the Rainbow in association with the traditional fiery ring.

followed later by the goddess Juno. Ferdinand is now in that mythical Celestial Paradise wherein the perfected Soul, emancipated from the cycle of incarnations, lives for ever; and indeed, at this very moment he exclaims:

> Let me live here ever:
> So rare a wonder'd father and a wise
> Makes this place Paradise.
>
> (Act IV., Scene 1.)

Furthermore, we are expressly given to understand that this beholding of the gods is directly related to and confirms his " contract of true love " with Miranda. In other words, it is an apocalypse; for it marks his union with the Wisdom or Truth that is fully acquired only through revelation.

Amid much that is vague and uncertain, there is one record bearing upon the pagan Mysteries which it is hardly possible to doubt or misunderstand. Hippolytus declares in the plainest terms that the most solemn and sacred rite in the ceremonies of Eleusis was that of mowing down in silence a ripe ear of corn; and he is no less explicit that this rite was reserved for the *epoptes*.* Now, Lucian clearly implies in his Treatise on Dancing that the matter of the Mysteries was expressed by means of *ballets d'action*.† Taking these two testimonies together, we may fairly infer that the Eleusinian Degree of *epoptes* comprised not only a vision of the deities (including Ceres, chief

---

* *Refutation of Heresies*, V. iii.

† Mr. Andrew Lang, in his Essay on *The Bull-Roarer*, writes: " In Lucian's treatise on Dancing (Περὶ ὀρχήσεως, c. 15) we read: ' I pass over the fact that you cannot find a single ancient Mystery in which there is not dancing. . . . To prove this I will not mention the secret acts of worship, on account of the uninitiated.' Lucian obviously intends to say that the matter of the Mysteries was set forth in *ballets d'action*." There seems no reason to dissent from Mr. Lang's conclusion.

deity of the cultus), but also a reaping rite performed in a dance. The parallel with the case of Ferdinand is surely remarkable. For the Masque which marks his union with Miranda is a vision of the deities (including Ceres), and it closes with the advent of " certain Reapers " who join in a graceful dance.

What was occultly signified by the mowing down of the ear of corn remains a mystery; and, although an interesting and suggestive conjecture can be framed in accordance with the principles of the present study, the authentic records furnish no evidence tending to confirm it. In these circumstances, such conjecture would have little or no value as proof of my case with regard to Ferdinand.

With the philosophical speech of Prospero, which ensues upon the vision and of which the purpose is to awaken Ferdinand from the dream of the earth-life and its transient material splendours, the " revels " of the Greater or Ocular Initiation according to the pagan model are ended. I have left a certain amount of the textual evidence contained in the story of Ferdinand for consideration later in a separate section dealing with Miranda; and hence the brevity of the present section, as compared with that relating to the Court Party. But enough has, I think, been said to show that, if this part of the Play be treated as continuing the allegory embodied in the story of the Court Party, we find in the two narratives a full account of that Pilgrimage of Perfection which is called Initiation.

# CHAPTER III

## *THE FALL*

IN the *Genesis* version of the Fall of Man we read how Adam and Eve fell from that Lower Paradise which is the subjective plane of pure reason (AIR). Hearkening to the voice of the Tempter, they descended to the passional plane; for we are told that, when they had eaten of the Forbidden Fruit, " the eyes of them both were opened, and *they knew that they were naked* " (iii. 7)—an obvious intimation of the fall of their consciousness to the passional WATER. Thereafter the Lord God in His anger set them to " till the ground " and to live by the sweat of physical labour; and thus they fell (as I shall presently show) to the material or terrestrial plane of EARTH.

Such was the Fall, in its psychological aspect. The self-redemption of man consists in his recovery of the Lost Estate of inspired reason. To achieve this, the aspirant must expiate the original sin by a triumph over precisely the temptations by which the Fall was compassed. He must overcome that insidious Tempter who is Desire. I have already dealt extensively with this ordeal, but the consequences of failure have yet to be considered. Failure to resist the Tempter involves not only failure to achieve " Initiation," but also another lapse to EARTH. And this further lapse necessarily corresponds exactly to the original Fall.

It is now my intention to show that the story of Stephano and Trinculo expresses this conception with singular and suggestive precision, and that the Play is thus completed as a mythological cycle by the inclusion of a version of the Fall; but, as a preliminary to this demonstration, the case of Caliban must first be considered.

## 1. CALIBAN.

Much has been written on the subject of Caliban. He may be said, in fact, to present one of the most difficult problems of the Play. The proposition which I now submit is that *in Caliban we have a personification on mythological lines of the Tempter who is Desire.*

I have already dealt at some length with the aspect of the Tempter as Desire, and also with the various forms in which he is represented. In the *Genesis* story the Tempter is described simply as a Serpent. But the typical form which he assumes in myth and legend is that of a monstrous Serpent or Dragon, as in the myths of Cadmus, of Perseus, and of St. George. This creature is native to water, whence he emerges to assail his victim. And since the conception of the Tempter, as Desire, is entirely subjective in significance, the water whence the monster emerges must be understood to be the emotional WATER in the human composition.*

It is with the Tempter in his traditional form as a water-monster, more particularly as the Dragon, that I identify Caliban, basing the case upon a mass of textual evidence in the Play.

---

\* Note that there are two mythical Dragons, the higher and the lower. The higher Dragon is native to the WATER ABOVE (FIRE), which is the element of intuitional wisdom; hence the higher Dragon is held to be sacred, as by the Chinese. It is the " Serpent of Wisdom." But the lower Dragon, being native to the passional WATER BELOW, is evil. It is the Tempter who is Desire—" the great dragon, that old serpent, which is the Devil, and Satan."

# The Fall

Now Caliban, like the mythical Dragon, is explicitly a monster and implicitly amphibious; for, although he lives upon the Island, he has the appearance of a fish:

What have we here? A man or a fish? Dead or alive? A fish: he smells like a fish; a very ancient and fish-like smell. . . . A strange fish! Were I in England now (as once I was), and had but this fish painted, not a holiday fool there but would give a piece of silver; there would this monster make a man. . . . Legged like a man; and his fins like arms. Warm; o' my troth! I do now let loose my opinion; hold it no longer; this is no fish, but an islander (Act II., Scene 2).

There is no mistaking Trinculo's first impression, which is strongly emphasised. Caliban certainly has a fish-like appearance; and, notwithstanding Trinculo's considered opinion that " this is no fish, but an islander," he subsequently makes the only compromise which he finds possible in the circumstances, for we find him exclaiming to Caliban:

Why, thou deboshed fish thou . . . Wilt thou tell a monstrous lie, *being but half a fish and half a monster?* (Act III., Scene 2).

We may also note the odd suggestion of Trinculo that Caliban has *a tail* (III. 2. 12–13).

The obvious implication of all this is that Caliban, like the Dragon, is a water-monster. And it is noteworthy that Antonio, when he has reached a state of clear reason at the end of the Play, has no doubts whatever as to the element to which Caliban properly belongs, for he remarks:

One of them [Caliban
*Is a plain fish.*

(Act V., Scene 1.)

Antonio, of course, is right. But Trinculo, being incapable of clear reason, is wrong when he " lets loose " his considered opinion. That Trinculo is right in his first impression of Caliban will hardly surprise the psycho-analyst.

171

# Shakespeare's Mystery Play

Now, although Caliban is a water-monster, he does not reside in the water. Moreover, he is seemingly *a hybrid*, for he is " legged like a man, and his fins like arms," and he is described throughout the Play as a " monster." Furthermore, as I shall make abundantly clear, he plays in accurate detail the part of the Tempter.

Caliban has, therefore, four important points of resemblance to the Monsters of mythological tradition and initiation ritual; for—(*a*) he is native to water, (*b*) he resides, or is encountered, out of water, (*c*) he is of mixed species, and (*d*) he figures the Tempter. True to the tradition, he is met with by Stephano and Trinculo when, emerging from the water, they have wandered on the shore—that is to say, he is met with when in the course of the Reascent they have passed through WATER into MIST. This MIST is the Purgatorial Wilderness, the place of temptation and expiation. It is also, as we have seen, a place or state of darkness; so that Caliban is quite truly described by Prospero as—

This thing of darkness . . .
(Act V., Scene 1, line 275.)

This may be no more than a verbal coincidence. It is, perhaps, a remark that is conventionally moral rather than deliberately symbolical. In any case, the Tempter is pre-eminently a " thing of darkness." Indeed, he is the Prince of Darkness.

But, although Caliban has four important points of contact with all the mythical monsters, it is to the Tempter as the mythical Dragon that he conforms more particularly. We find him complaining to Prospero that—

Here you sty me
In this hard rock. . . .
(Act I., Scene 2.)

172

# The Fall

To which Prospero answers:

> I have used thee,
> Filth as thou art, with human care; lodged thee
> In mine own cell, till thou didst seek to violate
> The honour of my child.

(Ibid.)

These allusions have no bearing whatever upon the general action of the Play. Are they, like other side-strokes in the dialogue, introduced simply as clues for the sharp-witted reader? Let us see.

Now, until the very close of the Play, when the allegory has been completely set forth, no one is allowed to enter the Cell except Ferdinand after the Masque. The Court Party is invited only to " look in " when Prospero throws open the entrance. Moreover, the Cell is the abode of Prospero and of Miranda (the Celestial Bride). It therefore appears to be the " sanctum sanctorum "; in which case its archetype is Heaven. The expulsion of Caliban from the Cell is thus a version of *the Fall of Satan from Heaven.* In *Revelation* we are told that the great Dragon ("which is the Devil, and Satan ") was cast out of Heaven for persecuting a woman there, and that he was shut up in the bottomless pit and a seal set upon him (xii. and xx.). In like manner was Caliban cast out of the Cell and shut up into the rock. And when he complains of this to Prospero, he is reminded of his persetion of Miranda and is told—

> Therefore wast thou
> Deservedly confined into this rock. . . .

(Ibid.)

According to *Revelation* xii., the Dragon (" which is the Devil, and Satan ") was cast out of Heaven because he stood before a pregnant woman to devour her child when it was born. This offence attributed to Caliban

173

(though different) is well adapted to the occasion, and accords with the traditional character of Satan, viz., presumptuous irreverence. Of Satan it is generally declared that he fell from Heaven through ambition. In Talmudic legend it is said that he attempted to learn the ultimate secrets behind the veil.* Compare this with the cause of Caliban's expulsion from the Cell. Miranda is an allegorical figure. She is the Veiled Lady who is Wisdom, the Lady who unveils herself and " reveals her secrets " only to her tried and proved lover (the initiate). I have already dealt with the sexual allegory according to which Wisdom is the Bride of the initiate, to whom she unveils her " secrets " after the mystical marriage, the idea thus expressed being that of Revelation, as distinct from Inspiration. Caliban's attempt against Miranda represents the sin of Satan expressed in terms of this same sexual allegory. It is an attempt to rape the Veiled Lady—that is, to acquire the secrets that are veiled from all save the highest initiate. And it is doubtless in this sense that Dante describes Satan as " the first adulterer."†

Let any critic who demurs to this interpretation, deeming it extravagant or fantastic, ask what conceivable reason germane to the ostensible purpose of the Play can be assigned for Caliban's attempt upon Miranda. It has no bearing whatever upon the immediate action of the Play; nor can Prospero's reference to it be defended as an explanatory " aside," for it explains nothing, save on my hypothesis that *The Tempest* is an allegory constructed on the lines of ancient mythology and ritual.

Many commentators make excuses for Caliban and contend that he is not without a certain crude nobility. One might with equal reason argue that the Devil of the Gospel myth is an amiable and generous

* Cf. footnote, Rodwell's *Koran*, Sura xv. 18.  † *Inferno*, vii.

fellow, and that Bunyan's Apollyon is a kindly patron. A lenient view of Caliban can be based only upon some of the speeches he addresses to Stephano and Trinculo; and, as I shall show in the succeeding section, throughout his association with these two men he plays the traditional part of the Tempter. No fair words he utters to them can, therefore, be held to his credit. Nor need we be surprised that it is Caliban, the water-monster, who makes the most sensuous speech to be found in the entire Play:

> The isle is full of noises,
> Sounds, and sweet airs, that give delight, and hurt not.
> Sometimes a thousand twangling instruments
> Will hum about mine ears; and sometimes voices,
> That, if I then had waked after long sleep,
> Will make me sleep again: and then, in dreaming,
> The clouds, methought, would open, and show riches
> Ready to drop upon me, that when I waked
> I cried to dream again.
>
> (Act III., Scene 3.)

It would be symbolically correct to say, in the common idiom, that at this moment Caliban is " in his native element." The speech seems out of place in the mouth of Caliban, until we realise (what my subsequent argument will confirm) that he is deliberately using the sweet seductive tones of the Tempter whose " native element " is the sensuous or passional WATER.* Such speeches as this one are precisely what must be ignored in forming a judgment as to his real nature, which is wholly evil. And so long as commentators allow them-

* In the First Folio the name appears not only as Caliban, but also as Calliban. It is, perhaps, worth mention that the Greek word *kalliboas* means " sweet-toned " ; also that the name of Calypso, the seductive nymph of the Island of Ogygia, is derived from the root *kalyp-* or *kalyb-*. The story of the detention of Odysseus by Calypso is (as I shall show later) a temptation myth, in which Calypso plays practically the same part as I am here imputing to Caliban in *The Tempest*.

175

selves to be beguiled in his favour by anything Caliban says while he is acting the part of the Tempter, they cannot lay claim to any greater measure of discretion and discernment than those two credulous fools whom he brings to disaster.

It is not strictly true that Caliban's more pleasing aspects are revealed only during his association with Stephano and Trinculo. There are two exceptions. Speaking to Prospero (I. 2), he protests that there was a time—before his attempt upon Miranda—when he loved his master. It is equally true that Satan was not always evil. He was among the Sons of God,* being Lucifer the Light-Bringer; and he became maleficent only after his Fall from Heaven. And again, Caliban exclaims, when he is told that he may yet win Prospero's pardon:

> I'll be wise hereafter,
> And seek for grace. . . .
>
> (Act V., Scene 1.)

Well, there is a cynical saying that " when the Devil is sick, the Devil a monk would be." But the words of Caliban are, I think, intended in a better sense. Taken with Prospero's hint that pardon may yet be won, they seem to embody an important intimation. They convey that even for the monstrous Caliban, who represents the fallen Satan, there is (as he himself is aware) always the hope of salvation. They are a negation of the doctrine of eternal damnation. They reflect the teaching of the Kabbalah that even the agent of evil can and will one day be redeemed.†

Caliban, it should be noticed, is met neither by the Court Party nor by Ferdinand until the end of the Play,

* Cf. *Job* i. 6.

† *Zohar*, i. 45, 168; ii. 97. See *Ency. Brit.*, 9th ed., vol. xiii., p. 813. Nevertheless, Shakespeare declares elsewhere that for the fallen Lucifer there is no hope (*Hen. VIII.*, III. 2. 371).

when the initiation scheme has been wholly set forth. This is as the nature of the case imperatively requires. The temptation of the Court Party is figured by their encounter with the Strange Shapes. It is designed according to the Siren model, and the encounter with the Dragon is therefore unnecessary in the case of these men. Had the members of the Court Party met Caliban during their wanderings, they would have been obliged to fight with and vanquish him in order to achieve the Lesser Initiation. Such an incident would, perhaps, have made the purpose of the Play self-evident. As for Ferdinand, the phases of psychological experience represented by his adventures on the Island do not include the phase to which the traditional temptation belongs; hence he meets neither Caliban nor the Strange Shapes.

Thus far I have given only such part of the evidence in support of my view of Caliban as can be detached from the general scheme; and throughout the ensuing two sections a mass of further testimony will be forthcoming.

## 2. STEPHANO AND TRINCULO.

I stated at the outset of this chapter that, in the course of the reascent through the elements to the Lost Estate (AIR), the aspirant is required to expiate the original sin which caused the Fall; and that failure to resist the Temptation, which recurs in the MIST, or Wilderness, is followed by a relapse through the elements to the plane of EARTH, a relapse which corresponds exactly to the original Fall of Man. With the aid of the entirely new conception of Caliban which I have just put forward, it can be shown that all this is contained in precise detail in the story of Stephano and Trinculo. The fact that the encounter of these two men with Caliban is delicious

# Shakespeare's Mystery Play

and hilarious comedy does not exclude the possibility that a philosophic allegory is intended. Aristophanes' *Frogs* is the acme of comedy, but it deals none the less faithfully with the tradition of the monsters encountered in the dark purgatorial region after the crossing of the River Styx. Indeed, his account of the arrival of Dionysus and Xanthias in this region has a certain indefinable resemblance to the first scene in which Stephano and Trinculo appear in *The Tempest*.

Like the Court Party, Stephano and Trinculo emerge from the sea and wander upon the shore of the Island; that is, they " come up out of the water " into the Wilderness—out of WATER into MIST. Here they presently encounter the Tempter, in the person of the Dragon Caliban, by whom they are submitted to two of the commonest of the traditional temptations.

Addressing himself chiefly to Stephano, whose lead Trinculo follows throughout the Play, Caliban offers to " show him every fertile inch of the island " (II. 2), and insistently urges Stephano to " make himself lord of it " (III. 2). This corresponds, of course, to one of the testing ordeals suffered by Christ in the Wilderness, after He had " come up out of the water "; for the Gospels tell us that the Tempter showed Him all the kingdoms of the world and the glories of them, saying, " All these will I give thee." In a previous chapter I took occasion to point out that this temptation is of a sensuous character. It is an allusion to the desire (which every aspirant must overcome) for the power and pomp of exalted rank and proud possessions. Symbolically stated, it is an effort of the Tempter to draw the consciousness of the aspirant down from MIST to WATER.*

* See section on the temptation of the Court Party, wherein I remarked that Prospero's words concerning his brother (" So dry was he for sway ") imply that Antonio's desire for temporal power is a " thirst "—a craving for the sensuous WATER.

# The Fall

True, Stephano could neither exercise much power nor enjoy much pomp in a place with so few inhabitants; but the fact remains that he is offered the sensuous gratification of being king and lord of the Island. In other words, he is submitted to one of the oldest of the traditional temptations—that of temporal glory.

Perceiving the favourable effect of this offer, Caliban proceeds to press his advantage by another, the purpose of which is to bring the consciousness of his victims down to the sensual plane of MIRE. In this endeavour he makes a suggestive allusion to the beauty of Miranda:

> And that most deeply to consider is
> The beauty of his daughter.
>
> (Act III., Scene 2.)

The grossness of intention in these words is patent. The appeal is not even sensuous or passional; it is simply sensual. It is the downward summons to the MIRE.

In the Canonical accounts of the testing of Christ in the Wilderness, there is no mention of a trial of this nature. But, in making Caliban use Woman as a means of temptation, the Poet has the sanction of all tradition; and it is perhaps worth notice that there is a version of the Gospel myth in which the Tempter is represented as placing before Christ a beautiful woman, saying, " Take her as thou wilt, for her desire is unto thee. . . ."*

* See *The Gospel of the Holy Twelve*. This work is, of course, of somewhat questionable authority; but its present interest lies in the " Brief Commentary " with which it concludes. On this temptation by Woman, we read: " In all the ancient initiations woman was one of the temptations placed in the way of the aspirant." This comment, being made in connection with the testing of Christ, is tantamount to affirming what I have argued at length—viz., that Christ's Sojourn in the Wilderness was an initiation ordeal. Buddha, of course, was tempted by Woman.

179

# Shakespeare's Mystery Play

I do not establish the foregoing points by wrenching a few suitable phrases from a context that alters the meaning I have attached to them. It is, I think, impossible to miss in all Caliban's speeches to Stephano and Trinculo a note of subtle and skilful persuasion. When he promises to show them " every fertile inch of the island," he speaks of it in soft seductive phrases, ending with the appeal—" Wilt thou go with me ?" Whereupon Stephano exclaims:

I pr'ythee now, lead the way, without any more talking. Trinculo, the king, and all our company, else being drowned, we will inherit here (Act II., Scene 2).

Later on, we find Caliban saying:

Wilt thou be pleased to hearken once again to the suit I made to thee ? (Act III., Scene 2).

And a few lines farther on, he complains that Prospero stole the Island from him, and tries to move Stephano to action by means of an adroit and insidious challenge:

CAL. I say, by sorcery he got this isle;
From me he got it: if thy greatness will,
Revenge it on him—for, I know, thou dar'st;
But this thing dare not.
STE. That's most certain.
CAL. Thou shalt be lord of it, and I'll serve thee.
STE. How now shall this be compassed ? Canst thou bring me to the party ?
CAL. Yea, yea, my lord. . . . (*Ibid.*)

The follows the gross allusion to Miranda, which promptly arrests the interest of Stephano:

STE. Is it so brave a lass ?
CAL. Ay, lord; she will become thy bed, I warrant,
And bring thee forth brave brood.
(*Ibid.*)

Here, indeed, is the authentic voice of the Tempter ! Stephano, who has previously declared that he and

# The Fall

Trinculo " will inherit here," now succumbs completely to the double temptation:

> STE. Monster, I will kill this man [Prospero]. His daughter and I will be king and queen (save our graces!); and Trinculo and thyself shall be viceroys. Dost thou like the plot, Trinculo?
> TRI. Excellent.
>
> *(Ibid.)*

Observe that Stephano asks for approval, not from Caliban, but from Trinculo only, who assents heartily.

The double temptation (WATER and MIRE) has now succeeded. Yet, to leave the matter in no doubt, Caliban seeks a further assurance from Stephano:

> CAL. Within this half hour will he be asleep;
> Wilt thou destroy him, then?
> STE.                       Ay, on my honour.
> CAL. Thou mak'st me merry; I am full of pleasure.
> Let us be jocund: will you troll the catch
> You taught me but while-ere?
> STE. At thy request, monster, I will do reason, any reason.
>
> *(Ibid.)*

Evidently Stephano is now thoroughly under the subtle influence of Caliban. It is interesting to note that in all the foregoing passages Caliban alone speaks in blank verse, the others speaking in prose.

Another illuminating hint is found in the fact that, when Stephano strikes Trinculo, Caliban exclaims:

> Beat him enough: after a little time
> I'll beat him too.
>
> *(Ibid.)*

This is patently an allusion to the common maxim that the Tempter, if he be yielded to, soon ceases to be the servant and becomes the master—in formal terms, " the Tempter " becomes " the Destroyer," as we can readily understand if his prototype be Desire. The same idea is associated with the mythical

181

Sirens, which are said to destroy him who responds to their seductive summons. To the literalist, Caliban's words must seem curiously studied and needlessly menacing. But, if Caliban be the Tempter who is Desire, the words are entirely appropriate; for, although he may be servile and full of fair promises at the outset, "after a little time" it will assuredly be a case of "the devil turned master."

Still a further hint seems to be given in the strange words of the "catch" which Stephano "trolls" at Caliban's request:

> Flout 'em, and scout 'em; and scout 'em, and flout 'em;
> Thought is free.

(Ibid.)

There are points enough to prove my thesis, without my needing to strain after more. But consider the state of mind of Eve at the moment of her surrender to the Serpent's promptings. Did not the Serpent cause her to believe that the Forbidden Fruit " was to be desired to make one wise " (*Gen.* iii. 6)? Did she not yield to the Tempter in a mood of intellectual rebellion? And is it not an odd coincidence that, at the like moment in like circumstances, Stephano (of all people) should defiantly sing of the freedom of thought (of all things!)? This parallel may be noted for what it is worth as an explanation the astonishing of words of Stephano's song.

Now, having yielded to the double temptation, the purpose of which was to draw their consciousness down from MIST first to the sensuous plane and then to the sensual plane, Stephano and Trinculo should be represented as falling back first to WATER and then to MIRE.

This, indeed, is precisely what we find in the Play. It will be noticed that, as soon as the double temptation of which Caliban is the instrument is succumbed to and immediately after Stephano has sung his defiant song, Ariel (who is invisible to them) plays upon his tabor and pipe. And with what effect? As Ariel subsequently tells Prospero:

> So I charmed their ears,
> That, calf-like, they my lowing followed. . . .
>
> (Act IV., Scene 1.)

Their complete susceptibility to the charms of the music indicates that, out of the MIST wherein they had listened to the voice of the Tempter, Stephano and Trinculo (and Caliban too, for that matter, since he necessarily follows his victims downwards) have now fallen back to the sensuous WATER. It is just at this point that Caliban makes the sweetly sensuous speech (" The isle is full of noises, etc.") which shows his consciousness functioning upon the plane of WATER. Moreover, as an additional testimony, the last few lines of this Scene are enlightening:

STE. This will prove a brave kingdom to me, where I shall have my music for nothing.

CAL. When Prospero is destroyed.

STE. That shall be by and by: I remember the story.

TRI. The sound is going away: let's follow it, and after do our work.

STE. Lead, monster, we'll follow. . . .

(Act III., Scene 2.)

Observe that both Stephano and Trinculo, who (according to Ariel, IV. 1. 174) had been " always bending towards their project," now speak of abandoning it for the present. They display, in short, that infirmity of purpose which is of the WATER—" unstable as water, thou shalt not excel."

This, then, is the fall of the consciousness to the plane of WATER. It is shown openly, as a psychological change. The further fall to the plane of MIRE is shown symbolically, or environmentally. For, when Ariel describes how Stephano and Trinculo had followed after his music, he concludes:

> At last I left them
> I' the filthy mantled pool beyond your cell,
> There dancing up to the chins, that the foul lake
> O'erstunk their feet.
>
> (Act IV., Scene 1.)

This filthy pool corresponds to the filth-laden Cocytus described by Virgil. It is MIRE, symbolical of the sensual plane, which is the penultimate stage reached by the falling consciousness that has failed to ascend to the height of initiation.

So far as the Tempter is concerned, the Fall of Stephano and Trinculo is now accomplished. Appearing to his victims when they had " come up out of the water " into the Wilderness (MIST), Caliban has successfully recalled them first to those sensuous and then to those sensual things which it was their business, as aspirants to initiation, utterly to renounce. They have accordingly fallen back, first to WATER and then to MIRE. They have failed in that effort of renunciation of which the successful issue is called Initiation.

Now, the *Genesis* account of the Fall is written in terms of the four cardinal elements only; and the penultimate stage of the Fall is, therefore, WATER. But a full statement of the doctrine would be written in terms of the seven elements; and here the penultimate stage would, of course, be MIRE. In the *Genesis* version, therefore, the Serpent brings down Adam and Eve to the plane of WATER; but in the Play, which contains a full statement of the doctrine, Caliban brings down Stephano and Trinculo to the plane of MIRE. But in both cases it is to the penultimate plane only that the victims are lured down by the Tempter.

# The Fall

I come now to consider in some detail the Fall from the penultimate to the lowest plane (EARTH). It is my intention to show that, just as in the case of Adam and Eve the Fall to the plane of EARTH was the deliberate work of the Lord God Himself, who in His anger drove them forth to " till the ground " and live amidst material concerns, so, in like manner, the Fall of Stephano and Trinculo to the lowest plane of EARTH is the deliberate work of Prospero while he is " touched with distempered anger."

I refer the reader to the closing phase of Act IV., Scene 1, wherein certain " glistering apparel " is hung upon a line, and wherein Stephano and Trinculo— momentarily distracted by the garments—are assailed by " Spirits in the shape of hounds." Brief though this part of the Scene is, it is replete with subtle but unequivocal intimations.

Only by some very drastic interpretation, such as I am about to offer, can this episode be rescued from sheer fatuity. In a Christmas pantomime I once saw a clown blow a penny trumpet to distract the murderous attention of a fierce cannibal; whereupon a second clown, taking the cannibal off his guard, promptly hit him on the head. Is this the level of Shakespeare? Is the device of the penny trumpet any more ridiculous than the one by which Prospero distracts his assailants, upon whom he then sets savage dogs? Why should Prospero, the magician, resort to this elaborate and unconvincing device to protect himself against Stephano and Trinculo (for observe that Caliban, whom he has " prepared to meet," is not so readily diverted)? Why does he not summon the dogs as soon as his assailants appear, or before they appear? Why does he not charm them from moving, as he does the Court Party, or render himself invisible, as he does repeatedly throughout the Play? Here are obvious and insistent questions, which must occur to anyone whose critical faculty can assert itself even against the prestige of Shakespeare's name.

The answer is, of course, that the Poet has some ulterior purpose to fulfil in the construction of this Scene. Undoubtedly we are presented with an allegory, which it is our business to interpret. A certain distinguished English critic (who shall be nameless) writes:

> The sensualist and the fool, alike infirm of purpose, are easily led by the glitter of a little frippery to yield to the first temptation that may offer. They busy themselves with the gay clothes presented to their eyes, forget their plot, and then, by spirits in the shape of hounds, with noise of a hunt, they who have fallen below the level of the beasts as beasts are hunted.

So much, and no more! Is this all that the Poet means? If so, surely his purpose is attained at an utterly disproportionate sacrifice? Could nothing more plausible than the trick of the " glistering apparel " be contrived? We are invited to believe that this exceedingly strained and unconvincing episode is an attempt by the greatest dramatist of all time to allegorise—what? The sententious little homily which the English Professor has discerned? Such an explanation seems to be quite inadequate.

But, if it could be shown that some such episode is quite indispensable to the completion of a specific allegorical purpose, then no doubt its outward appearance of sheer inconsequence and absurdity might be held to be amply excused by the imperative need for its inclusion. And this, indeed, is exactly how the matter stands.

In the first place, the text implies that Stephano and Trinculo share between them the " glistering apparel." There is (quite properly) no indication that Caliban is to receive any of it; in fact, he expressly repudiates the garments. In the second place, Stephano and Trinculo do not don the apparel at once. The text is quite explicit that they are only carrying the clothes when the dogs appear; and the fact that at the end of the Play they come in wearing the garments suggests clearly enough that they put them on after the flight from the dogs, a point of considerable importance.

Now, if the Play be treated as an account of initiation, there is no difficulty about the " Spirits in the shape of hounds." They are *terrestrial daemons*—*i.e.*, daemons of the plane of EARTH, as the angels are daemons of the plane of AIR. Speaking of the howling dogs mentioned by Virgil in *Aeneid VI.*, Thomas Taylor writes:

> The howling dogs are symbols of material daemons, who are thus denominated by the magic oracles of Zoroaster (*Eleus. and Bacch. Myst.*, ed. J. Weitstein, Amsterdam, p. 24).

He also calls attention to the first hymn of Synesius, wherein *matter* is represented as *barking* at the Soul. Furthermore, he quotes from the MS. Commentary of Proclus on the first *Alcibiades*, to the effect that—

> In the most holy initiations, before the presence of the god, the impulsive forms of certain terrestrial daemons appear, which challenge the attention (of the aspirant) from undefiled good to matter.

And, as Taylor remarks, Pletho expressly asserts in his work on the Oracles of Zoroaster that these terrestrial daemons appeared in the shape of dogs. Their symbolical function, as we gather from the words of Proclus, was that of driving the consciousness down to the terrestrial plane. In this encounter it was clearly the duty of the aspirant to remain steadfast and to ignore the dogs, as Aeneas did.

But, unlike Aeneas, Stephano and Trinculo flee

incontinently when the dogs appear. Whereupon Prospero exclaims:

> Go, charge my goblins that they grind their joints
> With dry convulsions; shorten up their sinews
> With aged cramps. . . .
>
> <div align="right">(Act IV., Scene 1 <i>fin.</i>)</div>

The meaning of the allegory is now patent. The flight of Stephano and Trinculo from the " Spirits in the shape of hounds " is their surrender to terrestrial daemons. It represents the downward movement to the terrestrial plane. And Prospero's command leaves little room for doubt as to the validity of this interpretation: for, in the physical torments which Stephano and Trinculo suffer after their flight, their consciousness must indeed function perforce upon the corporeal or terrestrial plane, which is the plane of EARTH.

It is worth notice that the physical pain is to be inflicted by goblins. There are many different kinds of elfish creatures; but the goblins, like the gnomes, are generally conceived as being troglodytes. It is, therefore, a peculiarly apt and subtle fancy that the EARTHLY bodies of Stephano and Trinculo are to be tormented by goblins—by the evil little sprites that dwell within the earth.

And what significance, if any, attaches to the " glistering apparel " with which Stephano and Trinculo are dallying when they are assailed by the dogs? Consider the character of the garments. We find Stephano apostrophising one of them in somewhat curious terms:

> Now, jerkin, you are like to lose your hair and prove a bald jerkin.
>
> <div align="right">(<i>Ibid.</i>)</div>

Thus one, at least, of the garments is " hairy." Now, if it is hairy, it must be made of skin.

188

# The Fall

This simple deduction furnishes the required key. Stephano and Trinculo succumb to the Tempter (Caliban) and fall to a lower plane; whereupon Prospero, " in some passion that works him strongly," intervenes. He invokes terrestrial daemons, which drive them down to the plane of EARTH; and thereafter we see them clothed in garments of skin which Prospero himself has provided. So, in the Eden story, Adam and Eve succumbed to the Tempter and fell to a lower plane; whereupon the Lord God, in His anger, intervened. He drove them down to the plane of EARTH, and we read that—

Unto Adam also and to his wife did the Lord God make coats of skins, and clothed them (*Gen.* iii. 21).*

The parallel is complete, and its value is reinforced by the fact that both stories have the same internal meaning, as I shall now attempt to show.

There is a curious tradition, which we find in Gnosticism and in the Zoharic system and to which Dante makes several allusions, that Man had no fleshly body when he dwelt in the Lower Paradise or Eden before the Fall.† If Eden be understood as the Elysian abode of the Soul before incarnation, this tradition is literally true. In a different sense, it is

* According to the *Koran* (vii.), God said to Adam and Eve: " Get ye down, the one of you an enemy unto the other, and ye shall have a dwelling-place upon earth. . . ." Here we have that driving down to earth (EARTH) which is an important part of the parallel.

† Cf. *Purg.* xi., where it is said that Dante, being still in the physical body,

> bears yet
> The charge of fleshly raiment Adam left him. . . .

Elsewhere (*Parad.* vii. 25, Carey's trans.) Dante speaks of Adam as being still unborn before the trespass—*i.e.*, Adam had no physical body.

See also Bouillet's translation of Plotinus (*Les Enneades de Plotin*, Paris, 1857), vol. i., p. 527, where it is said that this idea was entertained by Philo and by Origen, as also by the Kabbalists.

true even if Eden be understood as the rational plane; for, when the consciousness is in the AIR of inspired reason, it is quite outside the lower elements—*i.e.*, outside the emotional and physical vehicles. In either case, it may legitimately be said that the Fall from Eden involves the donning of the WATERY and EARTHLY bodies.

Whichever way we choose to interpret it, this tradition is implicit in the actual text of the *Genesis* narrative. Before the trespass, Adam was in the AIRY body.* After he succumbed to the Tempter, he put on the WATERY body, aptly symbolised by the apron of fig-leaves.† Lastly, he was driven down to the terrestrial plane to "till the ground," and was then clothed in the physical or EARTHLY body, symbolised by the coat of skin—as in the figure used in *Job* (x. 11): "Thou hast clothed me with skin and flesh."

This is no dizzy flight of special pleading for the purposes of my *Tempest* thesis; for the only point of immediate relevance—namely, that the "coat of skin" represents the physical or EARTHLY body—can be independently established by several authoritative references. Origen, for example, says that the garments of Adam and Eve after the trespass are *our fleshly bodies;*‡ and this opinion was certainly held

---

* When Adam was placed in Eden, the Lord God " breathed into him the breath of life " (*Gen.* ii. 7). Adam was now in that state of being divinely inspired (breathed into) which throughout this study I have argued to be the state of man in Eden.

† As an apron, it was worn on the passional or WATERY parts. In *De Is. et Osir.* xxxvi. Plutarch says of the fig-leaf that it was interpreted as a watering of all things, and that it was supposed to resemble the phallus in shape. Adam " knew that he was naked," and donned the fig-leaf—that is, he fell to the passional plane and donned the passional body, which may be understood in either of the senses indicated above.

‡ Cited by Isaac Myer in *The Quabbalah*, p. 309.

190

by the Valentinian Gnostics, for Valentinus himself says that the coat of skin is *the (physical) body*, and St. Irenaeus remarks likewise that it is " the visible body."* And Theodoret, yet more explicit, declares: " Adam is clothed in *the fourth man*—that is, in *the Earthly man ;* this is what is to be understood by *the tunic of skin.*"†

The case of Stephano and Trinculo conforms to this Gnostic and Kabbalistic interpretation of the *Genesis* myth. The donning of the " coats of skin " by these two men, after they have been driven down by the terrestrial daemons, signifies the return of their consciousness into the physical body. It is the completion of their Fall to EARTH. And, very properly, the closing feature in the story of Stephano and Trinculo is their entry in the last Scene, clad in the " glistering apparel " and racked with physical pain.

As for Caliban, he represents Desire; and Desire, being purely subjective, cannot be said to assume a physical body. Hence, Caliban does not share the " glistering apparel," and he declares quite definitely: " I will have none on 't." Here we may note that the *Koran* distinctly suggests that the Tempter is clad in a superphysical garment, and is therefore not physically visible.‡ Furthermore, the physical EARTH being lower and grosser than the passional and sensuous WATER to which the Tempter is native, Caliban naturally shows a better judgment than Stephano and Trinculo in the matter of the " coats of skin," ex-

* Bouillet, *Les Enn. de Plotin*, vol. i., pp. 527 and 517.

† *Ibid.*, p. 517. Theodoret's idea may be pursued as follows: The " fourth man " is the EARTHLY man, symbolised by the tunic of skin. The " third man " is the WATERY man, symbolised by the apron of fig-leaves. The " second man " is the AIRY man, which Adam may be said to have put on when God breathed into him. And the " first man " is the FIERY man.

‡ *Koran*, vii. 26. See footnote thereto in Sale's version.

claiming: " Let it alone, thou fool, it is but trash "—a point that has been much debated by commentators.

It remains to inquire why Shakespeare describes these " coats of skin " as " glistering apparel," as if to imply that they are in some sort fine and splendid garments. I suggest that he may have done so in accordance with tradition. For the " coats of skin " which Adam and Eve assumed after the trespass, and to which the " glistering apparel " has been shown to correspond, are described in the *Koran* (vii. 25) as " splendid (fair) garments " ;* in the Onkelos and Palestine Targums (*in loc.*) as " vestments of honour "; and in the *Zohar* as " robes of glory."†

Additional evidence confirming that the story of Stephano and Trinculo is a version of the Fall, on the general lines I am suggesting, is furnished by Stephano's allusion to the impending baldness of (one of) the garments:

STE. Now is the jerkin under the line; now, jerkin, you are like to *lose your hair* and prove a bald jerkin.

(Act IV., Scene 1.)

It is certainly very curious indeed that, according to a tradition mentioned by Yahya, the Fall of Adam and Eve involved *a loss of the hair*.‡ How Shakespeare could be familiar with this, I do not here discuss. But it is not easy to escape the conclusion that Stephano's seemingly foolish and irrelevant words refer to the same symbolical idea; for, having regard to the oddness of his remark and to its occurrence in a context which has all the other features of

* Rodwell gives " splendid " and Sale gives " fair."

† See A. E. Waite's *Secret Doctrine in Israel*, pp. 100-101.

‡ See footnote in Sale's *Koran*, vii. There is a great deal more in Yahya's contention than Sale appears to suspect. I do not now examine it; but the case of Samson and Delilah may be cited as another instance of a loss of the hair being associated with temptation and a fall from the favour of God.

a version of the Fall, the supposition of sheer coincidence is wellnigh inadmissible.

Let me now restate the proposition with which this part of the case was opened. The Lesser Initiation consists in the recovery of the Lost Estate of Man, and can therefore be achieved only by an expiation of the " original sin " which caused the Fall. In the course of his reascent, the aspirant must overcome the Tempter, and failure to do so involves a relapse which corresponds precisely to the original Fall of Man.

Such, I suggest, is the purport of the story of Stephano and Trinculo. I fully realise that this suggestion implies a considerable understanding on the Poet's part of unfamiliar subjects; but, if my theory be rejected, there is much in the Play that remains obscure or meaningless. Particularly is this the case with the episode of the dogs and the " glistering apparel "—an episode which every intelligent person must recognise as allegorical, and of which the reader who refuses my interpretation ought to offer another and a better, one that is more probable, equally supported by the text, and equally consistent with some comprehensive view of the Play as a whole.

### 3. Sycorax and Setebos.

Let us now briefly consider the two evil characters who, although they do not actually appear upon the stage, are mentioned somewhat pointedly in the dialogue. Of Setebos practically nothing is told us; but Sycorax, the mother of Caliban, is quite effectively delineated by the frequent references to her. The Poet's description of her has no bearing upon the immediate action of the Play, being introduced apparently for the sole purpose of shedding light upon the nature of Caliban. It furnishes, therefore, an interesting and important test of my thesis; for, unless I have been presenting a wholly mistaken view of *The Tempest*, we ought to find that Sycorax conforms, like Caliban her son, to some authentic mythological figure.

I submit that in Sycorax we have the typical Evil Woman of mythology, often expressly represented as the antithesis of that Immaculate Woman who is the " Celestial Bride "; and that the text of the Play ascribes to Sycorax the peculiar attributes with which the mythical Evil Woman is commonly endowed.

This Evil Woman appears in the *Zohar* as Lilith " the Prostitute," antithesis of Shechinah (the Celestial Bride). In *Proverbs* she is an harlot called the " Strange Woman," who is explicitly the antithesis of Wisdom.* In *Revelation* she is the Great Whore who rode upon the back of the scarlet beast.† Egyptian records are imperfect and inadequate; but, if analogy holds, the Evil Woman is found in Nephthys, dark sister of the sacred Isis. She is the Hebrew Tehom, and the Chaldean Omoroca or Thalath, whose Greek counterpart we shall presently find is Hecate.

Here it may be observed that Sycorax, like this Evil Woman, is *adulterous;* for she comes to the Island in a pregnant condition, and of her offspring Caliban it is parenthetically declared (V. 1. 273), that " he's a bastard one."

The mythical Evil Woman, with whom I identify Sycorax, is evidently a personification of the passional element (WATER). The name of the Hebrew Tehom signifies "the Deep," and that of the Chaldean Thalath signifies "the Sea." Of the Great Whore of *Revela-*

* *Prov.* ii. 16; v. 3; vi. 24; vii. 4-5.
† *Rev.* xvii. The condemnation of the sinful City of Babylon takes the form of a direct identification of it with this mythical Evil Woman.

# The Fall

*tion* it is said (xvii. 1) that she " sitteth upon many waters." And in *Proverbs* the association of the " Strange Woman " with water (as a symbol of passion) is implied in the exhortation against her, wherein it is written, " Drink waters out of thine own cistern . . . and rejoice in the wife of thy youth."*

Now, the Chaldean Thalath ruled over—and by her name (" the sea ") was identified with—the water that gave birth to the monstrous hybrids. Similarly Hecate, whom Dr. Warburton argues to be the Greek counterpart of Thalath, is invoked by Aeneas when he

---

* v. 15-20. In *Proverbs* we have ostensibly a warning simply against the actual prostitute; but, undoubtedly, the passage is allegorical and should be understood as a warning against the passional WATER in the widest sense. In chapters ii., v., vi., and vii. the reference is to the " Strange Woman," who is an harlot, whose ways are " movable " (v. 6), and whose house is a house of death (ii. 18; v. 5; vii. 27); wherefore, it is said, turn from her as from forbidden waters " and drink waters out of thine own cistern " (v. 15-20). Subsequently the reference is to the " Foolish Woman," whose house is likewise a house of death, and who entices with the words " Stolen waters are sweet " (ix. 13-18). Clearly the " Strange Woman " and the " Foolish Woman " are the same, and both represent the passional WATER. Both are contrasted with the pure Woman who is Wisdom—as the antithesis of Wisdom is Passion, which is Folly. This point will be further treated, *sub voce* " Miranda."

Of the " Strange Woman " it is said (v. 3-4) that her lips drop as honey but her end is bitter. So, too, the sensuous or passional WATER is " sweet-bitter." It is sweet with the sweetness that cloys. It is sweet in the drinking, but it is bitter in the after-taste. *Mare* (the sea) is generally held to signify " sweet-bitter " or " bitter-sweet." Cf. *Ruth* i. 20.

Venus (Greek Aphrodite, from *aphros* = sea-foam) is associated with the sea and with sexual passion. She may, therefore, be said to represent WATER in one of its aspects. Being young and beautiful, she is the passional WATER in its initial sweetness—as Sycorax, being old and hideous, is the passional WATER in its ultimate bitterness. In Browning's *Pippa Passes* we have an example of the sweet " stolen water " turning bitter in surfeit and aftertaste—of the lovely Venus and the hateful Sycorax in one and the same adulterous woman (Ottima). Cf. Shakespeare's *Sonnet* CXXIX.

encounters the monsters in Purgatory; and Apollonius Rhodius declares that she was actually the mother of Scylla, the evil water-monster.* And in like manner Sycorax is the mother of the monstrous Caliban, as it is the passional WATER that gives birth to Desire (the Dragon).

According to the Berosus fragment preserved by George Syncellus, the name Thalath not only signifies " the sea," but is also equivalent to " the moon," doubtless on account of the connection between them.† Hecate, whom Apollonius Rhodius calls " the night-wandering," is likewise associated with the moon. Thalath—and Hecate, too, for that matter —being essentially evil, she cannot be associated with the moon in the manner of the sacred Isis, but rather in an inferior and evil sense. In the Play we find Prospero declaring, with what seems to be unnecessary particularity, that Sycorax could control the moon and the tides of the sea; for he remarks of Caliban:

> His mother was a witch, and one so strong
> That could control the moon, make flows and ebbs,
> And deal in her command without her power.
> (Act V., Scene 1.)

If this passage be introduced to explain the nature of Caliban, it is a striking confirmation of my thesis.

* " . . . the hideous lair of Scylla, Ausonian Scylla the deadly, whom night-wandering Hecate, who is called Crataeis, bare to Phorcys . . ." (*Arg.* iv. 827 *seq.*). Phorcys, it may be added, was a sea-deity.

Citing Schol. Apoll. Rhod. *Arg.* iii. 859, Warburton remarks that horrid or terrifying visions were called Hecatea. Arguing that Hecate corresponds to Thalath, he continues: " The ancients called Hecate ' diva triformis '; and Scaliger observes that this word Thalath . . . signifies ' tria '."

† Ἄρχειν δὲ τούτων πάντων γυναῖκα, τῇ ὄνομα Ὀμορωκά. Εἶναι δὲ τοῦτο χαλδάϊστὶ μὲν Θαλάθ, Ἑλληνιστὶ δὲ μεθερμηνεύεται Θάλασσα, κατὰ δὲ ἰσόψηφον Σελήνην; Georg. Syncel. Chronogr., cited by Warburton.

# The Fall

Note the curious qualification in the last line, which makes the case of Sycorax precisely that of the Chaldean Thalath.

What we know of Thalath is severely limited; but Hecate, her Greek counterpart, is associated with evil spells and sorceries. So also is Sycorax:

> This damned witch, Sycorax,
> For mischiefs manifold, and sorceries terrible
> To enter human hearing, from Argiers,
> Thou know'st, was banished. . . .
>
> (Act I., Scene 2.)

Again: Thalath ruled the "darkness" that gave habitation to the monstrous hybrids, as Hecate ruled that dark region which Virgil calls "the place of Night" and which is the proper station of the monsters. And the evil charms of Sycorax pertain to darkness and night:

> All the charms
> Of Sycorax, toads, beetles, bats. . . .
>
> (*Ibid.*)

Shakespeare often uses the Dove and the Raven as figures for Good and Evil.* True, we find no mention in *The Tempest* of the Dove; but Sycorax is pointedly associated with the Raven. Caliban exclaims:

> As wicked dew as e'er my mother brush'd
> With raven's feather from unwholesome fen. . . .
>
> (*Ibid.*)

Note the reference to evil water, as well as to the raven. But, what is of much greater significance, the Greek word *korax* means "a raven." It also means "anything curved." Compare:

> The foul witch Sycorax, who with age and envy
> Was grown into a hoop. . . .           (*Ibid.*)

---

* *T. Night*, V. 1. 134; *2 Hen. VI.*, III. 1. 76; *Romeo*, III. 2. 76; *Sonnet* CXIII. 12, etc.

# Shakespeare's Mystery Play

In both cases the name of Sycorax reflects her nature.

Crooked (curved) is a common synonym for evil. The prefix *Sy*- means "pig."* The evil Hecate, to whom the evil Sycorax corresponds, was frequently represented with the head of a boar; and the Egyptian Osiris was sometimes depicted as stabbing with a spear a curved pig or boar, to represent his triumph over evil. (Compare *sy*, "pig," and *korax*, "curved").†

Two considerations must be borne in mind in judging the value of the foregoing argument—namely, (i) that, while the Poet's description of Sycorax can have no other purpose than that of explaining the nature of Caliban, it can hardly be very enlightening to the literalist, and (ii) that not only do the points dealt with above strikingly confirm my view of Caliban, but also they exhaust practically all that is told us of Sycorax, so that they certainly are not made by accentuating some convenient parts of the text and suppressing many others.

Two points I have not explained. It is declared (I. 2. 269) that Sycorax was blue-eyed, and also that she was born in Argiers (Algiers?). The former point is perhaps of little account. But the reference to her birthplace is somewhat strangely phrased (I. 2. 260-1); and although the whole character of the Play suggests that we have here some significant intimation, I confess I am at a loss to explain it. In any case, in respect of her banishment to a solitary island

* *Sys* = pig or swine. The terminal *s* is dropped in compound words. Thus: *boter* = herdsman; *sybotes* = swineherd; *sybosion* = herd of swine.

† There is a curious association of these words in the *Odyssey* (xiii. *prope fin.*), where it is said that the *swine* are beside the rock *korax*. Mythologically, swine are always evil. Compare the Gospel story in which the evil spirit passes into the Gadarene *swine*, which thereupon rush into *the sea*.

off the coast of Italy, Sycorax resembles the mythical Circe, evil sorceress and wanton.

Shakespeare often speaks of " the devil's dam."* Mythologically (as I have shown), she is represented as an Evil Wanton, generally associated with the sea; and her prototype is the passional WATER whereof the Dragon Desire is born. Shakespeare's phrase " the devil and his dam " is simply a version of the familiar phrase " the devil and the deep sea." In the Play Caliban is the devil as Tempter; and Sycorax, who is described as his " dam," corresponds to Tehom (" the Deep ") and to Thalath (" the Sea ").

Now, the term " devil " is not easy to define accurately, because it is always rather loosely and vaguely used. It is not used with a single meaning even in *The Tempest;* for Prospero calls Caliban " a devil, a born devil" (IV. 1. 188), and later "a demi-devil" (V. 1. 272). Elsewhere Caliban is not "the devil," but the son of " the devil " by Sycorax:

> Thou poisonous slave, got by the devil himself
> Upon thy wicked dam. . . .
> (Act I., Scene 2.)

If the word " devil " were not used with several different meanings throughout the Play, these lines might, perhaps, be deemed awkward to reconcile with my thesis. Yet they are not, in any case, wholly irreconcilable with it. I suggest that in this passage the Poet regards " the devil " as the Evil Power, which begets Desire (the Tempter) through the passional WATER. A distinction between the Devil and the Tempter is not unusual; and it is sometimes argued that the serpent which tempted Eve was only an agent

* *Merry Wives,* IV. 5. 108; *Com. Errors,* IV. 3. 50; *Shrew,* I. 1. 106; *ibid.,* III. 2. 158; *K. John,* II. 1. 128; 1 *Hen. VI.,* I. 5. 5; *Tit. Andr.,* IV. 2. 64; *Othello,* IV. 1. 153. In the second of these references it is a *courtesan* who is called *the devil's dam,* and a few lines later she is connected with *sorceries.*

of the Evil One. Another idea, and one that Milton uses, is that the Devil spoke through the serpent, the latter being the cover behind which the Evil One hid himself. Curiously enough, the Greek root *kalyb-* means cover and involves the idea of hiding. Certainly there are different aspects of "the Devil"; for he is variously described as the Tempter, the Destroyer, the Adversary, and the Accuser.

It is not positively declared that Setebos was the consort of the adulterous Sycorax and the father of Caliban; but, as the "god" of the infamous Sycorax (I. 2. 373), he could hardly be other than the Evil One himself. Relationships are always somewhat obscure or inconsistent in mythology, and the point is not of great importance. The fact remains that Setebos, as the "god" of Sycorax, is evidently the hostile Evil Principle, and it is (shall we say?) an odd coincidence that the Egyptian word *seteb-* means "what is hostile." Setebos corresponds, therefore, to the evil Set of Egyptian myth, whose consort was Nephthys, dark sister of Isis. It is not easy to determine the true Zoharic doctrine as to the distinction (if any) between the Evil One and the Tempter, for the references are as conflicting as they are numerous. But broadly we may say that in Setebos, Sycorax, and Caliban we have an evil trio corresponding to the Zoharic Samaël (the Evil One), Lilith his consort (the "Adulterous Woman"), and the serpent who is the active agent of temptation.

Setebos is mentioned only twice, and quite casually, in the Play; and the view of him here put forward cannot be independently established by direct textual evidence. Rather it is a corollary to the rest of the case. I am only concerned to show that Setebos has a counterpart in the general tradition, and that the inclusion of him completes the Play as a mythological synthesis.

# CHAPTER IV

## *THE POWERS OF REDEMPTION*

IT remains to consider the individual cases of
Prospero, Ariel, and Miranda. The respective
parts played by these three characters in the
Poet's comprehensive allegory have to a large extent
been indicated, explicitly or by implication, in the
course of the argument up to this point; but it is only
in the case of Miranda that anything in the nature of
independent proof has been given. From her position
in the general design of the Play she is clearly (in
one aspect) a personification of Wisdom or Truth;
and an analysis of the direct textual allusions to her
has amply confirmed this view. So far as Prospero
and Ariel are concerned, what they represent in the
allegory has up to the present been taken for granted
practically without proof or even comment, because it
is almost self-evident from the relation in which they
stand to the other characters and to the numerous
incidents I have interpreted. Nevertheless, if what
has hitherto been tacitly assumed on these general
grounds can now be proved independently by reference
to such parts of the text as bear directly upon Prospero
and Ariel, it is obvious that the basis of my theory will
thereby be widened and immensely strengthened.
To this end I shall proceed to examine a number of
passages that have not yet been dealt with, and shall
also give some further evidence relating to Miranda.

# Shakespeare's Mystery Play

## 1. PROSPERO.

In so far as the Play corresponds to the pagan rites, Prospero may be regarded as the counterpart of the hierophant, or initiating priest. But in the wider scheme I have latterly been treating he figures the prototypical Supreme Being, whom, indeed, the pagan hierophant was deemed to represent.

We have seen that the expulsion of the dragon Caliban from the Cell of Prospero is a version of the Fall of Satan from Heaven; which must imply that Prospero is equivalent to God. We have seen, too, that he stands in relation to Stephano and Trinculo precisely as the Lord God stood to Adam and Eve. Consider now the seemingly limitless range of Prospero's power:

> I have bedimmed
> The noontide sun, called forth the mutinous winds,
> And 'twixt the green sea and the azured vault
> Set roaring war. . . . The strong-based promontory
> Have I made shake, and by the spurs plucked up
> The pine and cedar. Graves at my command,
> Have waked their sleepers, oped and let them forth
> By my so potent art.
>
> (Act V., Scene 1.)

These are superhuman works. In fact, Prospero claims quite definitely that he possesses the power of mighty Zeus himself, for not only does he say that he can make lightning, but he declares that he has actually employed the god's own thunderbolt:

> To the dread rattling thunder
> Have I given fire, and rifted Jove's stout oak
> With his own bolt.
>
> (*Ibid.*)

For what purpose, save that of allegory, does the Poet thus exalt him to the very topmost pinnacle of superhuman power? Furthermore, although the storm

202

# The Powers of Redemption

which beset the " men of sin " is repeatedly stated in quite unequivocal terms to have been decreed and created by Prospero,* his minister Ariel expressly attributes it to Destiny and the powers of retribution:

> You are three men of sin, whom Destiny
> (That hath to instrument this lower world
> And what is in 't) the never-surfeited sea
> Hath caused to belch you up. . . . I and my fellows
> Are ministers of Fate. . . .
> The powers, delaying, not forgetting, have
> Incensed the seas and shores, yea, all the creatures,
> Against your peace . . . and do pronounce by me
> Lingering perdition, worse than any death
> Can be at once, shall step by step attend
> You and your ways; whose wraths to guard you from,
> Which here, in this most desolate isle, else falls
> Upon your heads, is nothing, but heart's sorrow,
> And a clear life ensuing.
>
> (Act III., Scene 3.)

Here it seems to be plainly intimated that Prospero himself is that Omnipotent Judge whom sinners cannot evade, who can pass sentence of " lingering perdition," but whose mercy can always be won by repentance. For Ariel, who declares himself to be the mouthpiece of the Judge, owns no other master than Prospero and knows full well that by him the ship-wreck of the travellers was contrived.

With the case of Ariel I deal fully in the ensuing section. But here we may note that this messenger and minister of Prospero, who is as capricious in character as the " mutinous winds " of which his master speaks, is explicitly stated to belong to the element of *air* : yet he assumes during the wreck the form of a *flaming fire* :

> I boarded the king's ship; now on the beak,
> Now in the waist, the deck, in every cabin,
> I flamed amazement: sometime I'd divide,

---

* Cf. I. 2. 1-2; I. 2. 26-9; I. 2. 194-5; V. 1. 6.

And burn in many places; on the topmast
The yards and bowsprit would I flame distinctly,
Then meet and join.

(Act I., Scene 2.)

So, likewise, it is said in *Psalms* that the messengers (angels) of God are *winds* (spirits), and His ministers a *flaming fire.**

In the larger design of the Play, therefore, the relative status of Prospero is evident enough. He represents the Supreme Being whose benign influence governs the lives of men. Sorrow and misfortunes he does, indeed, ordain; yet his sole purpose is thereby to bring sinners to repentance:

They being penitent,
The sole drift of my purpose doth extend
Not a frown further.

(Act V., Scene 1.)

His very name is suggestive of that Beneficent Power which works for the true happiness of mankind (*prospero*="I make happy"). Against him the dragon Caliban conspires with Stephano and Trinculo, as the fallen Satan conspires among men against the God he hates. Cast out by those whose thoughts are set on their own temporal ends, Prospero does not at once restore himself and maintain (as he could do) his sovereignty by a pitiless use of his superhuman power; but ("delaying, not forgetting") he patiently achieves his own reinstatement by leading them through tribulation to penitence and amendment. This done, he is all-forgiving, and gently bids them " Please you, draw near."

I have argued that *The Tempest* is an account of Initiation, conceived as a reversal of the Fall of Man. And what, in essence, is the Fall but the dethroning

* *Ps.* civ. 4. The Greek ἄγγελος, whence the word angel is derived, means actually a messenger; and πνεῦμα means both spirit and wind.

204

of the Most High from the human heart? In the Play we have a Ruler of supernatural power who has been exiled and forgotten by " men of sin "; and, with Prospero as with God Himself, the means whereby he regains his rightful kingdom are precisely the means whereby those who had dethroned him achieve Initiation.

There is one passage to which I desire to call particular attention, because it strongly confirms my view of Prospero while seeming to exclude it. I refer to the passage wherein he narrates to Miranda how they were driven from Milan and came to the Island. At this point Prospero speaks as an actual man, the exiled ruler of a temporal kingdom. Neither the manner nor the matter of his utterance is here consistent with the allegorical character I have imputed to him. And yet, if we study the text more closely, we find that by one deft stroke the Poet has almost openly declared his purpose at the very moment when he most conceals it.

Let us consider all the circumstances. In the first place, is there any need to assume that some measure of concealment was desirable? I suppose it is unnecessary at this stage of the case to point out that *The Tempest* is a theological heresy, judged by the standards of Shakespeare's day. It deals, like the allegories of Dante and Bunyan, with the pilgrimage of perfection; but it carries implications which these others do not. It is a synthesis of the main features of all mythology and ritual, whether Christian or non-Christian. It tells the story of man's upward struggle partly in Biblical terms and partly in terms of pagan myth and ritual. It not only presupposes, but actually demonstrates, that there is one universal tradition underlying all religious and semi-religious concepts. In short, having regard to the manner in which its theme is handled, *The Tempest* is an almost perfect essay in what we should call to-day Comparative Religion.

The Play therefore anticipates by at least two hundred years the evolution of theological criticism, and reveals in its author a degree of philosophic emancipation to which he might well have hesitated to give full and free expression in his own age. If (as is not improbable) Shakespeare were conscious of the general implications of *The Tempest*, he could not be wholly insensible of the charges to which it might expose him. He would certainly be aware that to proclaim (as the Play does in effect) the existence of a close affinity between the pagan myths and ritual on the one hand, and the mysteries of the Christian religion on the other, would be to " use strange fire at the altar of the Lord." We have good grounds for believing that Francis Bacon perceived this affinity; and, what is more, he admits that he deliberately refrained from dealing freely with the subject. What, then, were the seemingly imperative considerations that induced him to " interdict his pen all liberty in this kind " ?* If (as his own guarded language suggests) Bacon deemed it advisable to avoid as far as possible the frank and gratuitous discussion of questions involving anything in the nature of theological heterodoxy, would Shakespeare be altogether heedless of such considerations ? No doubt they would operate less forcibly in his case than in the case of Bacon, who, as a prominent statesman, would be under additional

* Cf. *Wisdom of the Ancients*, final paragraph on " Prometheus ": " And thus I have delivered that which I thought good to observe out of this so well-known and common fable; and yet I will not deny but that there may be some things in it which have an admirable consent with the mysteries of Christian religion. . . . But I have interdicted my pen all liberty in this kind, lest I should use strange fire at the altar of the Lord."

obligations of prudence; but the fact remains that what Bacon did not think it " good to observe " Shakespeare would hardly find it wise to assert. There was, however, this distinction between the case of the philosopher-statesman and that of the dramatist: that the latter could (and, I think, did) set forth in a veiled allegory what the former would not present in open argument.

On the assumption, therefore, that Shakespeare was aware of the more important implications, if not of all the implications, of the comprehensive allegory presented in *The Tempest*, we may reasonably suppose that he took some pains to conceal its inner meaning, leaving the Play to be interpreted by those in his own or a later age who could see behind its outward forms and appreciate the breadth and significance of its theme. And this conclusion is not only suggested by all the circumstances of the case, but is also strongly supported by direct textual evidence within the Play. How, then, does the Poet dissemble his real purpose?

His method is simple and effective. Putting his spiritual theme in a secular framework, he describes Prospero as the exiled Duke of Milan. Thus Prospero plays a double rôle. In the inner design of the Play he figures the Supreme Being; but in its outer design he is the human ruler of a temporal kingdom. When he narrates to Miranda how they came from Milan to the Island, he speaks in his nominal—as distinct from his allegorical—rôle. And it is certainly very significant that, before making this speech (and at no other point in the Play), Prospero, with a most marked gesture, takes off his magic garment:

> 'Tis time
> I should inform thee farther. Lend thy hand,
> And pluck my magic garment from me. So:
> Lie there, my art.
>
> (Act I., Scene 2.)

This magic garment, which invests him wirh supernatural powers, is the badge of Prospero's allegorical
character. Laying it aside, he ceases for the moment
to represent the Supreme Being, and descends to
ordinary human rank. In other words, the allegory
is temporarily suspended while Prospero, in his nominal
rôle as the exiled Duke of Milan, deals with the
circumstances which form the ostensible basis of the
Play.

Is there a better reason, is there indeed any other
reason at all, why Prospero should so ostentatiously
remove the mantle at this particular moment, and at
no other in the Play? If not, even my severest critic
must admit that in respect of this point, as of so many
others, I might fairly claim judgment by default.

## 2. ARIEL.

As the chief messenger and minister of Prospero,
Ariel plays in the cosmic allegory the part which is
assigned in the Old Testament to the Angel of the Lord,
in the New Testament to " the Spirit," and in the
pagan mythology to Hermes.

The exact status of these three powers—and particularly that of " the Spirit " in the New Testament
—has always been somewhat difficult to determine;
but that they all represent very much the same idea
is evident from the general resemblance between them.
They all belong, like Ariel, to the element of air;
and, further, they all perform the same function.
The " Angel of the Lord " is certainly one, and seemingly the chief, of those messengers (angels) of God
which, according to the passage already cited from
*Psalms*, are winds. The winged Hermes, chief messenger of Zeus, is likewise associated very closely with

# The Powers of Redemption

the wind.*  And " the Spirit," not only by its name
but also by the manner in which it is said to appear,
is practically identified with the wind.†  Broadly
speaking, the difference between the ordinary messengers and the typical chief messenger seems to be
that, whereas the former are simply the agents of
inspiration, the latter has a more comprehensive function.  It can and does descend lower than the plane of
AIR, to which the ordinary messengers are confined.
In the pagan myth it was Hermes (reputed the patron
of travellers) who descended from on high, and gave
to Perseus the wings which enabled him to mount up
into the air.  When the Children of Israel had crossed
the Red Sea, the Angel of the Lord was sent down to
lead them through the Wilderness to the Promised
Land.‡  In the Gospel myth it was " the Spirit "
which descended upon Christ after He had come up
out of the baptismal water, and which led Him up to
wander in the Wilderness.  And, similarly, it is Ariel
who brings the travellers up out of the sea to wander
in the maze of the " desolate isle."

No personal qualities are ascribed in the Bible
either to " the Angel " or to " the Spirit," both of
which seem to be conceived rather as an emanation
of God.  But Hermes, like all the figures in the pagan
mythology, is distinctly personalised.  Of the three,
therefore, Hermes would furnish the Poet with the
most clearly defined model for Ariel—in fact, with

* Roscher, in fact, identifies him entirely with the wind (*Hermes
der Wind-Gott*).

† The Greek *Pneuma* and the Hebrew *Ruach* both mean spirit or
wind.  Cf. *Acts* ii. 2-4, where " the Spirit " is said to come as a
rushing mighty wind.  Note also that those to whom it comes see
" tongues parting asunder, like as of fire "; and compare this with the
appearance of Ariel during the wreck as a fire that divides and burns
in many places.

‡ *Exod.* xxiii. 20 ff.

the only model that could serve. And what does comparison reveal? Ariel, although his native element is the air, can traverse the other elements:

> Grave sir, hail! I come
> To answer thy best pleasure; be 't to fly,
> To swim, to dive into the fire, to ride
> On the curled clouds: to thy strong bidding, task
> Ariel, and all his quality.
>
> (Act I., Scene 2.)

Hermes likewise, being sent by Zeus to command the release of Odysseus by the nymph Calypso, passes through all the elements (*Odys.* v.). But such tasks he performs reluctantly and at the " strong bidding " of Zeus; for, having crossed the sea and descended into the grotto of Calypso, he declares to her:

> 'Twas Zeus that bade me come hither, by no will of mine; nay, who would of his free will make his way through such unutterably vast salt water?
>
> (*Od.* v.)

The same unwillingness and need for compulsion is shown by Ariel, to whom Prospero, enforcing him, exclaims:

> Thou think'st it much to tread the ooze
> Of the salt deep;
> To run upon the sharp wind of the north,
> To do me business in the veins o' th' earth,
> When it is baked with frost.
>
> (Act I., Scene 2.)

It is one of the chief features of Hermes that he can translate himself in a flash from place to place. So with Ariel:

> I drink the air before me, and return
> Or e'er your pulse twice beat.
>
> (Act V., Scene 1.)

Furthermore, like Hermes, Ariel can render himself invisible and assume any form he pleases. Like

# The Powers of Redemption

Hermes, he is of a restlessly active, prankish, fickle, and capricious disposition. In a word, Ariel is essentially *mercurial.*

But, while he is thus personalised according to the model of the mythical Hermes, Ariel must be understood (like Caliban) in a purely subjective sense. This much is obvious from the psychological view I have presented of the Play and of the universal myth upon which it is based. How, then, shall we designate in this sense the spirit which drives man up from passional things to wander in the lonely wilderness of atoning effort, seeking the lost Word of God; which upholds him against the siren memories (or desire) that beset him in his weariness and discouragement; which, if its admonishing voice be faithfully obeyed, keeps him in the straight and narrow way of repentance and renunciation, and so brings him at last to the promised land of self-mastery and redemption?* In the widest sense of the term, this immanent spirit may be called Conscience, the impelling, guiding, and accusing messenger of God, which urges and sustains mankind in the long pilgrimage of religious endeavour.

Such is the part performed by Ariel in the Play. He is the antithesis of Caliban, as Conscience is the antithesis of Desire. It is Ariel (invisible) who unavailingly gives the lie direct to Caliban when the latter successfully tempts Stephano and Trinculo. It is Ariel who leads up the members of the Court

---

* Cf. *Exod.* xxiii. 20-21: " Behold, I send an Angel before thee, to keep thee in the way, and to bring thee into the place which I have prepared. Beware of him, and obey his voice; provoke him not; for he will not pardon your transgressions; for my name is in him." Similarly, Hermes is the patron of travellers and the guide through Purgatory (Wilderness). In the pagan initiations the candidate was led and instructed in the ceremonies by the Hierocceryx, who represented Hermes (cf. Mr. Dudley Wright, Phil.B., F.S.P., in *The Eleusinian Mysteries and Rites*).

Party to wander in the maze of the desolate isle, seeking " the lost Son "; who deprives them of the tempting banquet proffered by the siren shapes; and whose accusing speech (" You are three men of sin, etc.") causes them to renew their quest in a frenzy of remorse. Nor can we mistake his character when he says:

> But remember,
> For that's my business to you, that you three
> From Milan did supplant good Prospero;
> . . . for which foul deed,
> The powers, delaying, not forgetting, have
> Incensed the seas and shores, yea, all the creatures,
> Against your peace . . . and do pronounce by me,
> Lingering perdition, worse than any death
> Can be at once, shall step by step attend
> You and your ways; whose wraths to guard you from,
> Which here, in this most desolate isle, else falls
> Upon your heads, is nothing, but heart's sorrow,
> And a clear life ensuing.
>
> (Act III., Scene 3.)

Here is the authentic voice of Conscience, the divine agent against whom, as Ariel says, the swords of the Court Party can avail them nothing. There remains to be noted that, in the case of Ferdinand, it is Ariel who leads him up into the Elysium where happy spirits dance upon the yellow sands, and that it is Ariel, as Prospero says, who brings about his union with Miranda (the Celestial Bride).

Now, as the guide and sustainer of man in the upward struggle, Conscience is a friendly messenger. It corresponds to the Angel of the Lord, which guides and sustains the pilgrim in the wilderness. But to wrong-doers and backsliders Conscience assumes an opposite character. To them it is Satan, resisting them as the Adversary and tormenting them as the Accuser. A clear instance of this same inversion in the case of the Angel of the Lord is furnished in

# The Powers of Redemption

the Old Testament myth of Balaam, where it is said:

> And the Angel of the Lord placed himself in the way for an adversary (Hebrew, *satan*) against him (*Num.* xxii. 22).*

Moreover, it might quite well be contended that the inversion by which Conscience becomes Satan is implied by Shakespeare when he makes Benedick say:

> If Don Worm, his conscience, find no impediment. . . .
> (*Much Ado*, V. 2. 86.)†

Why "Don Worm"? Satan, as the Serpent or Tempter, is sometimes called the Worm—for example, by Milton in *Paradise Lost* (ix. 1068). Furthermore, hell is described in *St. Mark* (ix. 48) as the place "where the worm dieth not." In the subjective interpretation of hell, what is this "worm" that does not die? It is the Adversary (Satan), whether as Conscience which the sinner fails to overcome, or as Desire which the aspirant fails to vanquish. And the torment of the psychological state which is hell consists in the very fact that this Worm—whether as Conscience or as Desire—does not die. In short, it is true in the universal psychology that the Accuser, no less than the Tempter, can be the tormenting Adversary (Satan).

The case of Ariel in the Play is treated by the Poet quite in accordance with the foregoing principle. Ariel represents Conscience; and, as such, he corresponds to the Angel of the Lord, to "the Spirit," and to Hermes. But when he acts the part of Accuser to the "men of sin," he becomes Satan the Adversary; and at this point he very appropriately assumes the form

* Cf. verse 32: "Behold I am come forth for an adversary (*satan*), because thy way is perverse before me."
† Cf. *Rich. III.*, I. 3. 222: "The worm of conscience still begnaw thy soul!"

213

# Shakespeare's Mystery Play

of one of the traditional monsters or devils of Purgatory—namely, *a harpy.*

This latter aspect of Ariel explains his relations with Sycorax, of which Prospero tells us something in a considerable digression. I have already dealt in detail with the case of Sycorax, and shown that she occupies a definite place in the scheme which underlies the Play. I pointed out that she has nothing whatever to do with the action and that she need not have been mentioned at all for the purposes of the ostensible story; and the same is true of her relations with Ariel. Why, then, are they so carefully explained, if not to throw light on the allegory? Is there any significance in Prospero's digression?

Now, as Conscience Ariel resisted the will of the wanton Sycorax. To her he is Satan, the Adversary who " goes out to withstand her, because her ways are perverse before him."* And what did Sycorax do? Prospero, reminding Ariel, says:

> And, for thou wast a spirit too delicate
> To act her earthy and abhorred commands,
> Refusing her grand hests, she did confine thee,
> By help of her more potent ministers,
> And in her most unmitigable rage,
> Into a cloven pine.
>
> (Act I., Scene 2.)

Whence comes this curious fancy of the cloven pine? I suggest that the Poet here makes a carefully studied allusion to the proverbial notion of putting " the devil in a cleft stick." We have already seen that the term " the devil " is used with several different meanings in the Play; in fact, it is always somewhat elastic. And certainly the proverbial character of " the devil," as a hostile and tormenting power, is as appropriate in one sense to Conscience (the Accuser)

* Cf. *Num.* xxii. 32 (Revised Version).

214

# The Powers of Redemption

as it is in the contrary sense to Desire (the Tempter). The notion of putting "the devil in a cleft stick" no doubt expresses the idea of the mastering of vexatious Desire by the seeker after God; but it expresses equally well the idea of the mastering of vexatious Conscience by the hardened evil-doer. And it is in the latter sense, as the inhibition of Conscience, that the notion occurs in the story of Ariel and Sycorax.

And what are those " more potent ministers " who are said to have assisted Sycorax to imprison Ariel? On this point we are given no specific guidance in the text; but an answer to the question is suggested by the fact that all the main features of *The Tempest* have been found to have their counterparts in mythology. And, indeed, the allusion to these " more potent ministers " suffices to make this part of the Play correspond in form—as I think it clearly corresponds in significance—to the myth of the Sin of the Angels.

Quite simply in *Genesis* vi. 1-4, and with a mass of illuminating detail in the *Book of Enoch* vi. ff., it is related that the angels of God, descending from on high, lusted after the " daughters of men," by whom they begat giants and monsters.* The full myth contains many subtle and profound intimations, with which it is impossible to deal exhaustively within the compass of this present volume; but briefly it may be said to describe that thwarting of the divine will which occurs when the dynamic impulses, in the course of their descent from God into the world of action,

* According to *Genesis* and *Enoch*, the angels lusted after the women and descended from above in order to enjoy them; but the *Book of Jubilees* (iv. 15 and v. 1 ff.) declares that the angels were sent down to the earth by God to instruct mankind in right-doing, and descending to do so began to lust after the " daughters of men " (see Dr. Charles's footnote to *Enoch, in loc.*). For reasons that will presently appear, I think the latter version is undoubtedly the sounder.

215

become perverted in the sensuous medium symbolised by the " daughters of men " and so beget the evil desires symbolised by the monsters. In other words, the myth of the Sin of the Angels may be said to deal with the genesis of evil desires as it occurs in universal experience.

That all this is implied, consciously or otherwise, in the story of Ariel and Sycorax seems to follow as a corollary to what has already been written. I have shown by means of textual evidence that Sycorax personifies the evil aspect of that sensuous element which is represented in the myth by the " daughters of men ";* that Caliban her son is the mythical monster which represents the grosser desire; and that Ariel corresponds to the holy Spirit which is the will of God, striving in the heart of man as Conscience.†

What, then, are the " more potent ministers " who aided Sycorax to thwart and inhibit Ariel? Obviously they correspond to the sinning angels of the myth just recited; for it is expressly implied in *Genesis* (vi. 2) that when the angels had become allied with the " daughters of men " *the Spirit ceased awhile to strive.* Moreover, the " more potent ministers " are said to have assisted Sycorax, the sorceress, to confine Ariel into a cloven tree; and, according to *Enoch*, the

---

* It is true that Sycorax is described by Prospero as a " foul witch," old and hideous, whereas the angels loved the " daughters of men " for their elegance and beauty. But, although Sycorax was hideous to Prospero, she must have been alluring to someone, for she became pregnant. Compare the case of the " blue-eyed witch " Sycorax with that of the " blue-eyed witch " whose evil beauty drew down and perverted an angel from Heaven in Browning's *Pauline* (lines 96–123).

† Note that the term " conscience " is used in the widest sense to signify the upward-impelling, guiding, and accusing spirit. Ariel is, of course, a typical archangel; and, as such, he is equivalent to the seven archangels mentioned in *Enoch*—viz., Gabriel, Michael, Remiel, Uriel, Raphael, Raguel, and Sârâqael. The terminal *el*, common to all these names, denotes " strength " or " of God (the Mighty One)."

sinning angels taught the " daughters of men " sorcery, incantations, and *the dividing of trees.*[*]

Whether Shakespeare deliberately intended to reproduce the myth of the Sin of the Angels is not a question of ultimate importance. But I may perhaps emphasise the fact that, if my general view of *The Tempest* as an account of the spiritual redemption of man be correct, this interpolated story of the inhibition of Conscience (Ariel) and the birth of evil desire (Caliban) out of the sensuous imagination (Sycorax) forms a fitting prologue to the main action of the Play.

## 3. MIRANDA.

The bulk of the evidence relating to Miranda was given in the earlier part of this study, where the grounds for regarding her as a personification of Wisdom were considered at some length. There still remain, however, some further points with which it was not then convenient to deal.

It has since been argued that, in the Eleusinian rites, the Wisdom for which the aspirant goes in quest was represented by the mythical Persephone. Like Wisdom in the empirical initiation, Persephone had

---

[*] *Enoch*, Archbishop Lawrence, 3rd ed., pp. 5–6   For what it may be worth, I suggest that the tree was split *by lightning*. According to *Ps.* civ. 4, the ministers of God are a flaming fire, and hence they may be imagined as coming down to earth in the form of lightning. (Cf. Dr. Charles's Introduction to *Enoch*, 2nd ed., p. xciii, quotation from *Acts of the Disputation of Archelaus with Manes*, ch. xxxii.: " Angelorum quidam, mandato Dei non subditi, voluntati eius restituerunt, et aliquis quidem de caelo, *tanquam fulgur ignis*, cecidit super terram, alii vero infelicitate hominum filiabus admixti, a dracone afflicti, ignis aeterni poenam suscipere meruerunt.") According to the myth of the Fall of Satan—a myth which differs somewhat in conception and in form from that of the Sin of the Angels, seeming to signify rather the transmutation of spiritual desire into evil lust through impatience with the divine discipline—Satan fell as lightning from Heaven (*St. Luke* x. 18).

to be diligently sought for;* and, like Wisdom, she figuratively became the "bride" of the initiate in the ceremony which constituted revelation.† In so far, therefore, as the Play conforms to the rites of Eleusis, Miranda should correspond to Persephone, daughter of Zeus.

What, then, is the general character of Persephone? In the First Epistle of St. Paul to the Corinthians it is said concerning the planted seed that—

> That which thou sowest is not quickened, except it die.
> (xv. 36.)

And, as with the Egyptian Isis (to whom also Miranda corresponds), Persephone was held to be *the deity who presided over the quickening of the dead seed.* So with Miranda, of whom Ferdinand remarks:

> The mistress which I serve *quickens what's dead.* . . .
> (Act II., Scene 1.)

True, this line is not positively enigmatical. It reads more or less naturally in a simple context. Nevertheless, there is a peculiarity in the phrasing which is singularly appropriate if Miranda be the counterpart of Isis and of Persephone.

Now, although Persephone is often broadly described as the power that presides over the springing corn, yet in the myth around which the Eleusinian cultus revolved she is rather the planted seed itself;‡ and

---

* During the wanderings on the shore at Eleusis. At this stage Persephone was called *Pherrephatta*—cf. *Prov.* i. 28; *ibid.*, viii. 17; *Ecclus.* vii. 23 ff.

† That is, in the Greater Initiation. At this stage Persephone was called *Kore*, which means not only "the maid" but also "the bride."

‡ Porphyry (*De Antro Nymph.*, c. 6) describes her as the guardian of the planted seed. Yet, according to Thos. Taylor, Eusebius (*Eveng. Praeper.* iii. 2) cites Porphyry as saying that Persephone is the seed placed in the ground. Thus we find both views expressed by one and the same writer.

# The Powers of Redemption

her annual descent into the dark realms of Pluto, where she sleeps for a portion of the year, is the sowing of the seed in the earth, where it remains dormant for a period. But it does not follow from this, as many have supposed, that there is nothing more in the story of the lost Persephone than an agricultural myth. Indeed, there is another and a subtler meaning, based upon the analogy between the sowing of the seed and the process of incarnation. For Persephone, as the seed buried and sleeping in the earth, represents the divine essence (or "Soul") buried and sleeping in the physical body (EARTH).

The Soul, says Olympiodorus, descends Corically (after the manner of Persephone) into generation; and Sallust remarks that the rape of Persephone by Pluto implies the descent of the Soul.* I had occasion in the first part of this work to discuss the ancient doctrine that the Soul falls asleep when it goes down into the physical body; and the analogy between this doctrine and the myth of Persephone's descent into the realms of Pluto is further emphasised by the passage already quoted from Plotinus, who, speaking of the Soul, says that her descent into matter is a descent into Hades, where she falls asleep.† From this sleep the Soul is awakened in Initiation.

Consider now the case of Miranda. Like Persephone, she is a lost maiden, fallen from high degree. When she is first informed of her once high estate, she can summon only one dim and tentative memory of it:

> MIR.                    Had I not
> Four or five women once, that tended me?
> PRO. Thou hadst, and more, Miranda.
> (Act I., Scene 2.)

---

* Olympiodorus, Comment. *Phaedo* Platonis; Sallust, *De Diis et Mundo*; both cited by Taylor in *Eleus. and Bacch. Myst.*

† See Part I., Chapter II., third section, hereof.

# Shakespeare's Mystery Play

And Claudian says that Persephone, before her fall, was attended by a large company of nymphs.* This, point is, perhaps, a trifling one; but it is curious, to say the least, that the only circumstance Miranda is represented (quite needlessly) as recalling should be one that is a salient feature of the Persephone myth. Supplementing this, and far more formidable as evidence, is the fact that Prospero presently exclaims to her:

> Here cease more questions.
> Thou art inclined to sleep; 'tis a good dulness,
> And give it way—I know thou canst not choose.
> [*Miranda sleeps.*
> (*Ibid.*)

Why should she fall asleep so suddenly at midday, despite all the unusual happenings on the Island, and only a moment after she has declared that Prospero's strange disclosure was " beating in her mind " ? Above all, why is she *unable to choose?* To these questions, which cannot go unanswered, the literalist has no adequate reply to offer. But if the present hypothesis be accepted, the difficulty vanishes; for, if Miranda be intended to correspond to the Persephone of the Mysteries, it is obvious that at an early stage in the Play the Poet must somehow contrive to show her as plunged in a deep sleep.

It will be noticed that Miranda herself subsequently explains that " the strangeness of the story [of her identity] put heaviness in me." But even to the most casual reader this must seem utterly unconvincing—in fact, it is quite contrary to all reasonable expectation. Yet, if the present view of Miranda be correct, her words are not altogether inappropriate. For no simple

* *De Raptu Proserp.*, which professedly deals with the Eleusinian rites. In *Purg.* xxxi. 106-8 it is said that the same was the case with Beatrice before her descent into the physical body.

# The Powers of Redemption

assertion as to its high origin can alone suffice to arouse the Soul from the ignorance and stupor of the earth-life—a stupor that is deepened, rather than dispelled, by " the strangeness of the story." Moreover, if Miranda here represent the Sleeping Soul of the un-initiated, we perceive why it is that Prospero, having planned for the travellers just such a series of experiences as culminate (in the case of Ferdinand) in full initiation and " awakening," declares to her with regard to what he has done:

> I have done nothing but *in care of thee*,
> (Of thee, my dear one; thee, my daughter.) . . .
>
> *(Ibid.)*

In the esoteric design of the Play, therefore, Miranda has precisely the twofold significance of Persephone in the Eleusinian rites. Like Persephone in the psychological aspect of the Mysteries, she figures the Wisdom which the initiate seeks, and ultimately weds; and, like Persephone in the eschatological aspect of the Mysteries, she figures the fallen and sleeping Soul which it is the object of initiation to awaken and restore.

Numerous instances could be given of the occurrence of these traditional ideas in the popular and enduring fairy-stories. For instance, there is a striking resemblance between the story of the Sleeping Beauty and the myth of Persephone. In the former, the Princess is playing with a spinning-frame when, pricking her finger, she falls into a heavy stupor, and remains sleeping for a long period in her castle while a thick and dark wood grows up around it (cf. wood=*silva*=matter). In the myth, Persephone is weaving a tapestry when Aphrodite persuades her to pluck a narcissus flower (cf. *narke*=torpidity; hence " narcotic "=inducing stupor); and in that moment

221

she is seized by Pluto, who carries her down into the earth, where she falls asleep.* These two stories are not only similar in outward form; they also appear to express the same idea. They both serve to allegorise the fall of the Soul, by way of generation, into the physical body, where it remains in deep sleep. And the awakening and return of Persephone, like the awakening of the Princess in the fairy-story, represents the awakening of the Soul in Initiation. In short, Persephone is the Greek equivalent of the Sleeping Beauty; and Miranda, the Sleeping Princess of the Play, corresponds to both of them.''

A variant of this same theme of the fallen and oblivious Soul is found in the many stories that tell of a lost Princess, living in ignorance of her high estate until one day a Prince arrives to take her as his bride. Here the idea of sleeping is replaced by that of self-ignorance; but the meaning, of course, is the same. To this latter version also the case of Miranda corresponds; for during the action of the Play she is informed for the first time that she is an exiled Princess:

> Thy father
> Was Duke of Milan, and his only heir
> A princess—no worse issued. (*Ibid.*)

The Poet has strongly emphasised the fact that Miranda, like the Princess of the fairy-stories, is ignorant of her high origin. Prospero says:

> I have done nothing but in care of thee
> (Of thee, my dear one; thee, my daughter) who
> Art ignorant of what thou art, nought knowing
> Of whence I am. (*Ibid.*)

---

* See Claudian, *De Raptu Proserp*. Note the part played in the myth by Aphrodite, goddess of sexual love. Moreover, it may be added that spinning and weaving are often held to be emblematical of generation on its feminine side.

# The Powers of Redemption

And Miranda herself exclaims:

> You have often
> Begun to tell me what I am; but stopped,
> And left me to a bootless inquisition,
> Concluding, " Stay, not yet."

(Ibid.)

And, as in the case of the Princess of the popular stories, it is only when her Prince has arrived that Miranda learns who and what she is.*

Although it has no immediate relevance to the case of Miranda, I may here make a suggestion inferred from the symbolical figure in which the seed represents the Soul.† The seed is sown in the ground; after a period of dormancy, it is quickened; it sends forth a shoot which rises up out of the earth into the air, where it flowers; thereafter the seed falls again in due time from the air down into the earth; and the same process is repeated. This cycle of sowings is roughly analogous with the cycle of incarnations, which latter takes place between the " elements " of EARTH and AIR.‡ Now I have shown that the seed lying dormant in the ground actually was held to typify the Soul sleeping in the physical body; and it is hardly likely that, while this part of a simple and expressive analogy was definitely and widely recognised, the other part of it was entirely overlooked or ignored. In other words, since the ancients regarded the planted seed as emblematical of the Soul in the body, it would be reasonable to conclude that they regarded the flower which blooms in the air and turns to face the sun as emblematical

* This theme of the lost Princess is the subject of *The Winter's Tale*. Perdita (the Latin *perdita* means literally " the lost maiden ") corresponds to Miranda; and the Prince who comes to her is called Florizel, which is the name often given to the Prince in the fairy-stories.

† This, of course, is quite a common figure, not confined exclusively to the pagan Mysteries. Cf. 1 *Cor.* xv. 36-45.

‡ Cf. Part II., Chapter I., section on " Natural Symbolism."

of the disembodied and purified Soul which dwells in the sphere of AIR and looks upwards to the divine radiance above. In the case of the cereals, with which the rites of Eleusis were more especially concerned, the equivalent of the flower is the ear; and the mowing down and gathering of the Ear of Corn would aptly represent the release of the perfected Soul from the cycle of incarnations.

There is no doubt that this escape of the Soul was occultly intimated in the Orphic initiations;* and, in so far as the Eleusinian rites in their eschatological aspect had reference to the supposed experiences of the Soul both here and hereafter, the ascent from AIR to AETHER which constitutes the Third Degree must (in accordance with tradition) have implied the Soul's escape from the cycle. No direct evidence from ancient records can be cited to prove that such was indeed the occult significance of the reaping rite which Hippolytus says was performed before the *epoptes* in the Third Degree at Eleusis; but, in the absence of any other interpretation whatever, the suggestion I have made may, perhaps, be deemed worthy of consideration.

Now, between the view of Miranda considered in the first part of this study and the view put forward in the present section, there is a seemingly important difference. The inconsistency, however, is apparent rather than real; and it may here be briefly explained. From what has already been said, it is clear that the experience which constitutes Initiation may be conceived in two different ways—viz., either (*a*) in a subjective sense as the awakening of the Soul, or (*b*) in

---

* Cf. Cheetham, in Second Hulsean Lecture: " The aim and end of the Orphic initiations is . . . to prevent the Soul from re-entering into the never-ending series of forms of earthly life to which it might otherwise be destined."

an objective sense as the finding of Wisdom or Truth. There is no need to enter into any of the subtleties of the psychologist on the precise relation between subject and object in order to prove that these two conceptions have ultimately the same significance, for the point is practically self-evident. If, therefore, the Play have the meaning I ascribe to it, then it must be consistent with both of these equally valid conceptions of Initiation; and Miranda, in whose interest everything was contrived by Prospero, must personify —(a) in one sense the Soul of the aspirant, and (b) in another sense the Wisdom or Truth which he seeks.

Assuming that the conjecture I have made as to the meaning of the reaping rite recorded by Hippolytus be correct, we may say that Miranda, in her aspect as the awakened Soul, personifies that which in the Eleusinian Mysteries was represented by an *Ear of Corn*. But, whether as the awakened Soul or as Wisdom, she personifies that which on the authority of wide tradition may be represented by a *Fountain of Water*.

I have already had occasion to remark that there are two mythical dragons, the evil dragon being native to the passional WATER BELOW, and the sacred dragon being native to the divine WATER ABOVE (AETHER). A similar antithesis is found in the two mythical women, of whom one is reputed wanton and the other immaculate. Examples of this antithesis are presented in the Greek Aphrodite and Aphrodite Ourania, in the Hebrew Lilith and Shechinah, in the Biblical Strange Woman and Wisdom, and (if analogy may be invoked in default of definite records) in the Egyptian Nephthys and Isis. The same antithesis is found in the Play in Sycorax and Miranda, who represent respectively the Wanton Woman and the Immaculate Woman.

# Shakespeare's Mystery Play

Dealing in the previous chapter with the case of Sycorax, I showed that the mythical Wanton Woman personifies the passional or sensuous element in man (*Nephesh*), which is symbolised by the WATER BELOW. Obviously, then, the mythical Immaculate Woman who is her antithesis personifies the divine element in man (*Neshamah*), which is symbolised by the WATER ABOVE. It is this divine element, or aethereal Soul, which is awakened in Initiation.

Such is the subjective view of the two women; but the concept assumes a somewhat different allegorical form when it is expressed in the objective manner. The Wanton Woman then represents that for which the passional nature of man craves, as the tempted aspirant thirsts in the Wilderness for the WATER BELOW; and the Immaculate Woman represents that for which the divine nature of man craves, as the pilgrim Dante thirsted for the WATER ABOVE, in the person of Beatrice.* In this objective sense the Wanton personifies sensuous or passional pleasure, and the Pure Woman personifies wisdom or truth—as the antithesis of the Strange Woman of *Proverbs* is expressly said to be Wisdom.† Both women are symbolically depicted as a well or fountain; but, whereas man drinks of the former the " sweet-bitter " passional water, of the latter he drinks that " living water " which is the Light of God.‡

Between these two waters there is a curious and significant difference. The lower water quenches the thirst and becomes distasteful in surfeit; but of the

* *Purg.* xxi. 1; *ibid.*, xxxi. 127-9 and 139-41. In the last of these three passages Dante, alluding to Beatrice, speaks of his drinking at the well of living light.

† Cf. long footnote in earlier section, " Sycorax and Setebos."

‡ Cf. *Wisd. Sol.* vii. 26, in which the Woman Wisdom is declared to be " an effulgence from everlasting light." Beatrice is a well of living light (*Purg.* xxxi. 139-41, just cited); and the Bride of Lebanon is a fountain of living water (*Song* iv. 12 and 15).

226

higher water man is never sated. Thus it is said of the Strange Woman (WATER BELOW) that " her lips drop as honey, but her end is bitter "; whereas Wisdom (WATER ABOVE) declares that " they that drink me shall yet thirst."* The latter idea is associated also with Arduizur, the Persian Beatrice or Miranda; for her name is that given to a spring called *Fountain of Light*, whose keeper says: " Whoso drinks of this water will be parched by unquenchable thirst."† This difference between the two waters confirms the interpretation I have given. For every man knows that indulgence in passional pleasure quenches the thirst for it, and brings a temporary feeling of satiety; whereas thirst for wisdom or truth is not at all diminished, but rather increased, by the drinking. It may be remarked that a play upon this symbolical figure is involved in each of the last two of Shakespeare's *Sonnets*, wherein the Poet, paying extravagant tribute to his mistress, implies that she differs from all other women in this, that the more he drinks of the water, the more ardently he desires it.

The case of the Persian Arduizur has just been mentioned, and I may perhaps with advantage give here a summary of the myth as Schuré narrates it. The youth Ardjasp encounters a veiled virgin beside a spring. Her name, she tells him, is Arduizur, which is the name of the spring itself, and means " Fountain of Light"; and she adds that he who drinks of this water will be parched by unquenchable thirst. He, unthinking, drinks at the spring; and later, losing the maiden as it seems for ever, thirsts ardently for her. He takes counsel of the venerable priest Vahumano,

* Of the Strange Woman, see *Prov.* v. 3-4. Of Wisdom, see *Ecclus.* xxiv. 21. Compare also the case of Beatrice in *Purg.* xxxi. 129.

† Ed. Schuré, *L'Evolution Divine du Sphinx au Christ*, Perrin et Cie, Paris, 1912), p. 186.

who renames him Zarathustra (Greek, Zoroaster), and sends him to dwell in solitude in a cavern on the mountain-side. Here Zarathustra remained for ten years in lonely meditation. The daemons of the destroying Ahrimane, temptations and terrors, assailed him in the forms of hideous creatures and winged serpents, which filled him with self-doubt and fear for his mission. Zarathustra prayed fervently; but Ormuz came not, and the monsters grew yet more horrible. The shade of a veiled woman now appeared to him, bending over him with burning breath, then leaving him, still veiled and mute. Three nights later Ormuz, the Word, came at last to the seeker in a voice of thunder that was yet a melodious murmur. Zarathustra now returned to preach with a new and strong authority to his people, whom after many years he finally led to victory over their enemies. This work completed, he retired to his cavern, still mourning his lost Arduizur and praying that he might find her again. At last one day standing upon the mountain-top, he felt the chill shudder of death pass over him. He perceived a great luminous arch in the sky; and his soul, wrenched from his body, soared upwards. Above and beyond the luminous ring, he beheld a woman draped in light. "Who art thou, O wonder?" he cried. She answered: "I am Arduizur. It was I that came to thee in thy solitude. I am thine own divine soul. Let us now drink the cup of immortal life at the fountain of light." And Arduizur, sinking into his arms as the wife yields to the husband, gave him to drink of the cup. In that moment Arduizur had vanished, absorbed in him. Subject and object were united and identic. She lived in his heart; she looked through his eyes; henceforward they were one; and together thus they gazed upon the splendour of the Most High.

# The Powers of Redemption

Such is the essence of the myth of Arduizur, as told by Schuré. It needs no comment at this late stage of my argument. It contains every salient feature of the tradition with which *The Tempest* deals; and Arduizur is clearly the equivalent of Beatrice and of Miranda. Observe that not only is she that for which Zarathustra seeks and thirsts, but also she is his own divine soul, which is exactly what I have argued with regard to Miranda in her relation to Ferdinand.

From the foregoing evidence it is clear that, whatever may have been the actual practice in the ancient rites, the choice between divine and passional things, which are the alternatives presented to the aspirant in the self-conflict involved in Initiation, is mythologically depicted as a choice between—(a) two opposite kinds of water, and (b) two opposite kinds of woman.

Of the choice in terms of water there is an example in the story of Christ's encounter at the well with the woman of Samaria. Contrasting the water she is about to draw with the living water He can give, Christ says: " Whosoever drinketh of this water shall thirst again; but whosoever drinketh of the water I shall give him shall never thirst " (*St. John* iv. 6–18). At first sight this appears exactly to invert the traditional distinction between the lower and the higher waters; but the words of Christ have to be studied in relation to their context. The woman of Samaria comes to draw that ordinary water which is the symbol of Passion. Whereupon Christ, knowing that she has had five husbands and one who is not her husband, utters a parable to her. He tells her in effect that whoso drinks the water of Passion is satisfied for a time, but presently thirsts again for it, whereas whoso drinks of the living water of Truth shall never thirst for the water of Passion. In other words, He tells her in effect that Truth releases mankind from bondage to Passion, as it is written that Wisdom delivers us from the Strange Woman.* The context of Christ's words leaves no doubt as to His meaning. It is the lower thirst (not the higher) which is quenched by the living water; for the Woman of Samaria demands this higher water in order that, thirsting no more for the lower, she need not periodically return to the well.

Of the choice in terms of woman there are many examples. The case of Wisdom and the Strange Woman has already been amply dealt with. A parallel to this is found in the mythical Choice of Hercules, which describes how Hercules, going into a solitary place to meditate, was approached by two women— one, of modest mien and clothed in white, being called Virtue, who bade him follow the hard path of labour that led to her abode; and the other, of bold mien and so clothed as to reveal her bodily charms, being called Vice, who bade him walk with her in easy paths and enjoy all the pleasures of the senses.† Again, in the story of Odysseus' escape from the arms of Calypso, a choice on the part of Odysseus himself is implied in the fact that the wanton Calypso (Passion) released him at the bidding of the messenger Hermes (Conscience), who was sent by Zeus to perform this task at the instance of Pallas Athene, goddess of wisdom.‡ Yet another, but somewhat more complicated, account of the choice is found in the mythical Judgment of Paris, which relates how Paris, being called upon to choose between Juno and Minerva (Pallas) and Venus, brought

* *Prov.* ii. 16.

† Cf. Prodicus, in Xenophon's *Memorabilia of Socrates*, II. i. 21 *et seq.*

‡ *Odyss.* v. It is obvious that Pallas Athene, who grieves over the bondage of Odysseus to Calypso, plays here the part of Arduizur and of Beatrice, as the divine Soul of the wanderer.

much misfortune to mankind by preferring the wanton Goddess of Love to the Queen of Heaven and the Goddess of Wisdom. All these myths deal in their several ways with the fundamental choice involved in Initiation. Each is a version of the traditional allegory in which the alternatives of Good and Evil, Truth and Passion, Wisdom and Folly, are represented as a pure woman and a wanton; and of this same allegory *The Tempest* contains a version in the contrast between the immaculate Miranda and the wanton Sycorax.

True, nowhere in the Play is there any question of a specific choice between Miranda and Sycorax. Even in the case of Ferdinand, the implied choice is between Miranda and a number of sweet-tongued ladies. But these latter (as I have shown) represent those many pleasures of the senses which hold down in bondage the winged spirit of man; and, as such, they have practically the same significance as the evil Wanton whose " lips drop as honey." It is not surprising that the one great theme of Initiation should be expressed in several different ways in mythology; and we can hardly expect such a synthesis as is presented in *The Tempest* to be both comprehensive and unfailingly consistent. The Play contains the broad lines of every type of initiation myth. In the wanton Sycorax, mother of the monstrous Caliban, we have the Evil Woman according to one version of the tradition; but the story of Ferdinand, like the story of Dante which it resembles in so many respects, conforms to a different version of the same essential idea. The contrast between the peerless Miranda and the honey-tongued ladies who have often held Ferdinand in bondage has its analogy in the contrast between the idealised Beatrice and the siren women Dante has loved. It represents the contrast between the pure ideal and the many pleasures of the senses; and it has, therefore, the same ultimate meaning as the contrast between the Celestial Lady and the Wanton. Thus the story of Ferdinand, while it makes no mention whatever of Sycorax in antithesis to Miranda, does by implication contain that choice between two different kinds of woman which is one of the traditional modes of symbolising the fundamental choice involved in every initiation.

# CHAPTER V

## *CONCLUDING REMARKS*

THE answer which I have to offer to the problem of *The Tempest* has now been fully stated. It meets the many and obvious difficulties of the text. It rests upon such a vast amount of internal evidence as must quite exclude any suggestion that I have picked out a few convenient passages and exploited a few unimportant coincidences. And, far from being a " cranky " theory, it imputes to the Play not merely a high purpose, but the very highest and most comprehensive to which the genius of the Poet could be addressed.

Let the reader put aside whatever preconceptions he may have, and ask himself on what strictly rational grounds a theory possessing these three pertinent qualifications can be rejected. It is not definitely negatived by any Shakespearean fact that is established beyond the possibility of dispute; and, however unorthodox the theory may be, it involves no initial improbability substantial enough to outweigh the immense mass of evidence in its favour. Does it, indeed, involve any initial improbability at all ? I cannot think it does. Broadly considered, the meaning I have ascribed to *The Tempest* is certainly not one which is in the smallest degree peculiar in itself and inconsistent with the history of the drama up to Shakespeare's time, nor is it one which makes the Play utterly unlike any other masterpiece of art or literature. There is nothing odd or fantastic, nothing that the trained intelligence immediately and instinctively resists, in the essential idea I have sought to establish—namely, that Shakespeare wrote a dramatic version of the one theme which has appealed unfailingly to the imagination of mankind through all the ages. There is nothing contrary to reasonable expectation in the argument that such a work must inevitably be found to contain points of resemblance (whether intended by the Poet or not) to those parts of the Bible, of the pagan mythology and ritual, of the writings of Dante and Virgil and others, which demonstrably deal with the same great theme. Nor can it be denied that there is a singular fitness in the suggestion that the zenith of the drama, as represented by the climax of Shakespeare's power, was marked by a Mystery Play corresponding very closely to the ancient religious ceremonies with which the early art of the theatre was allied. And although the view of *The Tempest* which I have put forward does undoubtedly differ fundamentally from the ordinary view, I cannot conceive that any competent critic will treat the simple fact of its novelty as constituting, in itself, a really valid objection. Surely, then, my theory has no strong presumption against it on general grounds at the outset?

As a matter of fact, to those who can forget their own preconceptions for the moment and approach this question of initial probabilities in a truly judicial frame of mind, it may even seem that the balance is in my favour. Consider in broad outline all that this study implies. I have contended, in effect, that there is one epic theme which is immemorial, changeless, and universal—namely, the story of the upward struggle of the human spirit, individual or collective, out of the darkness of sin and error, into the light of wisdom and truth. I have shown that this psychological theme, or some aspect of it, underlies all authentic myth and

ritual; and it is undoubtedly the subject of numerous
works of art and literature. I have also argued that
the successful issue of the upward struggle constitutes
what is called Initiation, whether empirical or ritual—
the former consisting in success which is actually
achieved in experience, and the latter in success which
is merely simulated in formal ceremonies. My argument further implies that, while the countless allegorical versions of this same theme often differ considerably in respect of detail, certain strongly marked
generic features persist through them all, for the two
reasons—(*a*) that the series of subjective experiences
involved in the ascent " out of darkness into light " is
in its essential nature the same for all men, and (*b*) that
of these experiences the main ones have from the
earliest times been described by means of allegorical
figures which are so appropriate and expressive that
no radical and permanent deviation from them has,
or could have, occurred.* In other words, I have

---

* The earliest versions of the theme are found, of course, in the
myths of antiquity. Observe that it is important to distinguish
between the genuine myth and mere legend. The genuine myth is a
kind of mystery play dealing in the form of dramatic narrative with
truths that are valid, actually or potentially, for all sorts and conditions of men. It is an allegory which expresses some aspect of human
experience so truthfully, and by means of figures that appeal so irresistibly to our instinctive sense of fitness, that it lives on unchanged
from age to age. It may or may not form part of the body of religious
dogma professed by those who cherish and perpetuate it; but in either
case it has a permanent value which the evolution of theologico-
philosophical thought cannot impair. It cannot die, because it is
true for all men; nor can it suffer radical change in the course of
transmission from generation to generation, because the aesthetic
instinct, individual or collective, of those by whom and to whom it
is passed on recognises, consciously or unconsciously, the appropriate-
ness of its imagery and neither desires nor permits any essential deviation in this respect. Hence, in presenting allegorically any given
aspect of universal experience, the artist inevitably reproduces to
some extent, intentionally or otherwise, not only the substance, but

contended that the existence of those curiously persistent resemblances which the science of Comparative Religion has noted cannot be adequately explained unless the concepts which recur through all mythological and religious systems can be shown to typify certain enduring realities common to all mankind, and that these prototypical realities are to be found in the permanent facts of the universal psychology of aspiration. And I have endeavoured to establish that it is these same facts of subjective experience which form the ultimate theme of *The Tempest*.

Now, the questions I wish to put to every reader of independent and well-qualified judgment are these: Can we be satisfied to regard *The Tempest* as a pure fantasy without any dominant and controlling idea behind it; or must we regard it as an allegory having some inner significance which transcends its immediate and obvious purpose as a stage play? Can we say of it, as can be said of any pure fantasy, that it is entirely self-sufficient, needing no explanation at any point? Must we not admit, on the contrary, that it contains a very large number of strange and suggestive features— in respect both of action and of dialogue—which challenge us to look behind its peculiar outward forms

---

also the form of such genuine myths as deal with the same subject; and the degree of resemblance is directly proportionate to the aesthetic merits of his work. Thus, when Bunyan sought to portray the struggle of the aspirant with Desire, he automatically reproduced the myth of St. George and the Dragon in his story of Christian and Apollyon. And, indeed, could he have improved upon the myth in his effort effectively to personify Desire? Would a bird, or a dog, or a lion have served? Is anything but a Serpent or Dragon tolerable at all as a figure for Desire?

With regard to this question of automatically occurring resemblances, consider the import of the last footnote in my section entitled "The Way to Salvation." Does anyone suppose for a moment that Bunyan knew, or could know, anything whatever about the Egyptian initiations?

# Concluding Remarks

for some intelligible and paramount idea that unites
and explains them all? In short, must we not regard
it as an allegory? And if we conclude (as undoubtedly
many people have always felt constrained to do) that
much, if not all, of the text has some inner significance,
can we declare that the orthodox commentators have
put forward any really adequate interpretation—or,
indeed, any interpretation at all—of the Play as a
whole? Are we to believe that one of the maturest
works of the greatest poet of all time, a work which is
strongly allegorical in character and full of obscure
passages, is simply an indeterminate mixture of moral
platitudes, topical allusions, and autobiographical
intimations?* Is it not much more likely that an
elaborate and sustained allegory by a man of Shakespeare's intellectual calibre and sense of artistic propor-
tion has some fundamental unity of thought behind
it, and deals throughout with something of common
and constant value? In other words, is it not probable, rather than improbable, that *The Tempest* (if

* This, as every fair-minded reader will admit, is not a travesty of
the conventional view of *The Tempest*. The orthodox commentator
considers particular aspects of the Play and isolated portions of the
text, and offers a series of *ad hoc* interpretations. These interpretations are all more or less arbitrary. They are put forward without
any apparent regard for the important question of unity; and, however plausible they may seem, they lack weight because they are fragmentary and disconnected. Thus the orthodox commentator will
interpret (for example) the story of Stephano and Trinculo in a sententious moral vein; he will point to the union of Miranda with
Ferdinand, and remark that the Play was probably written to celebrate
the marriage of Princess Elizabeth with Prince Frederic of the Pala-
tinate; he will explain other conspicuous features by saying that the
Play was undoubtedly inspired very largely by the colonising enter-
prises of the time; and he will affirm also that the Play is Shakespeare's
swan-song, and that a number of passages in the text are allegorical
allusions of a purely personal nature. He may, and often does, say
all this and more of the same kind; but he offers no adequate and consistent interpretation of the Play *as a whole*.

237

it have any underlying significance at all) is the expression of a definite and coherent moral philosophy? If so, does it not demand a consistent and comprehensive interpretation, such as I have formulated? And, quite apart from the fact that no other all-inclusive theory of any kind has yet been forthcoming, could a better and more likely interpretation be suggested than one which implies (as mine does) that the Play is a version of the universal epic, that it deals with something which has appealed to all the purest aesthetic genius of the world, something which is enshrined in all that is best and most enduring in ancient myth and ritual, in religious concepts and ceremonies, in art and literature, and in popular tradition?

In no vital respect does my theory go beyond the scope of these very pertinent questions. It is, therefore, a theory of which the essential principles are well within the bounds of reasonable probability. And, although many of the textual comparisons I have made—more especially in the early part of this work—may appear at first sight to involve an eccentric and improbable view of the Play, they bear a definite logical relation to the ultimate and quite simple proposition for which I contend; for (as I have frequently emphasised) if the Play be indeed a version of the universal epic, it must of necessity resemble to some extent every other version of the same theme, including all authentic initiation ceremonies. Whether, in the case of any or all of the comparisons I have made, the resemblance is striking enough to warrant the positive conclusion that the Poet deliberately accentuated it, is a point upon which individual judgments may perhaps differ. In fact, I do not insist that all these correspondences are the result of conscious intention on the Poet's part. But I do maintain that my general view of *The Tempest* as a cosmic allegory not only explains the occurrence of such parallels, but also furnishes the comprehensive interpretation of which the Play seems to stand in need.

From the foregoing considerations it would appear that my theory cannot be rejected solely on the grounds of initial improbability. If any reader still think otherwise, I can do no more than inquire of him how the numerous and very remarkable parallels I have shown are to be accounted for, and by what utterly amazing freak of complex and sustained coincidence it happens that practically the whole of the text can be invoked in support of an entirely mistaken conception of the Play.

One other objection can be confidently expected, and may here be briefly dealt with. A certain type of critic, expressing a very common prejudice and taking little or no heed of the quantity and quality of the evidence I have been able to adduce, will endeavour to cut short all argument by saying that we ought to be content to accept a work of art as such, that it does not need to be elaborately explained, and that attempts to read into it meanings which the author may never have intended result from misguided ingenuity and a lack of aesthetic sensibility.

But can an objection of this sort be justly maintained in the present instance? I do not think it can. The critic in question would certainly agree that truth may be as important a factor as beauty in the success of a work of art as such; and he would doubtless admit that we may quite properly inquire how far any given work corresponds to the facts of human life and experience. Presumably he would also agree that to prove a work to be the perfect expression of unchanging realities is the highest tribute that can be paid to its artistic merit. Surely, then, this critic cannot reasonably complain of my treatment of *The Tempest?* For while I do not dispute the delicate and haunting beauty of the Play, I have shown (what no other commentator has shown) that it is in every respect true to human experience; and not only that it is true, but that it is permanently true; and not only that it is permanently true, but that it is universally true. What more can be said of any masterpiece of art?

Let me illustrate my standpoint by an entirely different example. Take the case of *Peter Pan*. Everyone recognises that *Peter Pan* is a supreme work of art; and the critic in question would say that we " ought to be content to accept it as such." Perhaps we ought; but, none the less, we may reasonably require the expert critic to explain the secret of its extraordinary success. To say that it appeals to all sorts and conditions of people because it is " a work of art " is no explanation at all. What makes it " a work of art "? Its beauty, its truth, or both? Does it appeal with irresistible power because it is an exquisite creation of the fancy? Assuredly; but is this the only conceivable reason which can, or need, be offered?

Now, suppose (for the sake of argument) I were to suggest that the overwhelming success of *Peter Pan* as a work of art is due in some measure to the fact that the story presents a perfectly truthful picture of the mutual relations of man and woman. Suppose I were to say that Wendy, loving the little house and the motherless (unborn?) human babies better than all else she encounters in her dream-flight with Peter to a land of imagination, personifies the mother-soul of woman; and that Peter, whose shadow is caught and held in Wendy's room while the real essence of him escapes to the realms of his higher and more lasting desires, personifies the questing spirit of man. Suppose I were to say that the heart of every woman goes out in instant understanding to Wendy for the sweet

# Concluding Remarks

mother-nature of her; and that in Peter every man perceives with a thrill of recognition (conscious or unconscious) the true reflection of something indefinable within himself, something which the soul of woman may perchance accompany, but can never capture and subdue; something wayward and wistful which, refusing to grow up to worldly and domestic responsibilities, follows the elusive light of a fairy Tinkabel whose very life is preserved by the simple assertion of faith.*

Suppose I were to say all this, as well I might; what then? Could I be charged with having exceeded the bounds of legitimate criticism? Could it be said that, in the effort to explain the secret of its universal appeal, I had treated *Peter Pan* as something other than a work of art? Surely not. Nor would the value of such an explanation be dependent upon proof of deliberate design on Barrie's part. Indeed, that is a question which need not arise at all, a question which could arise only if the suggested explanation were found to be supported by a large number of textual peculiarities not otherwise intelligible—as is the case, I think, with my interpretation of *The Tempest.*

For the general reasons which have now been stated,

* According to this view, the fairy light (Tinkabel) corresponds to what I have called the Celestial Bride. It is the elusive ideal which the questing spirit of man pursues: Beauty for the poet; Truth for the philosopher; Service for the statesman; Discovery for the adventurer; and so on. The reader will recall how the languishing fairy Tinkabel revives at the response to Peter's desperate and passionate appeal: "Say you believe in fairies!" Peter, between Wendy and Tinkabel, is a perfectly truthful representation of the imaginative spirit of man.

Approaching *Peter Pan* from another angle, I might (for the sake of the present argument) suggest that the story of Peter and Wendy is a version of the myth of Eros and Psyche, in that both deal with the same fundamental realities.

241                    Q

as well as for the particular reasons furnished by the detailed evidence, I submit my theory in reference to *The Tempest* with every confidence that it will survive the usual critical tests. Nevertheless, it is well to recognise frankly that a thesis so much at variance with conventional Shakespearean opinion must inevitably encounter a certain amount of unreasoning scepticism and unconscious prejudice, even in the best-intentioned of its judges. I shall, therefore, conclude this study by calling attention to the very significant appeal which the Poet himself has made to his readers.

There has already been occasion to point out that Prospero virtually declares a sustained interpretation to be both possible and necessary in respect of the series of incidents which befalls the Court Party. But the Poet's direct challenge to the reader is contained in the Epilogue, the whole of which is an earnest plea (spoken by Prospero) for liberation.

The obvious and generally accepted view is, of course, that the Epilogue is simply the conventional " plaudite," somewhat expanded for the purpose of intimating Shakespeare's intention to write no more; and, if the Play itself were nothing but a gossamer creation of pure poetic fancy, there would be neither need nor warrant for any other view. But we can hardly think that the Play and the Epilogue are entirely different in character and in significance. If the former be an allegory, so also in all probability is the latter. I do not deny that the Epilogue serves the ostensible purpose of a " plaudite," any more than I deny that what precedes it serves the ostensible purpose of a stage play. But I do suggest that, if the Play be indeed a sustained allegory which requires a coherent interpretation, some hint to this effect is likely to be concealed in the Epilogue.

From no standpoint is the Epilogue, which is

# Concluding Remarks

spoken by Prospero in the first person, consistent with his part in the drama. It can be reconciled neither with his nominal character as the magic-working Duke of Milan nor with his allegorical character as the Supreme Being; and those commentators are undoubtedly right who insist that Prospero here represents Shakespeare himself. But, while I agree so far, I dissent from the ordinary view that this closing speech contains simply the Poet's intimation that his labours as a dramatist are ended. I suggest rather that Shakespeare, having written a profound allegory, designed the Epilogue for the express purpose of pleading for *release* in the special sense of *interpretation*.

The grounds for this opinion are several. For example, it is with much creaking of the machinery that the idea of " release " is introduced at all. Among the many persons in the Play, Prospero is the obvious one to speak the Epilogue, since he is supposed to have contrived the events that make up the drama. But to put a plea for liberation into the mouth of Prospero, who has already promised the travellers a speedy voyage to Naples and signified his intention to accompany them,* involves so severe a strain upon what has gone before that the Poet must have been prepared to make no small sacrifice in order that such a plea should appear. In other words, we may fairly conclude not only that it is Shakespeare himself (rather than Prospero) who pleads for release, but also that there is some deep and genuine feeling behind the appeal. Moreover, it is his readers (or audience) who have the power to set him free or keep him bound. And again, if we do not release him, his purpose fails.

Let us now run through the Epilogue, regarding it as a plea by the Poet for liberation, a plea which

* Cf. *Tempest*, V. 1. 307-311, 314-16.

243

# Shakespeare's Mystery Play

is made in the semblance of a conventional " plaudite,"
and which is further obscured (save from the penetrating eye of intuitive imagination) by the inclusion of a
few references to the moninal plot of the Play:

> Now my charms are all o'erthrown,
> And what strength I have's mine own,
> Which is most faint: now, 'tis true,
> I must be here confined by you,
> Or sent to Naples.

But is it true?  It certainly is not true that Prospero,
in his aspect as the Duke of Milan, is prevented in
any way from quitting the Island, in its aspect as his
exile home.  But, according to my view of the Play,
it assuredly is true that the Poet, having exerted his
skill to the utmost in the composition of this allegory,
must now be " here confined " by us (his readers),
or set free through interpretation.

> Let me not,
> Since I have my dukedom got
> And pardon'd the deceiver, dwell
> In this bare Island by your spell;
> But release me from my bands
> With the help of your good hands.

By what spell is Prospero, Duke of Milan, held
prisoner upon the Island?  By none that we have
heard of before; indeed, he has already expressed his
intention to depart forthwith.  Moreover, the spell
that is now said to be capable of detaining him issues
from the reader (or audience).  Nor is it easy to
conceive in a literal sense how Prospero, the powerful
magician of the Play, can be so bound that it is for us
(the readers or audience) to release him.  Here are
glaring defects in the lines I am dealing with.  If
there be no purpose in the Epilogue sufficiently
important to override considerations of mere consistency, then these are faults which are wellnigh

Concurrent...

# Concluding Remarks

unpardonable, because they need not have been committed at all. On the other hand, they are faults which would be very largely excused by a demonstration that they are the inevitable consequence of an effort to further some paramount purpose. It is too much to claim that complete consistency is imparted to the lines by the assumption that the Poet himself is now speaking through the mouth of Prospero; but the hypothesis, when supplemented by my general view of the Play, does at least enable us to find some intelligible meaning in the words. For have I not shown that the Poet is tied by the bands of his own discreet dissimulation, a captive whom it is for us (his readers) to release by interpretation? Is it not true that we (his readers) can confine him, by the heavy spell of our uncomprehending literalism, within the bare and narrow limits of his nominal story, an exile from his intellectual kingdom? Observe, too, how the Epilogue continues:

> Gentle breath of yours my sails
> Must fill. . . .

If this mean that the actual vessel in which the Duke of Milan—notwithstanding the bands that hold him!—is about to accompany the travellers home must be propelled by the readers of the Play, there is here a marked straining for the sake of an effect that is extremely artificial and not a little bizarre. But such is not, and cannot be, the meaning; for Prospero, speaking as the Duke and magician at the close of the last scene, has expressly laid upon Ariel the duty of furnishing "auspicious gales" for the homeward journey.* It seems clear, therefore, that the words must be understood in some other than a literal sense. Now, if they be metaphorical, the first fact to remark

* Cf. V. i. 314-17.

# Shakespeare's Mystery Play

is that Shakespeare several times describes the work of his pen as a bark floating upon the water.* Moreover, precisely the same figure as in the present case is found in *Sonnet* LXXXVI., wherein the striking phrase " the proud full sail of his great verse " is somewhat enviously applied to the work of a rival poet. The context in which this phrase occurs enables us to analyse the metaphor with confidence. For the *Sonnet* goes on to affirm that the rival is " by spirits taught to write above a mortal pitch "; which obviously means that his work is spiritually inspired. It is by this inspiration (breathing into) that the sail of his verse is filled. What is expressed by the use of the same metaphor in the Epilogue under notice may be gathered from analogy with this quite clear example. The Poet pleads for such an interpretation of his Play as shall impart to it a spiritual meaning. The sails of his verse are spread, and it is for us (his readers) to fill them with the breath of our own genius. So, and no otherwise, can he pass from irksome limitations to the plenitude of his intellectual kingdom.

> Gentle breath of yours my sails
> Must fill, or else my project fails,
> Which was to please.

Here the Poet tells us frankly that he has some definite purpose, which must remain unrealised unless we " fill the sails " of his verse. True, he says his project was " to please "; but, having regard to all the circumstances, this may be declared to be a necessary and calculated understatement of the matter. Basing the case entirely upon internal evidence, I have argued that his deliberate intention was to allegorise something he was unwilling or unable openly to proclaim; and it would be strange indeed if he fully disclosed his design

* E.g., *Sonnet* LXXX.

246

at the very moment when he expressly lays upon the reader the task of elucidating it.  What he actually says here may perhaps satisfy the casual reader; but, if he really means us to believe that the purpose to which he alludes is simply and solely that of furnishing a few hours' pleasant entertainment, the more critical among us will take leave to inquire with respectful astonishment why the Epilogue so earnestly implores our saving aid in a matter of so little consequence.

> Now I want
> Spirits to enforce, art to enchant;
> And my ending is despair
> Unless I be relieved by prayer,
> Which pierces so that it assaults
> Mercy itself, and frees all faults.

These lines certainly have no relevance to Prospero, Duke of Milan.  We can find in them no meaning whatever, unless we assume that the Poet himself is speaking through Prospero.  But, even when this assumption is made, two alternative questions must arise in the mind of any thoughtful reader.  On the one hand, if he be telling us in a general sense (as some have supposed) that his labours as a writer are ended because he now lacks the art and the power for further literary effort, how can we reconcil the present mood of diffidence and even pessimism concerning his works with the serene confidence in their lasting greatness which he frequently professes elsewhere, as in the *Sonnets?*  On the other hand, if he be referring in a particular sense to *The Tempest,* surely this dark talk of despair in connection with a work which he says was designed solely " to please " is somewhat high-flown and strangely exaggerated. Both of these points are disposed of by the theory I am offering.  For I have sought to show that the Poet not only needs, but is at this moment invoking, the spiritual aid of his readers to enforce the real and secret purpose of *The Tempest;* and, looking back upon his allegory and recognising its many outward imperfections, he may well say that " his ending is despair " unless the appeal he now makes to us " pierce " so that we forgive the faults in a full appreciation of all that he attempted.

> As you from crimes would pardoned be,
> Let your indulgence set me free.

Yet again, in closing, he asks us to release him. His words are at once a plea and a challenge. All the evidence points to the conclusion that what he asks for is interpretation; and, if the case I have formulated through these many pages be rejected, I know not in what manner his appeal may be answered.

PRINTED IN GREAT BRITAIN BY
BILLING AND SONS, LTD., GUILDFORD AND ESHER

9 781169 748606